Micro Social Theory

Brian Roberts

First published in 2006 by
PALGRAVE MACMILLAN
Houndmills, Basingstoke, Hampshire RG21 6XS and
175 Fifth Avenue, New York, N.Y. 10010
Companies and representatives throughout the world.

PALGRAVE MACMILLAN is the global academic imprint of the Palgrave Macmillan division of St. Martin's Press, LLC and of Palgrave Macmillan Ltd. Macmillan® is a registered trademark in the United States, United Kingdom and other countries. Palgrave is a registered trademark in the European Union and other countries.

ISBN-13: 978–0–333–99569–3 hardback
ISBN-10: 0–333–99569–4   hardback
ISBN-13: 978–0–333–99570–9 paperback
ISBN-10: 0–333–99570–8   paperback

This book is printed on paper suitable for recycling and made from fully managed and sustained forest sources.

A catalogue record for this book is available from the British Library.

A catalog record for this book is available from the Library of Congress.

10 9 8 7 6 5 4 3 2 1
15 14 13 12 11 10 09 08 07 06
Printed in China

Micro Social Theory

TRADITIONS IN SOCIAL THEORY

Series Editors: Ian Craib and Rob Stones

This series offers a selection of concise introductions to particular traditions in sociological thought. It aims to deepen the reader's knowledge of particular theoretical approaches and at the same time to enhance their wider understanding of sociological theorising. Each book will offer: a history of the chosen approach and the debates that have driven it forward; a discussion of the current state of the debates within the approach (or debates with other approaches); and an argument for the distinctive contribution of the approach and its likely future value.

Published

PHILOSOPHY OF SOCIAL SCIENCE: THE PHILOSOPHICAL FOUNDATIONS OF SOCIAL THOUGHT
Ted Benton and Ian Craib

CRITICAL THEORY
Alan How

STRUCTURATION THEORY
Rob Stones

MARXISM AND SOCIAL THEORY
Jonathan Joseph

MICRO SOCIAL THEORY
Brian Roberts

Forthcoming

FEMINIST SOCIAL THEORY
Sam Ashenden

STRUCTURALISM, POST-STRUCTURALISM AND POST-MODERNISM
David Howarth

DURKHEIM AND THE DURKHEIMIANS
Willie Watts Miller and Susan Stedman Jones

Further titles in preparation

This book is dedicated to the memory of Evan and Mary

Contents

Acknowledgements

I would like to thank Dr Rob Stones, the editor of the *Traditions in Social Theory* Series, and Palgrave for the patience and help I received in the completion of this book. The late Professor Ian Craib, the original series editor, was an important source of inspiration throughout the writing of the book. I would also like to thank Dr Peter Billing, Director, Center for Regional and Tourism Research, Bornholm, Denmark and Professor Mats Greiff, Head, History Studies, Malmö University, Sweden for inviting me to spend time in their institutions and for their warm welcome and support. Finally, I owe the greatest thanks to Mag, Rhiannon and Iwan for allowing frequent retreats to my study desk.

Every effort has been made to trace all copyright holders, but if any have been inadvertently overlooked, the publisher will be pleased to make the necessary arrangements at the first opportunity.

1

Introduction

Micro and Macro Social Theory

In using 'micro social theory' in this book we are primarily dealing with its part in sociological theory while recognising various influences on such theorisation outside the discipline of sociology. Micro social theory is commonly associated with interpretive, 'subjective', small-scale theories – even sometimes termed 'social psychological' approaches to the understanding of social life with attention to agency, biography or subjectivity, social interaction and social process. Micro social theory is also often contrasted with 'macro' approaches within the discussion of the 'micro–macro issue' in sociology. In fact, it can be argued that 'All fields of empirical enquiry face a macro/micro problem in some form' (Barnes 2003: 339). Thus, study in a particular discipline can either start with recognition of the distinct case and its features or from a view that specific instances are merely part of a broader conglomeration. Whichever the starting point, issues arise regarding how 'micro' and 'macro' 'things' can be connected, how the investigation of 'the one should be related to enquiries in fields that study the other' and the extent to which they can be studied separately (Barnes 2003: 339).

The terms 'micro' and 'macro' are commonly used within sociological discussion – they form part of the sociological 'language' but nevertheless need some exploration. A short answer to the nature of their usage is that they are associated with different kinds of theory and analysis – although they can be more related than first appears:

> Micro analysis or 'microsociology' concentrates on the more personal and immediate aspects of social interaction in daily life. Another way of saying this is that it focuses on actual face-to-face encounters between people. Macro analysis or 'macrosociology' focuses on the larger-scale more general features of society such as organisations, institutions and culture. As such, macro phenomena are more 'impersonal' since they often appear to be more remote from daily activities and personal experience such as emotions and self-identity. (Layder 1994: 1)

The distinction between 'micro' and 'macro' theory or the problem of how they may be related can be a 'shorthand' for a range of associated issues or important

1

'dualisms' in sociological theory. So, alongside the polarity of 'micro–macro' there are a number of others that have played an important role in social analysis, such as action–structure and individual–society, that it often seems to subsume or mask (see Layder 1994: 2–7; Jenks 1998; Robertson 1974; Parker 2000: 91). The distinction between micro and macro theorisation often refers to the difference of 'size' or 'level' – i.e. between society and situation. Also, usually a notion of 'structure' (commonly as institutions or as social stratification – class, gender, ethnicity, age, etc.) has been equated with the macro 'level', while 'action' has been equated with the micro 'level' (as social interaction; social situations and the activities of individuals). The former has had more 'static' connotations; the latter associated with change, choice, and social processes. In my view we can retain the micro–macro distinction while also allowing for 'structure' at both 'levels' – as part of individual and group interaction in social settings as well as in its more traditional usage.

Faced with this micro–macro issue, theorists have responded in different ways, for example, some emphasising micro analysis at a 'low level', some seeing micro phenomena as the 'building blocks' of macro phenomena or as the macro in miniature. Others have challenged the 'duality' itself (e.g. Giddens – see Chapter 8), or seem not to recognise its relevance (e.g. Foucault and postmodernist/poststructuralist writers – see Chapter 8). While yet another group argue that the distinction is important as the basis of continued theoretical debate, insight and development (see Robertson 1974; Parker 2000: 109). What is necessary, in my estimation, is for some differences to be recognised between 'social levels' – some notion of stratification – which is able to conceive in a complex, productive manner micro–macro; agency–structure; individual–society; process–stasis (and other) distinctions not as oppositions but rather each as tendencies towards polarities which intersect. Thus, in this manner, I would argue it is possible to distinguish separate 'orders' or 'elements' while also recognising interconnection. This view recognises that we can argue that there are 'dualisms' (or polarities) in social theorising between social interaction or situation and the 'wider' society, while also we can see interconnections ('a duality') between these levels. The macro and micro 'levels', I would argue, can be studied both 'in their own right' as well as operating together in a dynamic, interrelated way.

Much discussion has taken place in sociological theory regarding overcoming the 'traditional' separation between macro and micro theory. Two very influential theorists – Giddens and Foucault (discussed in Chapter 8) – have been commonly criticised by commentators for going too far in eroding the macro–micro distinction by seeing an essentially 'flat' society – without levels or 'stratification'- as witnessed, it is said, in Giddens's 'duality of structure' or Foucault's 'discursive practices'. Another charge is that their dissolution of the macro and micro distinction has led to an insufficient allowance for complexity, dynamism and sharpness in defining and relating aspects of social life (Layder 1994: 219). However, both theorists can be seen as reinterpreting the micro view (by taking account of a notion of structure) while retaining a notion of the macro–micro interrelation. A theorist such as Goffman (Chapter 5) is of considerable interest here – and we can see the value of his work to writers such as Giddens. While not extensively analysing power, domination or institutions, he can be said to continue the classical tradition of Marx, Weber and Durkheim. They were concerned with the arena of social action while maintaining the institutional and historical reproduction of social practices (but admittedly having differing views of the action–structure relation) (Layder 1994: 217–18). Again, the view taken in this book is that we can study society at the 'level' of social interaction, while taking into account social structuring (for example, class and gender) in social situations, as well as retaining a sense of both micro (social situation) and macro (societal) levels.

Of course, the micro–macro distinction may seem a rather remote concern of abstract theorisation and of little pressing relevance to many researchers engaged in the daily practical intricacies of their social studies. But differing sociological approaches do carry a variety of assumptions concerning, for example, the 'individual' or 'society' and are associated with broad methodological and epistemological stances, such as how 'reality' is conceived. As Barnes (2003) notes, macro-sociological theorists are intent to 'to establish the reality of the macro-objects they describe' and combat the perils of reducing the social world to the actions of individuals, for instance, as driven by economic interest or as a fragmented, shifting and unstable mass of differing elements. The difficulty for macro sociologists is that as general phenomena, 'macro-objects' are more difficult to grasp, unlike individuals and situations, which can be more readily accessible (Barnes 2003: 341–2). Macro theorists, in asserting the 'priority' of macro phenomena, may regard certain micro theory as merely seeing society as an accumulation of calculative actions by rational actors (e.g. rational choice theory; see Chapter 8), or an outcome of many interactions in varied social situations (Barnes 2003: 342).

I would strongly argue, regarding the micro–macro 'problem', that a number of important points need to be made. First, as Layder argues, empirical study and theorisation together must address the issue. Secondly, the phenomena concerned are not simply antagonistic, instead, while they can still be regarded as different parts of social life, they must be seen as interconnected and mutually influential (Layder 1994: 1–2). Thirdly, differences between micro and macro analysis lie with the latter's emphasis on 'distributional phenomena in society as a whole' (e.g. patterns of wealth, of gender and occupation), but these inequalities can also be understood at the micro situational level of interaction and experience (see Layder 1994: 5–6). Finally, again, a reason for the continuance of the micro–macro 'problem' may well be that many sociologists see the macro–micro distinction as a means of fighting off perceived attempts to reduce an understanding of the social world to individual actions or small-scale settings, such as a rational choice theory (see Chapter 8) based on individual calculations and society as their unforeseen consequence (Barnes 2003: 342).

In my view, critically, while micro–macro issues may seem far removed from social research practice (as Barnes suggests), it is not merely a problem 'within' but also 'for' theory as 'product of human theorizing activity' (Barnes 2003: 342). This is an issue encompassing how sociologists practise the discipline and how 'lay' people also make connections between different parts of their social life, including their own actions and institutions – in short, how they perceive, construct and act according to 'micro and macro orderings' (Barnes 2003: 342). A micro social theory as a starting point in theorisation, I would suggest, produces an essential focus for social theory by its positive contribution to an understanding of the 'acting' individual and the nature of social interaction. But the common criticism that micro social theory only 'deals' or 'begins' with 'individuals', as resting on 'individualistic assumptions' (i.e. 'society is made by individuals'), is much too simplistic – as will become clear in the book. It will become apparent that there is a wider 'social' or 'societal' dimension within micro social theory.

Interpretive Approaches

Micro social theory is commonly associated with 'interactionism' – an inter-pretive approach to social phenomena (although some other approaches will also be examined in Chapter 8) within sociological theorisation which has a very different idea of 'science', research practice and topics of study (than macro theory):

> the general interactionist perspective sees the social world as constructed by the social actors through their vastly complex interactions in concrete situations ... Society is not a separate level of reality outside of individuals determining what they do, as structuralists argued. Society is what individuals are and what they do. (Douglas 1984: 8)

While it is possible to give some common views of interpretivist perspectives, Douglas notes that particular examples 'differ considerably over the question of what *degree* of freedom individuals in our society have in constructing meanings and lives (Douglas 1984: 8). These 'sub-theories' within the broad theoretical perspective of 'interactionism' Douglas identifies as: 'symbolic interactionism' (including labelling theory, and he includes rather loosely perhaps, Erving Goffman's 'dramaturgical' approach); 'interactional conflict theory' (subcultural theories sometimes associated with broader conflict approaches – we can also place Chicago Sociology here); and 'sociological phe-nomenology' ('existential theory', 'ethnomethodology') (see Douglas 1984: 9). Here, Douglas is using the term 'interactionism' very broadly and (rightly) distinguishes it from one of its constituents, 'symbolic interactionism': often writers confusingly use these terms interchangeably. Another source of confusion is where 'sociological phenomenology', as in Douglas's usage, is too readily cast under 'interactionism' or even sometimes taken to be very closely associated with 'symbolic interaction'; certainly it has had theoretical and empirical connections with 'interactionism' and its 'sub-theories', but some caution is needed in ascribing commonalities (Atkinson and Housley 2003: 36). Without going into detail on the various theories given by Douglas, we can say that we need to be as much aware of how they differ, e.g. on conceptions of the individual ('self', 'member'), social interaction, social situation and 'social structure'. In this book symbolic interactionism, Erving Goffman's work, Chicagoan sociology, phenomenology and ethnomethodology (and some other approaches) will be addressed separately, not as all merely forms of 'interactionism', but as all part of micro social theory with both areas of similarity and difference.

A starting point for my examination of micro social theory is Benton and Craib's (2001) description of the interpretive tradition as less concerned with the status of positivism (a philosophy of the natural sciences) than advocating the view that the social sciences are qualitatively different from the subject matter of the natural sciences, necessitating rather different methods (Benton and Craib 2001: 75). As outlined by Benton and Craib we can describe micro social theory as a 'cluster' of approaches, which are unified by a concern with the '*instrumental* notion of rationality' (or the operation of human reason in gaining knowledge about the world). They examine the work of Weber and a number of associated interpretive approaches, including 'phenomenological sociology'; rational choice theory, which was influenced by nineteenth-century political economic theories; and perspectives surrounding American pragmatism (Benton and Craib 2001: 75–6). For these different approaches social science examines individual action as directed to achieving goals in this world – an 'instrumental rationality'. While rational choice theory, for instance, is very different in various respects from 'interpretive' interactional approaches, there is a similar model of a rational actor making decisions according to circumstances.

Micro Social Theory and Sociological Theorisation

The micro–macro issue, it can be argued, is implicated in what sociologists do in terms of both theorisation and research, including the sociological methods and interpretation adopted. It involves the connections between 'everyday life', and within it 'everyday sociological practice', and agency/biography, the nature of social interaction and the 'ordering' of social situations (e.g. as interaction and structural orders). The investigation of such interconnections is not merely important for sociological development. For Giddens, the 'sociological enterprise is now even more pivotal to the social sciences as a whole, and indeed to current intellectual culture generally, than it has ever been before', since we currently live 'in a world on a knife-edge between extraordinary possibility and global disaster' (Giddens 1987b: 17). Gone, it seems, are the optimistic social visions of the eighteenth- and nineteenth-century founders of sociology, nevertheless the recent controversies within the discipline have enabled a clarification of its current and possible role. These controversies, for Giddens, cannot be understood without reference to the methodological problems in sociological practice, which has been undergoing a re-evaluation.

We can agree with Giddens that the social sciences rely on 'lay concepts' but also that they develop their own 'conceptual metalanguages' to 'grasp aspects of social institutions which are not described by agents' concepts'. As he says, the concepts and theories produced by social scientists also 'leak out' and are used by 'lay' social actors outside the disciplinary endeavours. This circularity of 'conceptual metalanguages', he says, 'deserves careful consideration, for grasping its nature leads us to a major reappraisal of the practical influence of sociology upon modern societies' (Giddens 1987b: 19). We can add that the importance of micro social theory for sociological activity, given the current era of social transformation, is its general emphasis on the subjective, interactive aspects of life, the constitution of social life in its ordinary daily round, and its interrelation with institutional orders. The scrutiny of these areas has a vital part to play in examining the impact of and responses to important social changes. Social transformation is often described at the macro levels of global institutions and associated economic and social shifts (e.g. in trade and finance, cultural homogenisation and migratory disruptions) but crucially, it is also shaped, experienced and responded to at the 'micro' level by socially active individuals and groups.

This book fits the main approach of the Traditions in Social Theory Series. Micro social theory, including interactionism, symbolic interactionism, phenomenology and ethnomethodology, can be considered a tradition in sociological theorisation. More usefully, it can be considered to be a group or 'cluster' of theorists and theories, which are usually described and assessed together (Benton and Craib 2001). This is not to argue that there are not significant differences within the 'tradition' (especially, if we add, as I do here, 'rationalistic' approaches – see Chapter 8), but generally 'micro sociologies' can be contrasted with broadly 'macro' (or 'structural') theorisation. The book gives the development of the tradition, assesses current debates and examines its contemporary importance.

In my view micro social theory has definite strengths for sociological work – despite the criticisms that can be made of a focus on the micro 'level' or of the particular 'limitations' of specific theories. It has made a very distinctive contribution both to social theory and to substantive areas (e.g. as we will see in the discussion of community and place, and friendship and intimate relations and other 'empirical fields' in Chapter 9) – and has a future value in understanding contemporary social life.

My stance is that the current and likely 'future value' of micro social theory is very much related to the illumination it gives of the 'micro' details of individuals (e.g. the self) and their interactions as a focus for investigation and theorisation. But it also has continued importance in the way it 'reaches out' to the wider social world at the micro local, meso (intermediate) and macro (society) 'scales'. Here I am not trying to advocate or generate a broad micro social theory, but there are themes drawn out in each chapter which demonstrate the continued vitality of micro social theory as an arena of study in 'its own right' and as interconnected with other 'levels'. Micro social theory, very briefly, can be said to have the following relevances:

- the Chicago School's focus on groups, social distance and ecology (Chapter 2)
- the generalised other, role and society in Mead's work (Chapter 3)
- in the definitions of situation and of 'settings' of interaction further developed in symbolic interactionism (Chapter 4)
- the presentation of self, drama, ritual and game, and interaction order in Goffman's observations (Chapter 5)
- the background of shared knowledges and accountability in the phenomenological traditions (Chapter 6)
- the traces of wider structures in experience (gender inequality) in the micro writings of feminist writers such as Dorothy Smith, or of cultural categories in post-structuralist feminist writers (Chapter 7)
- the ideas on the formation and continuance of social relations according to exchange, rational choice, control, network, disciplinary power and structuration approaches (Chapter 8)
- and finally, prominent recent substantive work has developed important themes in micro theory, such as community and place; or focused on underdeveloped themes in social interaction such as time; or brought forward relatively neglected theoretical areas, such as emotion and body in relation to experience (Chapter 9).

We can see the continued importance of micro social theory as not merely an 'abstract' pursuit of theorisation, but as connected to research on the key areas – social interaction, experience and social context – that are fundamental to daily social living.

Outline of the Book

The chapters of this book are organised in a general chronological order to trace the developments of parts of the 'cluster' of theories, for instance, the origins and development of symbolic interactionism, or lines of influences between differing approaches when considering particular themes (e.g. interaction, experience). Inevitably, there are at points 'overlaps' between the micro theories considered.

Chapter 2: Chicago Sociology

This chapter outlines the work of Chicago sociology, particularly the work of R. E. Park and W. I. Thomas, which has had a wide influence on theoretical and substantive areas within sociology. It will outline the origins of the 'Chicago School', especially in pragmatism and Social Darwinism and its emphasis on ideas of community, social process, and ethnography and life history. The chapter includes: Introduction: Chicago School and Micro Social Theory; Origins: Pragmatism and Social Darwinism; Small and the First Generation; Robert Ezra Park; Natural Areas, Natural History, 'Naturalism'; Cultural and Natural Orders; Immigration and Race; Chicagoan Studies; Case Study: W. I. Thomas and F. Znaniecki (1958) *The Polish Peasant in Europe and America*; Critique; and Conclusion.

Chapter 3: Symbolic Interactionism 1 – Origins

This chapter outlines the origins, main ideas and 'perspective' of symbolic interactionism in the work of G. H. Mead (his social psychology and social philosophy), with specific attention to mind, self and society, and the act and social interaction. Mead's work will be placed in the context of his pragmatic philosophy as also associated with Dewey, James and others. It will also outline the criticisms of Mead's approach. The chapter includes: Introduction; Origins; What is 'Symbolic Interactionism'? George Herbert Mead – His Philosophy and Social Psychology; The Self, Mind and Society; 'I' and 'Me'; Play and Game; Role; Society; Case Study: Time; The Influence of Mead's Work; Critique; and Conclusion.

Chapter 4: Symbolic Interactionism 2 – Developments

This chapter outlines the development and diversity of symbolic interactionism with particular reference to the work of Herbert Blumer and certain substantive areas – included here are methods and methodological issues. Questions regarding the features of the 'social situation' in symbolic interactionist theory, and what is neglected or underemphasised, are addressed. The chapter includes: Introduction; The Development of Symbolic Interactionism; Herbert Blumer's Symbolic Interactionism; Blumer and Mead; Critique of Blumer; Varieties of Symbolic Interactionism; Qualitative Research and 'Interactionism'; Case Study: Deviancy Theory and Careers; Critique; New Developments; and Conclusion.

Chapter 5: Erving Goffman

This chapter introduces the distinctive perspective of Erving Goffman – sometimes called 'dramaturgy'. It will explore his ideas on the self, interaction and society and compare them with other approaches. It will also examine Goffman's 'methodology' and ask whether he can be described as, to some extent, a 'structural' theorist. The chapter discusses Goffman's main 'metaphors' and ideas – drama, game and ritual and notions such as co-presence and inter-action order. An assessment is made of his contribution to the micro–macro 'link'. The chapter includes: Introduction; The Origins of Goffman's Work; Drama; The Self; Interaction Order; Co-presence; Ritual – Regions and Frames; Case Study: E. Goffman (1972) *Interaction Ritual: Essays on Face-to-Face Behaviour*; Critique; and Conclusion.

Chapter 6: Phenomenology and Ethnomethodology

This chapter outlines the origins of the phenomenological approach (e.g. Husserl). It examines the work of Schutz and main concepts, e.g. intersubjective experience, typifications, and common-sense knowledge and the development of the approach (e.g. Berger and Luckmann) in later work. The chapter introduces the main ideas of the 'ethnomethodological' approach in the work of Garfinkel – e.g. members' 'methods', accomplishment of order, accountability and meaning, indexicality – and the differences between ethnomethodology and 'conventional' sociology. The chapter includes: Introduction; Phenomenological Sociology – Origins: Husserl and Schutz; Critique; Case Study: P. L. Berger and T. Luckmann (1971) *The Social Construction of Reality: A Treatise in the Sociology of Knowledge*; Ethnomethodology – Origins; Members' Methods; Accountability; Conventional Sociology; Ethnomethodology and 'Misconceptions'?; Critique; and Conclusion.

Chapter 7: Subjective Experience, Feminism and Sociology

In this chapter the feminist contributions to the examination of the relationships between research, theory and experience within sociology will be outlined. Feminist sociology as associated with feminist methods, experience and the 'personal', reflexivity, and gender will be overviewed and assessed. The chapter includes: Introduction; Varieties of Feminist Theory; Critique of Sociology; Experience, Reflexivity, Interdisciplinarity; Feminist Methodology; Case Study: The Family; Feminist Theorisation and Micro Social Theory; and Conclusion.

Chapter 8: Theoretical Developments in Micro Social Theory

This chapter reviews a range of theories which have been identified as at a 'micro level', especially those which have become increasingly prominent since the mid-1980s. The chapter includes an examination of the work of

Giddens and Foucault with reference to how they view 'micro structure' and the 'making' of the individual. Although not usually regarded as 'micro theorists' their influential ideas – in Giddens in terms of structure as 'emergent' or 'lived', in Foucault how knowledge/power 'flows' through particular contexts or institutional settings – are relevant to the micro situation. Also examined are theories that can be considered as 'micro' but do not fit the interpretive tradition (just as discourse and structuration theory do not) – rational choice, control theory, exchange theories and network theories. Even so, such theories could be seen to share a 'rational' model of the actor. The chapter includes: Introduction; Exchange Theory; Rational Choice Theory and Control Theory; Network Theory; Michel Foucault; Anthony Giddens; and Conclusion.

Chapter 9: Substantive Developments in Micro Social Theory

In recent years a range of previously relatively neglected areas of theorisation and empirical study have emerged within sociology – including place, time, friendship, body and emotion. This is not to say that these areas have not been present, or not deemed important previously by some writers, but that they have become the focus of a re-evaluation and re-emphasis in sociological endeavour. These substantive areas have important consequences for micro theorisation in terms of providing a new sophistication in how traditional concerns, such as role, situation and interaction are considered. The chapter includes: Introduction; Community and Place; Time; Emotions; Friendship and Intimate Relations; Narratives; Body; and Conclusion.

Chapter 10: Conclusion

The conclusion returns to the question of the micro and macro distinction in sociological theory and contrasts it with the issue of agency vs. structure. It points out the main themes arising in the book, such as the model of the actor and the conception of structure in micro social theory. It ends by emphasising the part played by the 'sociological imagination' – and the plea that micro theory should be also applied to the life of the micro theorist. The chapter includes: The Micro Social Theory Tradition as a 'Cluster'; Action and Structure; and Conclusion: Micro Social Theory and Sociological Imaginings.

Glossary

A range of useful definitions of terms used.

Further Reading

A broad review of the contemporary work and influence of interactionism can be found in P. Atkinson and W. Housley, *Interactionism* (London, Sage, 2003). B. Barnes gives a quite sophisticated discussion of 'structure and agency', with an extensive bibliography, in his 'The Macro/Micro Problem and the Problem of Structure and Agency', in G. Ritzer and B. Smart (eds.), *Handbook of Social Theory* (London, Sage, 2003). Jenks and others provide a chapter-by-chapter introductory discussion of key 'dichotomies' in sociological theory in C. Jenks (ed.), *Core Sociological Dichotomies* (London, Sage, 1998). Layder gives an extended and 'accessible' examination of the relations between micro and macro social theory in D. Layder, *Understanding Social Theory* (London, Sage, 1994). R. Stones (ed.), *Key Sociological Thinkers* (Basingstoke, Palgrave Macmillan, 1998); G. Ritzer (ed.), *The Blackwell Companion to Major Contemporary Social Theorists* (Oxford, Blackwell, 2000); and A. Elliott and B. S. Turner (eds.), *Profiles in Contemporary Social Theory* (London, Sage, 2001) give detailed biographical contexts and theoretical appreciations of a number of writers featured in this book (e.g. Goffman).

2
Chicago Sociology

Introduction: Chicago School and Micro Social Theory

The Chicago School may at first seem an unlikely subject for a discussion of micro social theory, since its work was centred on the city and urban processes. However, it was also concerned with particular social groups and social situations, social distance between individuals and the social effects of city life – and in its more specific concern for meanings and social interaction it was a major contributor to 'interactionism' (Fisher and Strauss 1979: 457). In the 1920s and 1930s sociologists at the University of Chicago compiled an enormous amount of material from a wide range of sources on urban life. Chicagoan sociologists also attempted to understand the relations between the individual, groups and urban processes, and institutions using in-depth ethnographic and other study; in doing so they generated influential theories of urban patterns and expansion (Short 1971a: xi). Thus, while the 'city' was the main unifying context of study, there were a number of common 'micro' themes around the development of situated meanings and social interaction, i.e. the attitudes and values arising from the experiences and the process of adjustment to industrial and urban life. For micro social theory the particular importance of Chicagoan sociology lies in its attention to the first-hand description and understanding of the 'life histories' of individuals and social groups, ideas on social distance and social processes, and the focus on the ecological setting.

Origins: Pragmatism and Social Darwinism

The term 'The Chicago School' can be used as a broad description of the sociological work at Chicago in the late nineteenth century up to the mid- to late 1930s. Under the leadership of Robert Ezra Park, the department at Chicago became the foremost sociology department in the United States. Some writers have questioned the notion of the Chicago 'School' as a united group establishing a tradition with a certain focus on urban life and social interaction – rather than the 'reality' of various individuals pursuing their own intellectual

12

and research interests, with disagreements and differing friendships. It is said there was a great deal of academic endeavour and general collaboration but not a unified theoretical and research approach. In this regard – while unsurprisingly there were often substantial differences between writers in temperament, research methodology and interest – perhaps it was more a loose grouping than a tight-knit 'school'. Nevertheless, this chapter will follow a common approach by other commentators who have used the term 'school' and have identified a dominant theme – a collaborative, adventurous, very productive focus on urban life, patterns and process and the social adjustment of individuals and groups to changing urban experiences (see Short 1971a: xi–xiv). The term can be considered to be a general shorthand for a group of individuals and the influence of their ideas centred on the city and social change, including certain substantive issues (e.g. crime and delinquency and other social problems such as race and immigration) and contributions to research methodology. Some commentators would include George Herbert Mead, who was not in the department, and his 'symbolic interactionist' disciples such as Blumer (Chapters 3 and 4) within the Chicagoan tradition of Thomas, Park and Burgess. This addition is due in broad terms to the importance of the general background of liberal pragmatist philosophy on Chicagoan study, in particular, the influence of Dewey, James and Mead.

The Department of Sociology founded at Chicago (1892) was possibly the first department devoted to sociology in the world. It was meant to have a practical focus, being close to the social issues affecting Chicago – a city that had experienced massive growth from a small settlement to a major industrial entity (with meatpacking, steel, railcar and other industries) within sixty or so years. Sociology was therefore to be oriented to the daily problems and experiences of the urban environment. Chicago was a centre for immigration with substantial Italian, Polish and other communities, and migration from the Southern states. The university, founded with support of John D. Rockefeller, Snr. and under President William Rainey Harper, was meant to have a more immediate, 'applied' outlook than the traditional institutions on the East Coast. Sociological study was not to be confined to an 'ivory tower' of retreatist scholarship.

It was the setting of the vibrant midwest city, with its fast-growing diverse population, variety of social movements and conflicts, and mass immigration which inspired the concerns and studies by Chicagoan sociologists. In its early period there was some influence of 'Christian Sociology' and social reform impulses in areas of social problems, civic principles, city conditions, education, and labour and ethnic relations. Despite a necessary caution in seeing a homogenous methodological and theoretical approach, it is perhaps possible to detect some central themes leading through the department's work – a set of liberal, demotic values and concern with objective but applicable knowledge, as seen in Park, Thomas and Burgess. There was a certain 'progressivism' (the possibility of gradual social progress), as highlighted by interests in social cohesion and control, communication and relations between social groupings.

Small and the First Generation

The sheer diversity, physical expansion and vivacity of the city held a fascination, excitement and anxiety. The growth of industrialism and associated life patterns and values put traditional organisations, the family, community and religion under strain – whether the new urban dwellers originated in the small towns of the Midwest or were recent immigrant groups from rural areas of eastern or southern Europe. Albion Small, the founding head of the department, and his colleagues of the 'first generation' were immediately faced with the urban problems of a rapidly expanding and diverse city. Small wrote (with G. E. Vincent) perhaps the first sociology textbook (*An Introduction to the Study of Society*, 1894) and founded the *American Journal of Sociology* (1895) after establishing the department. The Chicagoan issues concerning the basis of community, the threat of new values and individualism, and ethnic and national identity came at time of debate about national 'character' and the extent of immigration (i.e about one million people entered the United States in 1906). 'Social Darwinist' notions were prominent in popular publications in the early twentieth century, centring on the 'fitness' of populations, while evolutionary ideas were strongly represented across the emerging social sciences. Another influence on Chicago sociology was 'liberal pragmatism', as in the writings of James, Dewey and Mead, which was associated with principles of 'objective knowledge' and 'progressivism' in social organisation. These principles found expression in calls for social reform and were connected in practice to forms of community work, juvenile justice reform, and discussion of how difficulties in labour and ethnic relations could be met.

A 'second generation' was heralded by the arrival of Robert Ezra Park to the department. What became notable was the broad range of research studies undertaken by Park, Burgess and their colleagues. But by the close of the 1930s the position of Chicago sociology at the head of the discipline in the United States was under challenge from more general, societal theory (i.e. functionalism) and critiques of a restrictive methodological focus on the city, and more specifically, the use of 'human ecological' analogies and concepts. Despite its pioneering of statistical methods under Ogburn, Chicagoan sociology, and Park in particular, were also attacked for their stress upon qualitative methods, which came 'under pressure' from advances in statistical and attitudinal research. Even so, the 'decline' of Chicagoan sociology was relative and perhaps, at least in part, due to the expansion of sociology elsewhere; in fact, a further talented generation was emerging, including Louis Wirth, Everett Hughes and a number of brilliant students including Edward Shils, Howard Becker and others. The thread of concern remained on urban or city life – or perhaps more broadly industrial urban society, including its diversity and anonymity but also its vibrancy and the 'mixed' effects on individuals and communities.

Albion Small was joined in 1895 by William Isaac Thomas (1863–1947) as his doctoral student. Thomas later reflected that he felt he had passed through three centuries from his early life in rural Virginia to the twentieth-century city of Chicago. This passage alerted him to the connection between 'types' of individual and social change. He conceived himself as an extrovert leading an introverted life; in his classic book with Florian Znaniecki, *The Polish Peasant in Europe and America* (1958; originally published in five volumes, 1918–20), he outlined the bohemian, philistine and creative individual types in relation to urban experiences (Roberts 2002: 35; see Coser 1977).

Park met Thomas when the latter visited the Tuskegee Institute and was invited by him to the University of Chicago. Thomas's own background was in anthropology and he was influenced by Boas's examination of cultural diversity and, in particular, a movement away from biological assumptions concerning race and culture. His early publications included the pioneering texts *Sex and Society* (1907) and the edited volume *Source Book for Social Origins* (1909). However, he is most known for his classic study with Znaniecki, which employed innovative methodologies (such as the use of family letters, organisational records and life-history materials) and developed key theoretical ideas (e.g. attitudes and values) on how immigrant communities adapted to a new social environment. As Short describes, it was the work of the 'second generation' of sociologists at Chicago that was mainly to be credited for the vitality of the discipline in the department at the university and its influence more widely with in the United States.

> One of the most important factors permitting this development – in sharp contrast with the dominating influence at other universities of somewhat doctrinaire sociological scholars ... was the *openness* with which sociology was viewed, both in substance and in method. There was no 'party line,' save for the admonition to 'objectivity' and 'disinterested investigation' in the interests of a developing science ... Chicago's 'second generation' was even broader in its interests and methodological perspectives than was the first ... while there was general agreement on the justification of sociology in terms of its ultimate service to mankind, there were almost as many views concerning the means by which such service might properly be rendered by sociology as there were scholars to hold them. (Short 1971a: xiv, xviii)

Robert Ezra Park

Robert Ezra Park (1864–1944) was born in Pennsylvania but his family then moved to an area of Minnesota, which had a strong Scandinavian settlement. At first he studied engineering but then moved towards the study of philosophy. He was a student at the University of Michigan and at Harvard, where as a

postgraduate he came into contact with William James. His route to the academic profession was circuitous. He had a career in journalism in a number of
cities writing on social issues but he also studied in Germany, becoming
influenced by Simmel, before teaching philosophy at Harvard University. He
eventually became the secretary for Booker T. Washington, the leading civil
rights campaigner before the Second World War, at Tuskegee Institute. Park
travelled with Washington on a study tour of Europe and co-wrote *The Man
Farthest Down* (1984). He joined the Chicago Department in 1914, by then
middle-aged, was made a professor in 1923 and retired ten years later. He said
he 'really completed' his 'education at Harvard, Berlin, Strassburg, and
Heidelberg' in terms of finding a viewpoint and problem. His early focus was
an attempt to look at the newspaper sociologically and to describe it 'objectively and generically as an institution' (Baker 1973: 255).

In the period between the First World War and the mid-1930s Chicago
Sociology was the 'exemplar and pathsetter' forming the general sociological
view in the United States, founding the major journal, occupying the presi-
dency of the American Sociological Society (ASS), publishing the most influential books and training the main sociologists (Coser 1977). Small and Vincent's
early sociological textbook was followed by Park and Burgess's well-known
Introduction to the Science of Sociology ([1921]1969), which marked a shift
from conflict theory (e.g. in Small) to an influence from Simmel's formalism,
although they are both now better known for the study of the city, press, race
relations and the family (Martindale 1961: 252–4). Park and Burgess, in fact,
drew on a wide range of thinkers (including Cooley and Small), but the main
influence seems to be Simmel, who was cited the most with Thomas, whose
own *Source Book for Social Origins* (1909) provided a template, in a close second place. They did not outline specifically new concepts but rather a refor-
mulation of existing work with a strong accompanying emphasis on working
ideas for rigorous, intensive research (Braude 1970: 2). At the centre of the
book is the notion of social control as the problem for sociology. There is also
a focus on the idea of social processes – to be analysed in terms of social
involvement (or integration) and social forces.

A 'flavour' of Park's ideas and its sources can be gained by his idea of 'marginal man', which can also be seen as some reflection on his own life and the
anxieties and lack of direction felt by many of his generation:

> Something of the same sense of moral dichotomy and conflict is probably character-
> istic of every immigrant during the period of transition, when old habits are being
> discarded and new ones are not yet formed ... But in the case of the marginal man
> the period of crisis is relatively permanent ... the characteristics of the marginal
> man ... [are] spiritual instability, intensified self-consciousness, restlessness, and
> *malaise*. (Park 1928: 893)

Park adds that it is 'in the mind of the marginal man – where the changes
and fusions of culture are going on – that we can best study the processes of
civilization and of progress' (Park 1928: 893).

W.I. Thomas left the University of Chicago in 1918 but his influence remained, particularly in the work of Park, through a number of research areas (e.g. ethnic relations and migration) and an interest in first-hand research, city life, cultural groups and processes. The legacy was not an emphasis on systematic theorisation and, in fact, some of Park's formulation of 'human ecology' did not emerge until rather late in his work. Biographically their careers had some shared features: both came to the study of sociology from other areas, studied in Germany (although this was not uncommon) and seemed to experience a turning point through the realisation of their vocational interests in mid-life.

The varied career of Park, perhaps ironically, may explain his eventual academic work. He wrote that his observations as a journalist and his reform activities led him to seek more detailed understandings of events and be less apt to advocate immediate social reform without an adequate basis of knowledge. Indeed, he was suspicious of ready solutions and moralising. Park's sociology was a mix of interest in the communal basis of the small rural community while having an intense concern for the patterns and process of urban living – hence his focus on social bonds and social control. While not supporting immediate social reform without knowledge and a preference for detailed observation, he still had a view on social change which reflected a tension between the influence of evolutionary thought and conflict theory alongside pragmatism and progressivism. The result was a consideration of the role of adaptation in individuals and groups to social changes while holding a pragmatic, democratic view of communication. Although aware of self-interest, he argued that greater knowledge of social differences between groups would challenge existing arrangements; a new basis of co-operation would become established through a deeper recognition of events prior to political and social change. For instance, the crowd could be made more 'public' by more objective knowledge and communication, and thereby, the social distances between individuals and groups would be lessened. There was an interesting mix in Park's work between a pragmatist belief in progress and a more restrained idea of its possibility by social intervention due to Social Darwinism (e.g. Sumner and Spencer). Social Darwinism had a deep influence across sociology, psychology and anthropology during the period, but was also being modified. While inducing at least a sceptical attitude towards the possibilities of reform, pragmatists argued that a gradual, guided, social evolution was being realised. Early Chicagoan work emphasised an applied sociology and was close to social reform activities, but for Park communication and knowledge were necessary for social change. More specifically, Park owed a debt to W.I. Thomas and his anthropological approach (derived from Boas) in his orientation towards both the conflictual and adaptive aspects of social processes and fieldwork on urban life.

Park gave a number of sources for his study of urban life, including the new social and business surveys of consumer markets in the city and studies of rural communities. A key point in the urban research development of Chicago was Park's pioneering article 'The City: Suggestions for the Investigation of Human

Behavior in the Urban Environment' (1915) (published in the *American Journal of Sociology*) (see Park, Burgess and McKenzie, 1969, 1967). Park was outlining a very large research programme in the social 'mapping' of the city. It was followed by a proposal by Small that various university departments should co-operate in research activities. A second turning point in Chicagoan urban research was the huge study of migration by Thomas and Znaniecki (1958), *The Polish Peasant in Europe and America*, published between 1918 and 1920. While the former essay sketched a programme for research, the latter study offered a variety of materials – life history, agency records, newspapers and family letters – in conjunction with (often previously formulated) theoretical considerations (e.g. attitudes, values). In Park and Thomas there is a shared interest in individual adjustment to conditions (e.g. 'marginal man' in the former, and the character types of the creative, philistine and bohemian, in the latter) and the potential for change, as well as holding a very strong emphasis on the processes of group adaptation. Again, if there is a general strand that brings together Chicago sociologists it was a commitment to the study of the urban environment and to the emerging discipline of sociology as scientific study and its application for societal improvement – although there were obvious differences in how that might be achieved (Short 1971a: xviii).

Natural Areas, Natural History, 'Naturalism'

Park's various ideas on social groups and urban social processes were brought under the rather ambiguous notion of 'human ecology' in a series of later articles. The idea of human ecology demonstrated a legacy of evolutionary conceptions in his work in a number of ways, as indicated by his use of ideas such as symbiosis and biotic balance from the ecological study of plants (see Turner 1967: xxvi). From his close colleague Burgess there is an organismic or zonal model of the city as divided into different urban environments. This conception is based on an analogy with the individual plant organism with layers of development (e.g. onion rings or tree cross-sections), and gives a structural aspect to human ecological theorisation. These areas constituted 'natural habitats' in which differing species competed or symbiotically (compatibly) coexisted to meet the needs for food, light and space. Another key idea is that of 'natural history' (see Turner, 1967: xxiii) which provided a notion of process by drawing on the comparison with the individual life – birth, development, maturity, old age, etc. It is a stage model through which particular cases (e.g. immigrant groups) are seen to develop. Finally, there is a 'naturalistic' orientation (see Matza 1969) as a broad cultural approach which seeks to uncover cultural meanings and report social diversity; this is shown by an anthropological concern with fieldwork in the city. These three elements – natural area, natural history and 'naturalism' – were by no means fully reconciled under the heading of human ecology and may be responsible for some rather one-sided assessments of Park's and Chicagoan work (e.g. as environmental determinist).

The idea of the natural history seemed to have a wide role in Park's sociology. His view of sociology was as a science but one that drew on anthropological methods and was influenced by Simmel's formalism. Park considered that when the study of history becomes less concerned with eras and more with the comparison of institutions (e.g. churches), then natural history enters as a mediating link between history and sociology. With the formation of comparisons and concepts sociology as a science enters and a new means of understanding is developed. It was the interest in social change on the one hand and social control on the other that informed his attempt to understand city life. Park earlier, as a journalist, had begun to look beyond the exposure of social ills and towards a more intensive observation of the city and a conceptual framework. He wrote later:

> I expect that I have actually covered more ground, tramping about in cities in different parts of the world, than any other living man. Out of all this I gained, among other things, a conception of the city, the community, and the region, not as geographical phenomenon merely, but as a kind of social organism. (Madge 1963: 89)

Park's intent as a journalist and later in his article 'The City' (1915) was to develop a deeper understanding of urban life than descriptive accounts and a moralism that informed (he argued) much of social intervention. Nevertheless, it could be said that as he was slow to systemise his approach in human ecology, it retained substantial deficiencies. It would seem to be rather against the social psychology being developed by Dewey and James and in some respects their commitment to understanding the cultural meanings of groups. The use of natural history and ecological analogies to account for the 'natural order' brought such difficulties. Much is not fully outlined, such as the specific relationship between the natural and cultural orders and what is contained in each. For instance, to what extent are newspapers and cultural groups 'determined' in following the stages of the natural history? To what extent are the meanings of those involved important? It seems that social institutions and social classes or groups are being placed within a certain natural model of social structural developmental to some exclusion of their cultural aspects. A further issue is how the division of labour operates and the movement between 'natural areas' is accomplished as a group adapts. Finally, individual differentiation is apparent, but how this takes place in detail is not sufficiently outlined.

Cultural and Natural Orders

A central problem in Park's discussion of cultural and natural orders, despite his intention to be more theoretically sophisticated than merely describing urban spatial patterns, is the exact relationship between the ecology–natural and social–cultural domains. There seems to be more than an analogy being used with plant ecology, a comparison which itself would be simplistic; it is unclear to what extent the 'natural' is the basis for the 'cultural'. This lack of rigour probably accounts for the frequent criticisms of Chicagoan theorisation of an ecological or environmental determinism. In accounting for social problems the explanation is displaced to the 'natural area' or the 'natural' – thus the critique of society is lessened while having the merit of not blaming the population involved (as was common in contemporary debates around immigration).

Human ecology appears to give a 'scientific' understanding rather than a moralistic one in pointing to an imbalance between the social and natural orders in certain locations. It also neatly avoided the idea that social progress was not possible since intervention was bound to fail: if social pathology was located at the level of the 'natural area' it was possible, as could be demonstrated, for new groups to move through such areas to others less 'natural'. Here cultural processes of social adjustment are apparent and a new basis of accommodation between groups. While competition between groups seemed fundamental to a new basis for social order, it was perhaps temporary, and a new stage of relationships would take place despite possible conflict. Thus, there was some optimism – even where conflict arose it could be an indication of adjustment in the relations between groups. In a parallel manner to James's 'moral equivalents' to conflict, a new social adjustment could be found. The basis of this view can be questioned; for example, Merton criticises such ideas when saying that it seems that culture is a veneer through which destructive outbreaks occur (crime, violence) unless 'social control' was strong enough (see Merton 1957). A difficulty also remained on just how natural areas were formed, and here there seemed some differences within Chicagoan researchers. Were such areas to be defined according to geographical location, symbiosis and competition, cultural characteristics, social interrelations, political activity or the social order?

Park regarded the city as 'the natural habitat of civilised man' while seeing it as an ecological, economic and geographical phenomenon with cultural features. More specifically, it could be studied in a manner which was comparable to the work of anthropologists by detailed observation of its various communities. Park stated that natural areas were 'not planned' but resulted from 'tendencies' which cities attempt to control and correct. For Park, the moral order was important – the daily strivings of groups in their work and community as great as laws or traditions as such. The city was a 'social laboratory' for the scientific study of how the ordering of individuals, groups and institutions is accomplished. A key focus was the 'natural area' – as a 'region' which does not arise from 'design' but has a natural history and a characteristic function (as in the case of the slum) of receiving migrant populations. The city is to some extent and sense a huge 'organism' or 'constellation' of natural areas which sifts and sorts the population so that individuals are fitted into the most appropriate milieu. However, there seemed to be some change in Park's idea of natural areas: he appeared to move between a spatial conception of 'natural' boundaries (such as transport routes) and a more social view – or at least natural areas as containing 'communities'. A community, in the latter view, was an organic unit with a quite clear structure and 'phases in life' (young to old) like other 'organisms' (groups, institutions). Each area becomes differentiated according to its features and populations, e.g. slum and rooming districts, bohemian localities and broader residential areas, as groups migrate.

While the definition of natural areas and how they are formed is not completely clear so there are, in fact, a variety of meanings of natural history in Chicagoan work (Turner 1967: xxiii). A natural history is a sequence or evolution in the establishment of a form, e.g. an institution such as a newspaper. It is also an underlying set of natural, unplanned forces, which produces a particular phenomenon, such as the slum *or* a series of stages that inevitably follow each other in a clear line. In addition, it can be a broader conception as sustaining in an integrative and dynamic process, a social order; for instance, racial conflict is one stage in a longer series of adjustments in the social equilibrium of social relations (see Turner 1967: xxiii–xxiv). Such adjustments between conflicting elements (e.g. classes, racial groups) may create forms of relationship or reciprocity which vary in length of time but, in Park's view, social processes are a continuous means of providing social equilibrium.

Park's idea of the natural history as a set of stages contains four connected elements: competition, conflict, accommodation and assimilation (see Turner 1967: xxxii–xxxiii). Competition rests rather more on an unnoticed biological struggle (and economic struggle) than on a social phenomenon relating to mere contact; it is a source of prejudice and feelings for others rather than a social interaction. Conflict is associated with social control and the outcome forms the individual's location in the social hierarchy. Accommodation relates to the mores and customs of society and its normal state of social organisation. Finally, assimilation is a term often misunderstood, as one group accepting the culture of another or a simple 'like-mindedness'. Instead, the term indicated that a new balance or 'working arrangement' was being produced between groups, alongside the development of new types of social organisation, following changes in the outlook of groups (see Turner 1967: xl).

Immigration and Race

A reason for studying immigration for Park was to examine group formation according to national sentiment and how new groups fit into a position in American society. The natural history model would seem at least initially to be a more convincing explanation of immigration in Chicago than a more narrow focus on immediate race relations, conflict and discrimination following the migration from the southern States. For instance, Park accounts for the rise of segregation due to the 'agitation' during the Reconstruction period, which divided the races on political grounds. His stress is on the separation in the personal and social relations between master and slave and the following seg-regation in churches, schools and other organisations. Park's intent appears to be the examination of the natural history model of accommodation and assim-ilation and the passing of conflict into another phase rather than an analysis of the domination of one group over another for advantage and the effects of racism. His overall view is of a 'bi-racial' society or parallel class structures, specific to the United States, within each race, including business, professional and working groups (see Park 1967: 169–84; Smith 1988: 123–7). Some dis-tance, it is argued, emerged between the races as the values of freedom began to replace 'habits of servitude' and 'instincts'. In Park's view racial prejudice was not due to some individual foible or unusual attitude but rather it was an example of a more general set of attitudes held and developed by groups undergoing change (Park 1967: 172). Thus, while social distances continued between the races there had been crucial shifts in the basis of accommodation – and hence the form of social distance. As Turner explains:

> In the simplest of terms, accommodation prevails when social distances are known and every man is in his place; conflict breaks out when the distances are ill defined or people abandon their assigned stations. Racial conflict is not so much the rela-tionship among individuals as it is among persons conscious of their racial identities. The upshot of racial conflict is readjustment in the distribution of status and power between the races, which is translated into accommodation temporarily by devices such as accepting an 'etiquette' of race relations. (Turner 1967: xxxv)

Park's natural history model is a compromise between Social Darwinism and a pragmatist optimism of James and Dewey: racial conflict may therefore be a new more progressive stage in race relations marking a new accommodation and a new social equilibrium. A couple of further points are worth noting here with regard to individuals: first, individuals are related through social distance; but while opinions (apologies, justifications) are individual, attitudes are col-lective and similar. Park also made a distinction between racial antagonism, which refers to the extent of social distance and racial prejudice, which placed people into categories within a position in the social order (see Park 1967: 171–3). Again, the intent is to show that 'antagonism' does not imply irrepara-ble opposition between groups but instead, a shift in a traditional order to a new arrangement, since the rise in conflict indicates change and progress. So, racial conflict and antagonism do not necessarily imply a rising level of preju-dice but instead may show 'progress' is taking place (Smith 1988: 126).

The idea of social distance can be placed alongside the notion of antagonism – in its concern not with conflict but with the nearness of relationships. It is not 'instinct' as such which can account for racial prejudice and false categorisa-tions, but the strangeness of others and the insecurity it produces. Thus, where the physical characteristics are more dissimilar then the assumption is even greater that there is a different set of moral standards. A concomitant to the notion of social distance is the marginal man – a figure to whom we attribute categories of difference (see Turner 1967: xxxix–xl). Park argued that the 'races no longer look up and down: they look across' (Park 1967: 184). For Smith, this 'rather romantic view of a South which Park had known best only through the eyes of the black elite was contrasted with the fate of northern migrants' (Smith 1988: 127).

Park, in his sceptical view of progress, placed much weight on the role of the newspaper in raising issues and seeking greater communication at times of tension and conflict in the urban environment. This social and practical research interest is not surprising given that he was an ex-newspaper journalist, a concern which is reflected in *The Immigrant Press and its Control* (1922) and other work (see Bulmer 1981). In addition, he exhibited a Deweyan view of culture as founded on communication and its role in sustaining a social group's solidarity during times of transition.

In summary, a central strand of Chicagoan sociology between Small, Thomas and Park is the influence of a general evolutionist view (derived from Spencer) of the set laws governing natural and social phenomena that could not be contradicted by intervention. But this is challenged by another influence which held that, by a step-by-step rational process of investigation, knowledge could be gained and then communicated. This tension is present in Park's view of the modification of natural order at the social level – as a social evolution, as progress. It can be seen in his treatment of race where inherited 'temperamental qualities' led to the selection of aspects of the cultural environment and the search for 'a vocation' in a particular spatial context. But where the 'inner core of significant attitudes and values' was 'modified by social experience' of the wider environment (Smith 1988: 125). Like Thomas, Park felt that social progress still brought corresponding difficulties.

Chicagoan Studies

While it can be debated whether the Chicagoan sociologists constituted a 'school' or merely a loose group of some kind there is no doubting the productivity of the researchers in the department during the 1920s and 1930s on urban phenomena. The formulation of ideas on human ecology and in the encouragement of fieldwork on social problems, the generation of data on social, political and other patterns in the city and the contacts with outside welfare and other bodies were part of the common programme of urban study. Park was joined by E.W. Burgess as a collaborator, and money for research was provided by private foundations and the SSRC. Between the mid-1920s and 1930s 40 major studies were published; early studies included Nels Anderson's *The Hobo* (1923), Thrasher's *The Gang* (1927), Cavan's *Suicide* (1928), and

Zorbaugh's *The Gold Coast and the Slum* (1929). In the next decade Cressey's *The Taxi Dance Hall* (1932), McKenzie's *The Metropolitan Community* (1933) and Reckless's *Vice in Chicago* (1933) and other major studies were published. As the human ecological framework to guide research was not fully developed these studies used the 'slum' or 'disorganised area' and other areas as a general setting for the collection of materials such as those obtained by ethnography. Park's articles 'Human Ecology' (1936) and 'Symbiosis and Socialization' (1939) were only published after his retirement. Interestingly, perhaps, these ecological ideas, especially the life history and natural history, could be also applied to the Chicago school as an institution.

Park's sociological writings and research were to a large extent influenced by a tendency towards the disciplines of history and anthropology (Turner 1967: xx). While he founded a major exploration of urban life and social conditions he also had a particular preference for personal documents in uncovering social meanings:

> The value of a human document as a datum is that it brings the object that is under investigation closer to the observer. Like a magnifying glass, it brings into view aspects of the object that were before that time not visible or only partially so. (Park 1967: 27)

Park, like Thomas, argued that personal documents were valuable in achieving insights into how groups such as an immigrant community adjusted to the new society:

> The more we understand the attitudes and personal histories of individuals, the more we can know the community in which these individuals live. On the other hand, the more knowledge we have of the milieu in which the individual lives, or has lived, the more intelligible his behavior becomes. (Park 1967: 11)

Following Park's contribution, the theoretical attention to 'urban experience' was furthered by Wirth in his article 'Urbanism as a Way of Life' (1938). According to Smith, Wirth gave a 'broadly pessimistic picture of modern tendencies', despite advances in 'utility and efficiency'. Urbanism brings major disadvantages since 'anomie was generated by the substitution of secondary for primary contacts, the weakening of kinship bonds, the decline of the family, the loss of the neighborhood, and the erosion of traditional bases of social solidarity' (Smith 1988: 163). Nevertheless, sociologists

> could make a major contribution towards protecting and developing liberal ideals and practices ... to make democracy workable in modern urban industrial societies; for example, through the fashioning of effective planning techniques. (Smith 1988: 166)

Case Study: W. I. Thomas and F. Znaniecki (1958) *The Polish Peasant in Europe and America*

Thomas and Znaniecki's massive, but often neglected 'classic' was originally published in five volumes in 1918–20 and was the first major empirical study completed within the Department of Sociology at Chicago (Bulmer 1983: 470). It was financed by private funds to examine immigrant problems and was influenced by Thomas's interest in various social reform activities. The study contained over 2,000 pages and examined an important contemporary problem – the issue of large-scale immigration at a time of increasing debate surrounding eugenics, race relations and national character. It was concerned to make clear that social problems of the immigrant group arose from the difficulties in adapting to the industrial urbanism and values of American life (Roberts, 2002: 43). A very wide variety of materials, including 700 family letters between America and Poland, newspaper accounts, and court, emigration, social work and other records were obtained to pursue different elements of immigrant communal experience. The difficulties faced by Polish immigrants were considered according to the pressures of social demoralisation on the one side and the adaptive formation of a Polish-American culture and organisations on the other. *The Polish Peasant* stimulated intense debates on the how interpretation and theorisation had taken place from the materials, the relative merits of statistical and case methods, and the validity and reliability of 'personal documents' (see Plummer 1983: 45–6; Roberts 2002: 43). Herbert Blumer, a follower of G. H. Mead (see Chapters 3–4) concluded in his well-known 'appraisal' in 1939 that it was unclear to what extent the theoretical contribution depended on previous work – nevertheless, the conceptual development of ideas such as attitudes and values were commended (Blumer 1969: 117–26). Since its publication and following subsequent editions many writers have recognized the high standing of the study in sociological research due to its contribution to sociology in terms of human action and experience – despite its interpretive problems (Bulmer 1983: 474; Coser 1977: 518).

  The Polish Peasant showed the need to examine both objective and subjective (individual meanings) of social life, as in the relationship between certain social personality types and major societal changes; i.e. the Philistine with an unchanging set of attitudes, the Bohemian open to new influences and the Creative Individual who matched an evolution of freedom with a co-operation needed by modern society. Also, immigrant groups had to redefine their position given their new situation since pre-existing habits were now threatened due to the crisis of the group. How individuals and groups perceived these changes was of especial importance since, as Thomas said in his famous dictum, 'If men define situations as real, they are real in their consequences.'

Critique

A number of criticisms have been made of the Chicago School. First is the view that they had an antipathy towards quantitative techniques. This charge is often levelled at Park in particular. In fact, while Park did advocate qualitative methods, the life history as the 'perfect method' and ethnography, his human ecological approach was an encouragement to the use of statistics as well as the collection of other material 'facts' on the urban environment. Park's attitude towards statistics was that they should not displace other forms of data; his preference was for methods that revealed the subjective aspects of individual and group life in the urban environment. In fact, Chicagoan sociology collected a wide variety of data and pioneered social statistics.

Chicagoan work has been criticised, especially in the late 1930s for its use of the 'analogy' made between plant life and habitats and social life in city areas. In addition, charges were made of the inadequacy of the ecological model and its 'environmental determinism': it seemed that individuals and groups were driven by conditions of living (e.g. housing) to behave in certain way, due to an associated 'ecological fallacy', that the conditions of a given area lead all people in it to act in the same way (see Taylor 1973: 122–31). Plainly, the human ecological framework was deficient as an understanding of group behaviour and social structure. In general terms, it was dropped by later area studies but the attempt to identify the characteristics of certain areas has remained (e.g. in relation to crime). There is less truth in the charges of environmental determinism and ecological fallacy if the notions of natural area are placed alongside the other emphasis on naturalism, the meanings individuals and groups give to behaviour, and the ethnographic stance taken. Chicagoan work, in fact, demonstrates the richness, variety and vibrancy of urban locales and influenced much later work on deviancy and other fields through the application of life-history and ethnographic methods (see Matza 1969). It is this legacy that fed into later 'Interactionism' (Fisher and Strauss 1979; see Chapter 4). The charge of determinism due to non-social (or even certain social) forces used in explanation could have been reduced had Park maintained a close focus on the social aspects of competition and conflicts in urban processes, e.g. in the social competition for housing and other resources between groups within and between areas (see Bulmer 1981). Thus, as in his more empirical work on race relations, such a sociocultural emphasis can be found, rather than on the social disorganisation of a natural area and more quantitative definitions of urban life (e.g. rates of crime and poverty) in other Chicagoan work.

The difficulty in Park's work is that the conceptualisation of ecology appears to be used in various ways to understand the cultural realm – as analogical, descriptive and also in an explanatory manner. The attempt to systemise its usage perhaps had the disadvantage of not making sufficient allowance for the 'subjective' definitions of the situation and of wider cultural meanings. Park's problem lies in attempting to resolve a dual inheritance. He seeks to explain conflict and social problems, social control and social diversity while believing in human sociability, communication and rationality; thus, potentially destructive forces are made to originate in the 'natural' but are shaped and find an outlet in social processes (Taylor, Walton and Young 1973: ch. 4; see Merton 1957). Park, in drawing upon Small, Ward, Thomas and Sumner, was also taking on certain polarities: 'pragmatism versus Social Darwinism, optimism versus pessimism, reason versus tradition, emancipatory individualism versus communal solidarity' (Smith, 1988: 123). For Coser:

> It would be exaggerated to claim that Park furnished a finished system of sociology. He never had such an intention. He was content instead to develop a series of general ideas and sensitizing concepts that could appropriately guide the empirical work of his students ... Park's theoretical ideas were persuasive enough to develop a Chicago-based 'school' of urban ethnography and human ecology that still inspires a great number of contemporary investigations. (Coser 1979: 317)

Finally, Chicagoan sociology has been described as 'liberal' or 'liberal reformist' (a progressivism) whose radical edge in its critique of society was founded on knowledge of social conflicts in the city and the deprivation and suffering of the poor urban dwellers prior to the First World War. C.W. Mills attacked the liberalism implicit in such a 'situational approach' which neglected structure and a related professional ideology that was based on dealing with one case at a time (as in social work) and so supported a fragmented approach to social problems. Mills had the view that personal problems are also public issues (Mills 1970a: 14–15: see also Mills 1970b, 1964). He described the current of 'liberal practicality' as follows:

> To detect practical problems is to make evaluations. Often what is taken by the liberally practical to be a 'problem' is whatever (1) deviates from middle-class, small-town ways of life, (2) is not in line with rural principles of stability and order, (3) is not in concurrence with the optimistic progressive slogans of 'cultural lag', and (4) does not conform with appropriate 'social progress'. But in many ways the nub of liberal practicality is revealed by (5) the notion of 'adjustment' and of its opposite, 'maladjustment'. (Mills 1970a: 102)

This tradition, according to Gouldner and other radical critics in the late 1960s and early 1970s, had become part of the American ruling class or imperialist project – a more conservative ideology which was being maintained by workers within the state (see Gouldner 1970; Smith 1988: 17). Increasingly, career self-interest in research and other academic activities had blunted any original political critique. However, for others, the broad range of interactionism, which includes the legacy of Chicagoan work, still has a critical, sceptical edge when investigating society while containing a range of views and sociological orientations. For some, views of Chicagoan sociology may at least partly reflect the orientation of the critic:

> It is striking that there are quite different versions of the history of Chicago ... They reveal how different versions of the past can be constructed in order to represent and justify subsequent interests. (Atkinson and Housley 2003: 18)

Conclusion

The work of Robert Park and his colleagues is most noted for the attention given to city life and urban spatial patterns. While this undoubtedly was the central empirical focus surrounding it there were a number of related themes important for micro social theory: a view of situated social relations and human nature as shown in the various themes of communication (e.g. the immigrant newspaper); ethnic and national identity; race relations; immigration and population change; crime and deviance and community study – the daily experience of urban life itself. Park and his associates, in my view, provided an inspiration for subsequent sociological work not merely because of the practical studies they undertook on pressing issues but because of the fascination and pursuit of sociological understanding of urban life. Madge gives an insightful summary of the Chicago School 'around 1930' and its legacy:

> For the first time a start was made in the more or less systematic study of deviant groups with mildly antisocial features, such as the hoboes and the taxi-dance hostesses. Perhaps the abiding fact about the Chicago series is that it is unified by its field of interest rather than by its methods. Probably more than with any other school of sociology, there is a distinctive quality in Park's creation in Chicago, with its determined concern with locality, its faith in human betterment, and an intrinsically American hatred of deviation and radicalism which cohabits strangely with the school's grasp of the wonderful richness and variety of human institutions. (Madge 1963: 125)

The contribution to micro social theory of Chicagoan work is an emphasis on interaction and communication in the understanding of social groups, using such ideas as social distance (as in the study of group relations), the meanings given in social situations and the ecology of the immediate social milieu. Chicagoan sociology formed a powerful element within interactionism (as defined by Fisher and Strauss 1979) due to the attempt to see an evolutionary notion of adaptation when understanding social life as more a social process, by drawing on Dewey and James. The Chicagoans also championed the life history and ethnographic work, which provided a lasting legacy in qualitative research (commonly associated with interactionist theory). Additionally, they developed the collection and interpretation of various kinds of official and private documents, including the gathering and development of family letters, organisational records, census and other material. Thus, they had an eclectic approach to the methods to be used in understanding social life, an open approach that is now gaining increasing favour in methodological discussion and practice.

While the ascendancy of the Chicago School was challenged in the late 1930s and appeared to be in decline, its legacy emerged strongly in the 1960s, especially in the field of deviance. It also continued as an influence on the study of community and urban processes, the media and race, and ethnic relations. The emphasis on cultural meanings, social processes and social interaction, personality and situation – evident in their small-scale empirical studies – became major strands in the development of 'interactionism'.

Further Reading

The Chicago School is not commonly discussed in recent textbooks on social theory. However, there have been a number of overviews of its work, which discuss its organisation, leading figures, research output and issues surrounding its studies: M. Bulmer, *The Chicago School of Sociology* (Chicago, University of Chicago Press, 1984); R. E. L. Faris, *Chicago Sociology 1920–1932* (Chicago, University of Chicago Press, 1967); J. Madge, *The Origins of Scientific Sociology* (London, Tavistock, 1963), chs. 3, 4; F. H. Matthews, *Quest for American Sociology* (Montreal, McGill-Queen's University Press, 1977); D. Smith, *The Chicago School: A Liberal Critique of Capitalism* (Basingstoke, Palgrave Macmillan, 1988); 'The Chicago School: The Tradition and the Legacy', Special Issue of *Urban Life*, 11(4) (January 1983).

A short introduction to Park's work can be found in E. C. Hughes, 'Robert E. Park', in T. Raison (ed.), *The Founding Fathers of Social Science* (Harmondsworth, Penguin, 1969), while short autobiographies by Park and Thomas are available: P. J. Baker (ed.), 'The Life Histories of W. I. Thomas and Robert E. Park', *American Journal of Sociology*, 79(2) (1973): 243–60. A good starting point for studying Park's work is R. E. Park, *On Social Control and Collective Behavior* (Chicago, University of Chicago Press, 1967): see also R. E. Park, *Human Communities* (Glencoe, IL, The Free Press, 1952); and R. E. Park and E. W. Burgess (eds.), *The City* (Chicago, University of Chicago Press, 1967). A collection of Chicagoan writings is to be found in J. F. Short, Jr. (ed.), *The Social Fabric of the Metropolis* (Chicago, University of Chicago Press, 1971).

3

Symbolic Interactionism 1
Origins

Introduction

An immediate issue in the consideration of symbolic interactionism is the question of definition. There is some confusion in the use of the term by both its adherents and commentators: sometimes 'symbolic interactionism' is called 'interactionism', or even (neo)Chicago School or tradition (see Fisher and Strauss 1979). For some, interactionism refers the later Chicago-influenced writers such as Howard Becker and Erving Goffman. But these figures lead us back to E.C. Hughes, and then Thomas and Park, with concerns (according to one view) for 'fieldwork, urban sociology, and defend-the-underdog sociology' which avoided 'macrostructural emphasis in favor of its microscopic interactional one' (Fisher and Strauss 1979: 457). For yet others, symbolic interactionism refers to the specific legacy set by the writings G. H. Mead and his interpreter Herbert Blumer. Thus, there seem to be 'at least two interactionist traditions' with rather different, but often confused, intellectual groundings (Fisher and Strauss 1979: 458). Here 'symbolic interactionism' will be used primarily to refer to the original work of G. H. Mead (while recognising the contribution of other 'pragmatist' writers) and his follower and interpreter, Herbert Blumer. This strand of thought, when joined with the work of Chicagoan sociological writers (Park, Thomas, Hughes and others), constitutes the twin 'pillars' of the broader theorisation of 'interactionism' (see Fisher and Strauss 1979; Atkinson and Housley 2003). The contribution of symbolic interactionism, in this chapter drawing from Mead, lies in an array of insightful concepts, including the self, the generalised other, and role and society, used for the study of micro social interaction.

This chapter outlines the origins, main ideas and 'perspective' of symbolic interactionism in the work of G. H. Mead, with particular attention to his ideas on mind, self and society, and the act and social interaction. Mead's 'social psychology' will be placed in the context of his pragmatic philosophy as also associated with such writers as Dewey and James.

30

Origins

Usually, the work of George Herbert Mead (1863–1931) is taken as the starting point of symbolic interactionism. Mead's work originates in two broad currents of thought. First, his pragmatist philosophy derives from the ideas developed by a number of writers, including John Dewey, C. S. Peirce, Chauncery Wright and William James, during the latter years of the nineteenth century. Here, in broad terms, is the view that intellectual effort is part of cultural community – a processual view of the individual's knowledge in relation to the meanings of others – so that knowledge becomes a common project. Secondly, there is the current of evolutionary theory, which was so strong in the human sciences in the late nineteenth and early twentieth centuries. For instance, Mead took evolutionary ideas on the change of species and applied them to the shifts brought about by social processes to human life. The usage was allied to a pragmatic view which allows the pragmatist 'to challenge mechanical conceptions of action and the world and to restate problems of autonomy, freedom, and innovation in evolutionary and social rather than mechanistic and individualistic terms' (Strauss 1964: xviii; Desmonde 1970). The outcome is a 'view that reason, or rationality, creates the world to claim or assume that the division between knower and known has been bridged – not just in the human sciences but also in the natural sciences' (Benton and Craib 2001: 87). Mead's pragmatic principles regarding the place of reason led him away from those who emphasise the 'non-rational' side of human conduct. He reworked Darwin's notion of gestures 'in the light of human communication; and biological evolution emerges in the topmost species as something new and different – a true emergent' (Strauss 1964: xviii). Mead was not so much concerned with the detail of evolutionary mechanisms but with the attempt to 'socialise' evolutionary ideas within a pragmatic view of action. Thus, the general ideas on species change found in Darwin were altered to understand how social processes modified social forms.

A central point in pragmatism is the connection between thought and action, and its relation to the formation of scientific knowledge. A particular concern was the nature of research practice of the scientific practitioner – how was social intervention to take place? Was there a point in social evolution where the application of knowledge could lead to social improvement? The pragmatist intention was to avoid the systemisation and outline of schemas derived from Social Darwinism (especially Spencerian ideas) and also the empiricism of routine fact-collecting and measurement. Instead, the pragmatist approach involved the understanding of adjustment to changes in the particular situation, with the careful consideration of problems, and seeking solutions. Thereby, aided by communication, change would occur gradually at the wider social level. There is a parallel here, for Mead, with the routine decisions made by the business leader or administrator. Experimental, incremental adjustment was envisaged, founded on a more lasting, 'progressive' approach than hasty major changes resting on little evidence:

> The scientist's attitude is that of a man in a going concern which requires at various points readjustments and reconstructions. The success of the readjustments and reconstructions is found in the triumph over the difficulty, as evidenced by the fact that the concern continues to operate. He finds his tests in the parts of the whole which still operate. (Mead 1964: 48–9)

In Mead's view the mind and social experience are involved in experimental science. Within the thought of the scientist engaged in experimental and other scientific work and in the operation of the mind generally, there is always the awareness of the existence of selves and minds of the community of colleagues and others. This is a different view from one that sees the collection of facts and formation of scientific ideas and important theoretical systems separate from a social context. For Mead, in his 'The Nature of Scientific Knowledge', theoretical systems are developing within social process in institutions – within the activities of scientists – and as part of the problems they try to understand rather than as a clash of systems (Mead 1964). There remained something of a social evolutionary model in Mead, the implications of which have not always been fully recognised – the pattern of succession of theoretical systems was being replaced itself. As society, mind and self altered, so did the content and form of social ideas. The progress of any thought reflected how social individuals considered themselves and the social relationships they participated in.

Mead's portrayal of society's social structure and social organisation is rather thin – there is a 'liberal pluralism' where class relations are differentiated or, further, are merely one of a number of types of relationships, such as buyer and seller, with some relations more important socially than others. According to Mead, each relationship is 'socially functional' and each individual a 'socially functional' member of a group. In the 'ideal society' a 'functional differentiation' would still exist according to individual abilities and tasks. However, through greater social participation, old ideological conflicts (and the social disruption they produced) would be overcome. Mead believed that the future 'ideal society' could be approached by a combination of the 'economic' aspects of society and the 'communal' features of religion:

> Those abstractions can be put together in a single community of the democratic type. As democracy now exists, there is not this development of communication so that individuals can put themselves into the attitudes of those whom they affect. (Mead 1967: 328)

In summary, within the work of Mead there is a 'liberal pragmatist' view and a thread of debate with 'Social Darwinism'. As Mills (1970b) argues, Social Darwinism and instinctivist psychology posed a problem for a liberal view since such approaches supported traditional forms of individualism. Instead, pragmatists 'wanted to give mind, rationality, a place in nature and in the psychology of human affairs; and they wanted to see human nature as modifiable through the reconstruction of the social "environment", hence the importance they attached to communication and "mass education" ' (Mills 1970b: 42).

What is 'Symbolic Interactionism'?

While not underestimating the contribution of Dewey, James and other pragmatists to symbolic interactionism, Mead's work is usually seen as the connecting link between pragmatist philosophy and social psychology and sociology. The connections were cemented by Mead's student and follower, Herbert Blumer, who was his leading interpreter. For Blumer, the symbolic interactionist approach sees a 'human society'

> as people engaged in living. Such living is a process of ongoing activity in which participants are developing lines of action in the multitudinous situations they encounter. They are caught up in a vast process of interaction ... in making indications to others of what to do and interpreting the indications as made by others. (Blumer 1969: 20)

Individuals are 'formed, sustained, weakened, and transformed in their interaction with one another' as they join together in different associations and positions (Blumer 1969: 21). According to Meltzer et al. (1975) (broadly using the term 'interactionism'), Dewey, Mead, Cooley and Thomas gave prominence to the 'group' as composed of individuals sharing ideas and as a source of individual interpretation and conditions of behaviour. Here was also a concern for the development of the personality and self, which included due attention to the biological aspects of individual motivation in acting (Meltzer et al. 1975: 48). A further factor is the use of the term 'symbolic behaviour'. This involved more than language; it included other forms of communication – 'it was only with reference to certain specific aspects of the theory that language was elevated to a primary position in the symbolic element, e.g. Mead on self-reflexiveness'. The symbolic interactionists developed the idea of society as composed by 'shared meanings'; its influence on early research was through the focus on interaction as 'a crucial link between the individual and the social group' and 'in the adoption of the method of sympathetic introspection' (Meltzer et al. 1975: 50–1). Thus, there are a number of related processes: the construction of the self, its interrelation with the surrounding social setting – including the notion of social negotiation in the production of reality, and the mutual construction of meaning between social worlds – and the overall construction of society as a symbolic community.

Symbolic interactionist 'sociologies' can be seen as combining three related themes (Plummer 1991a: x–xi). First, 'that distinctly human worlds are not only material and objective but also immensely symbolic'. Unlike animals, human beings employ their 'elaborate symbol-producing capacity which enables them to produce a history, a culture and very intricate webs of communication'. Although we routinely create ' "accounts" to explain our actions and lives', we produce 'shared meanings' which 'are always open to reappraisal and further adjustment'. Second is the idea of 'process': 'Lives, situations and even societies are always and everywhere evolving, adjusting, emerging, becoming.' Hence, in this perspective, there is a 'focus upon the strategies of acquiring a sense of self, of developing a biography, of adjusting to others'. Finally, there is a focus on 'interaction' – rather than attention to self or society there is a concern 'with the joint acts through which lives are organized and societies assembled'. In short, as Plummer says, there is 'behind symbolic interactionist sociologies a pervasive imagery – of symbol, process and interaction' (Plummer 1991a: x–xi). Symbolic interactionism appears to have several characteristics: the formation and exchange of meanings; an emphasis on social process and the interrelation between individual and group; the social construction of social structure rather than as merely externally imposed; and a dedication to 'subjective' or 'naturalistic' methods of research practice.

For symbolic interactionists it is through interaction that meanings are negotiated in defining the social world. People act according to the meanings they have and as formed in the continuing interaction with others, which in turn informs new interaction. It is, therefore, the researcher's task to study such processes and meaning. In summary, symbolic interactionism constructs a particular sense of rationality, derived from its pragmatist roots:

> Pragmatism draws neither explicitly on the common-sense notion of means-end rationality of Max Weber nor on the more rigorous conception of rational choice theory, but talks more about the different rationalities that exist in different situations. There are many different means-end chains, varying from situation to situation ... the meanings and relations can be understood in the context of pursuing practical purposes in the world. (Benton and Craib 2001: 87–8)

George Herbert Mead – His Philosophy and Social Psychology

George Herbert Mead was a colleague of Dewey's at Michigan and Chicago, and he studied under Royce and in Germany. He was familiar with Cooley's idea of the looking-glass self. Mead was influenced by the experimental psychologist Wilhelm Wundt and a number of his ideas, although modified, appear prominently in his work (Deegan 2001: xxvi–xxxi). During his life his influence was through students taking courses on social psychology and philosophy and through various writings and articles in the fields of reform and education (see Deegan 2001). He has had a wide influence within sociology and some areas of social psychology; particularly from the 1960s onwards, he was read by sociologists in the fields of deviance and studying smaller institutional settings seeking to explore the formation and interchange of meanings, e.g. the giving and acceptance of 'labels' in welfare, education or policing. The work of Goffman on the 'presentation of self' (see Chapter 5) can be seen as a further 'instrumental' twist where individuals actively present themselves to others to 'manage impressions' rather than having an essential self (Benton and Craib 2001: 87).

For Mead, social psychology is the discipline that 'studies the activity or behavior of the individual as it lies within the social process; the behavior of an individual can be understood only in terms of the behavior of the whole social group of which he is a member' (Mead 1967: 6). Mead was intent to dispel individualistic theories that see an individual's experience as prior and forming social processes. Instead, the experiencing individual (in mind and self) must be seen as within a pre-existing society and part of social processes.

The Self, Mind and Society

A central concern in Mead's work is to find a middle path, to replace longstanding polarities by positing a dynamic set of relations – the individual as in relation with others and also related to the natural or biological. The individual's action is shaped by and, in turn, shapes society while subject to and channelling biological elements of nature. In this way, Mead sought to avoid theories that conceived the individual as determined by internal or external forces while portraying the individual as creative and an active social participant. He places particular emphasis on the 'mind' and 'reflexivity'. The mind is realised in the social process as part of the experience of individuals as he or she takes the attitude of the other (towards him or herself). There is an adjustment to the social process as the individual operates reflexively and thereby develops the mind (Mead 1967: 134). Individuals are able to take the role of others within action – to understand the view of another individual and change their actions in relation to how others may respond. Individuals have the ability to produce and respond to 'significant symbols' in communication. Through reflection or inner conversation thought takes place which prepares for the act in the social process involving others. In developing his own ideas on the self Mead was taking account of, while criticising, different traditions:

> Mead made three types of criticisms of the previous theories of the self: (1) either they presupposed the mind as antecedently existing to account for mental phenomena (Wundt); (2) or they failed to account for specifically mental phenomena (Watson); and (3) they failed to isolate the mechanism by which mind and the self appeared (James and Dewey). (Martindale 1961: 354)

Mead's starting point was the dynamic social process containing social acts; from this basis he attempted to overcome the 'mentalism of the introspectionists' and the limitations of Watsonian behaviourism (Martindale 1961: 354). In short, the restrictive dualism of 'mind' and physical being – found in previous theoretical 'subjectivism' and 'objectivism' – had to be overcome. Individuals could perceive themselves as objects and, through symbolic communication, particularly language, could respond to and anticipate others. Similarly, Mead developed the idea of 'attitudes' as both 'introspective states and the starting point of the act' (Martindale 1961: 355). Symbolic communication, particularly through vocal language, was centrally important. Where a gesture produces the same idea in the giver and receiver then a 'significant symbol' is present. The individual is able to take the 'attitude of the other' in his or her gestures. This is a conversation of significant gestures, which is prepared for 'internally' and takes place externally with others through the operation of the 'mind' in thought. Thus, the 'mind' is formed within a social process in the communication of gestures as significant symbols (Mead 1967: 47, 50).

For Mead, the self has a development – it forms within the 'process of social experience and activity' with others rather than being given at birth. However, in 'habitual action', like in the intelligence of lower forms of animal life, there is not a self, since no thinking is required as we merely adjust; it is not necessary for it to be organised within the self. The body 'can be there and can operate in a very intelligent fashion without there being a self involved in the experience. The self has the characteristic that it is an object to itself' (Mead 1967: 136). There are two stages in the self's full development. First, the self is formed by the organisations of certain attitudes towards him or herself through taking part in social acts, and secondly, by the organisation of the general social attitudes of the social group (or generalised other) (Mead 1967: 158):

> the individual's self is constituted simply by an organization of the particular attitudes of other individuals toward himself and toward one another in the specific social acts in which he participates with them ... at the second stage ... [the] ... self is constituted not only by an organization of these particular individual attitudes, but also by an organization of the social attitudes of the generalized other or the social group as a whole to which he belongs. (Mead 1967: 158)

Mead's emphasis is on the self as reflexive, as both subject and object, an object basically different from other objects. Intelligent rational conduct has to involve the individual taking an 'objective, non-affective attitude toward itself' – to become an object (Mead 1967: 137–8). He states that the origins of the thinking, reflective self are social: the self is 'cognitive' and its formation can be found in the internalised 'conversation of gestures' with oneself and others. Hence, Mead argues that the individual enters into experience of self 'only in so far as he first becomes an object to himself just as other individuals are objects to him or are in his experience'. Individuals become an object to them-selves by specifically taking the attitudes of others towards themselves within a shared context and experience (Mead 1967: 138).

A tension may be seen in Mead's discussion of the self between Social Darwinist and pragmatist influences – a pull between (biological) individuality and rationality. For Mills, Mead attempts to overcome this conceptual tension between the 'I' of a 'liberal' individual and the 'me' of sociologised conscience (Mills 1970b: 42, fn). Put rather differently (and simply), the self is poised between an evolutionary notion of the creative, open, spontaneous, but poten-tially conflictual, individual and group action and an 'instrumental rationality' which attempts both practical and progressive social outcomes:

> There is a limited resemblance here to the instrumentalism espoused by positivists, who have problems with the status of 'theoretical' entities that cannot be seen or measured. Such concepts are seen as useful fictions which enable us to achieve our purpose and organize our perceptions and knowledge. (Benton and Craib 2001:86)

In Mead's view, the individual has a self in relation to the selves of other group members, reflecting and expressing their broad outlook and behaviour. Even so, he also recognises that the self is not static or merely 'singular' but we have creative and multiple selves – according to social experience and setting, a dif-ferent self is apparent.

'I' and 'Me'

James's work on the self was a starting point for Mead's own discussion of the 'I' and the 'Me'. For Mead, the self has two identifiable parts or phases with-out which there would be no 'novelty' in experience or 'conscious rationality':

> the 'I' is always something different from what the situation itself calls for. So there is always that distinction, if you like, between the 'I' and the 'me'. The 'I' both calls out the 'me' and responds to it. Taken together they constitute a personality as it appears in social experience. (Mead 1967: 178)

The self is more than a mere organisation of social attitudes. The 'I' responds to the 'me' of the organised set of attitudes of others at the same time the 'me' reflects the 'I' – in this way Mead seeks to show the dynamic relation between the organic basis of the 'I' and the social as in the 'me'. Thus, there is a recog-nition of the 'organic' 'side' of the self which is often underplayed by inter-preters but is very much part of its dynamic or internal conversation. The 'I' is 'biologic', unpredictable, uncertain, creative and impulsive; it exists and responds in the immediate 'specious present', so we are only aware of it in 'memory image'. It is 'never entirely calculable'; only after experience is the individual aware of it since its response is uncertain rather than premeditated (Mead 1967: 175–6):

> The 'I' is a manifestation of human natural needs; it, or the energy behind it, is 'deeply embedded' in man's human biological nature. That is why Mead calls it the 'biologic I'... in a state of tension with social 'me.'... once minds and selves emerged, the two processes became interdependent. (Zeitlin 1973: 228, 230).

Mead uses the idea of 'impulse' rather than 'instinct' to allow for a more dynamic conception of the reflexive self – shaping impulses and guiding the 'I' through reflection and towards rational, conscious action. Thus, human beings are not simply driven by instincts (e.g. for food, shelter, sex) – or merely socially formed according to the one-way attitudes of others. Human action involves social situations in which individuals engage in reflection; he 'perceives a definite tension between individual, biological man and civilization' (Zeitlin 1973: 230). Mead says that the 'content' of self can be considered as 'selfish' (or the basis of 'selfishness'), but its 'structure' is social. He adds that when there is conflict due to different 'impulses' a resolution is made by the 'rational side' of the self (Mead 1967: 230, fn).

Mead portrays the self as acting with reference to others and immediate objects and as reintegrating them in memory. The activities of others bring a response in the individual, but there is also the other aspect of the 'me' – the reflective self – that is, evaluating and contemplating responses.

Play and Game

'Role-taking' is intimately involved in the formation of the self. Through play the child can take on various roles, such as parent, doctor or teacher, as experiences in the creation of the self. The child interrelates with significant others, for instance, in the family; in 'playing at' there is the operation of an imaginative consciousness which can prepare for different lines of action. Mead argues that a game differs crucially from play in that in the former the child must have taken the attitude of other players engaged in the same activity. Here, he is referring to the attitudes of the 'generalised other' of the organised group, which contributes to the individual's 'unity' of self. The 'team', and its activity as the generalised other, enters into the experience and thinking of the various members engaged in the social process and influences or exercises control over their behaviour. A result is the sharing of a common set of social meanings through organising the attitudes of group members into the pattern of attitudes of the generalised other.

It is also only by reflection and thinking that a variety of actions can be contemplated, future responses anticipated and action taken. Through 'abstract' thought the individual is able to take the attitude of the generalised other towards him or her self; whilst in 'concrete thought' it is taken as expressed by others towards him/herself with whom he or she is involved in a particular situation (Mead 1967: 155–6).

Role

Role and role-taking have an important position in Mead's work, which allowed for the connection between the personality and social group or community. The child within the 'game', as Morris says, has 'not merely assumed the role of a specific other, but of any other participating in the common activity; he has generalized the attitude of role-taking' (Morris 1967: xxiv). Here, Mead is exploring how individuals assess their own impulses and interests and the view of the group. It is through the processes of thought and reflection that seeing different ways forward solves problems faced in action. Although Mead has a cognitive, rational, instrumental view of action, it is far from simple, since he challenges the notion that individuals simply respond to outside stimuli from the surrounding world or preceding events, while positing a consciousness that is reflective and active in shaping action and the future (Zeitlin 1973: 236, 240–1). Mead says we have a sense of different possibilities owing to the differing relationships that we have with various people. Not only are there changes between how we are to different people but there are aspects of self that are merely there to relate to it. In short, we have separate selves according to shifting 'social reactions'; the 'appearance of the self' is a result of its place in the particular social process (Mead 1967: 142).

Individuals have various selves while maintaining some continuity. The self is formed in part by 'taking the role of others' – the conceiving of oneself through others' expectations, attitudes and their responses through symbolic communication (language and gestures) with both 'significant' and 'generalised others'. Within role-taking there is a sharing of significant symbols relating to a mutual experience; in this way, a degree of the society or social group is ingested by the individual through each interaction with others. The 'generalized social attitudes' make possible an organized self.

Society

For Mead, there are similar situations and associated common responses, which are combined to form the community or institutions. He says 'the institutions of society are organized forms of group or social activity – forms so organized that the individual members of society can act adequately and socially by taking the attitudes of others toward these activities' (Mead 1967: 261–2). In the full development of the self it is not enough for the individual to take the attitudes of others towards him/herself and to each other into the individual experience. The others' attitudes towards the organised society and differing social projects also must be taken in. It is through the operation of the generalised other that the community controls the behaviour and thinking of individual members of the community (Mead 1967: 155).

Mead's ideas on social structure are limited but he does describe two kinds of 'socially functional classes or subgroups' to which individuals belong. First, there are 'concrete social classes or subgroups' (e.g. political parties, clubs, corporations) which he regards as 'functional social units' where individuals are directly related to each other. Secondly, there are 'abstract social classes or subgroups' (e.g. debtors, creditors) to which individuals are less directly connected but which may carry possibilities for 'enriching' social relations between all the members of the whole, unified society (Mead 1967: 157).

Case Study: Time

Mead's philosophical work has been relatively ignored; it is his 'social psychological' writings which have been more apparent as within social psychology and sociology. But his work, including his social psychology, I would argue, can only be fully understood by putting it in this wider philosophical context. For example, a long neglected area has been Mead's work on time – our conceptions of the past, the present and the future. Recently, there has been an increasing interest in time in sociology and, in particular, Mead's work on the topic (see Adam 1990, 1995; Roberts 2002: 82–4; Mead 1932, 1964: 328–41). His emphasis is on the present or 'emergent event': the past is not recoverable 'as it was', it is not a view of the past as recoverable, but as a continuous construction through the present experience (see Adam 1990; Maines et al. 1983; Flaherty and Fine 2001). Thus, the past only influences as it is rewritten and selected according to the present, where the future is also coming about. As Mead says: 'The assurances which we give to a remembered occurrence come from the structures with which they accord' (Mead 1929: 237).

> Mead's theory of time conceived of the past and the future as expansions out of the present, rather than the common conception of a sequence proceeding from the past, to the present, to the future. The reconstruction of the past and the anticipation of the future arise from the same foundation, the reality of the present. The past, therefore, is not a fixed condition of a structured time period, but will vary in accordance with any particular present. (Petras 1968: 12–13)

In Mead's notion of time, even if we were able to collect all the information about a life or past event, the 'truth' would remain in the present. A later present would remake it through its 'emergent nature' (Petras 1968: 13). As Adam remarks, the 'reality' for Mead rests in the present: 'The present implies a past and a future, but they are denied existence. Any reality that transcends the present, he argues, must exhibit itself in the present' (Adam, 1990: 38).

A rather different, and generally overlooked, aspect of Mead's analysis of the past is his insightful linking of the changes in philosophical ideas with the historical development of the self (see Martindale 1961: 359). His ideas on the self came at a time of increasing psychological, anthropological and 'popular' interest in the inner workings of the individual personality. For Mead the self was becoming more 'social' or, to put it rather better, increasingly able to take the role of the other and act towards lasting social betterment due to increased social knowledge (see Maines et al. 1983). The discussion of time has become an important sub-area in social theory, with Mead's work a key reference for an understanding of how individuals perceive experiences of the past and present and act according to an anticipated future.

The Influence of Mead's Work

Mead's influence was relatively limited during his life to his students and some colleagues, such as John Dewey, at the University of Chicago. However, due to the dominance of Chicago sociology and the expansion of the discipline these students spread Mead's conceptualisation across the United States, thereby establishing his reputation and influence. In 1894 Mead, at the age of 31, was enlisted to the Department of Philosophy by John Dewey; but 'sociologists were soon learning social psychology from him':

> Mead's major impact on sociologists ... began in the 1920s when his advanced social psychology course became very popular. E. Faris, of the sociology department, also taught social psychology, an amalgam of his own views plus those of Dewey and Mead. Mead died in 1931, but Faris and Herbert Blumer continued the Meadian-inspired tradition. (Fisher and Strauss 1979: 459)

Blumer, as Fisher and Strauss point out, was also influenced by the Park–Thomas tradition of sociology. Along with Everett Hughes, Blumer passed both the Meadian and Park–Thomas legacy to an impressive range of students. These included Becker, Freidson, Klapp, Lindesmith, Davis, Goffman, Gusfield, Rose, Stone, Strauss and Turner, who were to make major contributions to areas such as deviancy, race, urban studies, collective behaviour, occupations and social interaction. They spread the interactionist legacy across the expanding number of departments of sociology in the United States, so much that it was 'no longer associated closely with Chicago itself' (Fisher and Strauss 1979: 460).

A key to this process of dissemination was the work of a number of students, such as Herbert Blumer, who used Mead's work to challenge existing forms of abstract conceptualisation divorced from the lives of individuals and the predominance of quantitative methods and behaviouristic accounts of individual action. As Joas states, the 'rich sociological research tradition' set by Blumer and others instead 'emphasized the openness of social structures, the creativity of social actors and the need for interpretation of the data of social science' (Joas 2003: 96). While only part of Mead's work, at least until more recently, was used in sociological theory, today his ideas have been considered by conflict sociologists, feminist sociologists, phenomenologists and others, indicating that he has gained a 'classic' status as a reference point for sociologists of many viewpoints (see Joas 2003: 96–7). In a wider context, given the inclusion of symbolic interactionism within interactionism, and the latter's pervasive presence, some have considered whether we are 'all interactionists now' in sociology (Atkinson and Housley 2003: 144–75). Such a view, obviously, needs to be considered with some caution according to the depth of influence in theorisation and research practice. An immediate problem with identifying the influence of Mead in particular on subsequent work is the actual meaning of symbolic interactionism. A symbolic interactionist approach to its own development, as Plummer points out, would highlight its changing meaning, shifting descriptions of its origins, the debates about its development, and so on (see Plummer 1991a, 1991b). There is also the issue of 'reading' Mead since much debate has also flourished on the 'authenticity' of the accounts and development of his ideas by his interpreters such as Blumer.

Another question is whether Mead is the founder of 'symbolic interactionism' or more widely 'interactionism', since there is the increasing recognition of the broader 'legacy' of pragmatism – as an influence on both Mead and later writers. So, for some, the work of Peirce, James and Dewey and others has to be taken into account. Within 'interactionism' there is the additional legacy of the Chicagoan sociology of Thomas and Znaniecki, Park and others – alongside anthropological theory and fieldwork methods (through Thomas), and Simmel's 'formalism' (through Park). A range of subsequent approaches including phenomenology, ethnomethodology (and conversational analysis), feminist thought and varieties of cultural studies and postmodern ideas could also be added to the diverse 'tradition' of interactionism (see Plummer 1991b; Denzin 1992, 2001; Meltzer et al. 1975; Atkinson and Housley 2003). Plummer, in attempting to find a common thread in 'interactionism', concluded that there is a certain odd unity in its impatience with traditional philosophical polarities, for instance between freedom and constraint, or holding a scientific approach while leaning towards reformism. Interactionism, broadly in origin, was not based so much on an attempt to pursue abstract issues but rather on a practical, contextual, 'progressive' approach to acting 'lived' experience (see Plummer 1991a: xiv).

Returning to 'symbolic interactionism', we can say that it is at base 'an interpretative approach' which has an underlying 'notion of instrumental rationality' shaping research practice and the view of the individual and social intervention or reform derived generally from the versions of pragmatism found in Peirce, James and Dewey. While subsequent symbolic interactionism has developed from these bases, it has also changed in emphasis (for example, losing its immediate connection or debate with evolutionary thought). But in assessing its core assumptions and deeper influence, these foundations in pragmatism and evolutionary thought should be made visible. It is also important in assessing the influence of symbolic interactionism to provide an historical context. For Meltzer et al., writing in the 1970s, its role in the formation and development of the idea of the 'group' and its questioning of the notion of instincts as motivating behaviour in the discipline had largely been forgotten (Meltzer et al. 1975: 52). Rather, the focus had been on the testing of the concepts of self, identity and role. They added that a 'resurgence of interest' in the theory had taken place due to a rise in interest in 'self-psychology' and 'identity', the recent development of role theory, and the use of 'reference group' in empirical research. But they argued that the revival might be more closely attributable to the development of 'ethnomethodology and dramaturgical sociology' (Meltzer et al. 1975: 52). However, today – after a period when symbolic interactionism seemed (at least for some) to be in decline – there appears to be some revival in its theorisation and interests (see Chapter 4).

Critique

There are a number of common criticisms of Mead's 'social psychology'. First, the rather different emphases and interpretations of his work appear to be due to some difficulty in understanding the meaning of his ideas, attributable to a lack of clarity in the definitions of key terms – and the rather piecemeal statements of his ideas. Secondly, because of the rather instrumental or cognitive view of the individual and action there are certain important gaps in his discussions. For example, as Meltzer et al. point out there is insufficient attention to the 'emotional and unconscious elements in human conduct' (Meltzer et al. 1975: 84). Part of the difficulty in appraising Mead and his legacy, of course, is that his ideas were not presented in a systematic way and posthumously published from notes. Also, the problems in 'reading' Mead are compounded by the need for extended empirical examples – and some methodological statements. Even though symbolic interactionism has led to a massive amount of research, in Mead's own writings there are 'no clear-cut prescriptions of either general procedures or specific techniques for enhancing its researchability' (Meltzer et al. 1975: 84). A more general question has also been asked of 'symbolic interactionism' concerning whether it is a 'theory' with testable propositions rather than perhaps a 'perspective' – a way of looking at the world according to certain ideas or assumptions. Yet, it can be said that, in 'rooting thought in communicative interaction and locating the self as an emergent in ongoing transactions between the person and the community, Mead prepared the ground for investigations of the concrete sociological links between social and thought processes' (Coser 1977: 311).

Conclusion

While there are difficulties in pinning down the exact or consistent meaning of many of the central ideas in Mead's work, his contribution to micro social theory has been very substantial. He was able to include the subjective understandings of individuals within social action and processes and in doing so, interconnect the individual and society. For Joas, 'Mead's grasp of the unity of individuation and socialization defines his place in the history of sociology' (Joas 2003: 96). In part, his contribution was an historical one – of its time in changing the assumptions of social theory – but his micro social theorisation is still relevant and referred to since he was inquiring into central issues within social psychology and sociology. He provided a view of the individual self within its social setting – including time and space, elements that have been generally neglected (until recently). As Meltzer et al. state:

> The primary function of Mead's philosophy was to provide a context within which the nature of self was bounded by time, as well as by space. The role of the future, in addition to the past, was recognized as an important variable in the motivation of behavior. With this idea, Mead added to the pragmatic notion that motivational elements are dependent upon societal as well as individual variables. The presence in two systems made men and women both determined and determiners. (Meltzer et al. 1975: 41–2)

It has been unfortunate that the main focus of attention on Mead has been on the self and its development within the micro situation, without considering sufficiently its wider societal and sociohistorical context and placing it within his broader social philosophy. Thus, in Mead's discussion, the self is not merely 'located' in the immediate micro social interaction; what has been much less observed is how the conception 'reaches out' to other, macro societal and historical contexts. The simple depiction of Mead's idea of the self as a 'social construction' has masked the fact that it can be understood at the micro and as related to macro levels.

Further Reading

The most commonly cited of Mead's books in sociology are: *On Social Psychology* (Chicago, University of Chicago Press, 1964) and *Mind, Self and Society* (Chicago, University of Chicago Press, 1967). Increasing attention is now being paid to his other, but much less available, more philosophical books: *The Philosophy of the Present* (La Salle, IL, Open Court, 1932); *Movements of Thought in the Nineteenth Century* (Chicago, University of Chicago Press, 1936); and *The Philosophy of the Act* (Chicago, University of Chicago Press, 1938). See also H. Joas, *G. H. Mead: A Contemporary*

Re-examination of His Thought (Cambridge, Polity, 1985); G. H. Mead, *Essays in Social Psychology*, ed. M. J. Deegan (London, Transaction Books, 2001) and H. Blumer, *George Herbert Mead and Human Conduct*, ed. and intro. T. J. Morrione and T. Morrione (Walnut Creek, CA, AltaMira, 2003). K. Plummer (ed.), *Symbolic Interactionism* (2 vols., London, Edward Elgar, 1991) provides key articles with excellent introductions to the foundation and development of the approach. A further overview is provided by P. Rock, *The Making of Symbolic Interactionism* (Basingstoke, Macmillan, 1979).

4
Symbolic Interactionism 2
Developments

Introduction

This chapter examines the development and diversity of symbolic interactionism with particular reference to the work of Herbert Blumer, its contributions in certain substantive areas, and methods and methodological issues. In addition, it notes the critiques of symbolic interactionism, and interactionism more broadly, and the various recent developments and reassessments of its origins. Symbolic interactionism, while initially (particularly through Blumer's work) very much grounded in the concepts of G. H. Mead, has witnessed a series of influences both from other theoretical developments in micro social theory as well as a 'rediscovery' of the wider tradition of pragmatism. The criticisms of symbolic interactionism have also had an influence on its recent development – as it has turned to discuss a number of overlooked areas and theoretical and methodological difficulties. Its contribution to micro social theorisation has been very extensive, in particular on the discussion of social contexts – the meanings given to social situations, the 'settings' of social interaction (for instance, deviancy and social organisations), and the exploration of the nature of social interaction itself.

The Development of Symbolic Interactionism

The issue of terminology again needs to be emphasised. To restate (from Chapter 3), 'interactionism' can be considered to be a wider body of theory than 'symbolic interactionism', including some but not all of the theory and methods undertaken during the 1920s and 1930s by Chicago sociologists (Atkinson and Housley 2003: 2). Thus, interactionism, following Fisher and Strauss (1979), has within it parallel but related traditions derived from some Chicago sociology and from the 'symbolic interactionism' of G. H. Mead (and his interpreter, Herbert Blumer). There has also been considerable debate regarding whether there is a unifying pragmatist inheritance within and between these strands, centred on the differences between Mead, Dewey and other pragmatists and the differences between Park, Thomas and Mead, and so on. For instance, Atkinson and Housley (2003) argue that in the development of Chicago sociology, it was Georg Simmel (rather than Mead) who was particularly important. In this view, it was not until after the Second World War, with the emergence of a 'new' Chicago School and the setting out of varieties of interaction, after Blumer's writings, that Mead became particularly important within sociological study. In fact, Blumer was influenced by both Meadian social psychology and Thomas and Park's version of interactionism (Atkinson and Housley 2003: 8). Thus, it seems, there are ample grounds for confusion over the term 'interactionism'. As noted by Atkinson and Housley, it has been seen more specifically as 'symbolic interactionism' including a number of key figures (e.g. Mead, Cooley and Blumer). It has been applied to the micro sociological study of social interaction and social encounters, such as face-to-face interaction (Goffman). Finally, it has also been used to describe or include the tradition from Chicago sociology which investigates urban life, deviancy and deviant careers, and ethnographic study of work and occupations (Becker and Hughes) (Atkinson and Housley 2003: 37).

Here we will take a 'simple' path, as before, and see two related traditions – symbolic interactionism and Chicago sociology – as constituting 'interactionism', while noting the broader influence of pragmatism and the connections with a range of other (often more recent) theoretical developments. Of course, within these two 'traditions' it can be argued that some writers are more important than others, for example, perhaps regarding Becker and Hughes as more influential today than Park and Thomas. Others may 'reinvent' the traditions by returning to their origins, for example, a later focus in symbolic interactionism has been towards pragmatist writers such as William James and Charles Peirce. In part, as new theoretical and substantive interests emerge, so the work of the 'founders' is being re-examined and reappraised. This review of founding pragmatist writings has included the work of Mead, particularly his more philosophical writings and subjects such as 'time' (see Chapter 3).

Herbert Blumer's Symbolic Interactionism

'Symbolic interactionism' was a term coined by Herbert Blumer (1900–87) in 1937 (Blumer 1969: 1). It was Blumer who was also mainly responsible for making Mead's ideas more available through his guides to a number of key ideas in several articles (see Blumer 1966, 1969). Blumer was a PhD student at Chicago and, therefore, well acquainted with its study of urban life and cultural groups. After some years of teaching there he moved to the University of California in the early 1950s. Blumer is a key bridge between Chicagoan sociological urban study and the social psychology of Mead. While not a particularly prolific author and researcher, he did engage in much empirical study and made very important theoretical and methodological contributions, other than his work on Mead, particularly on the nature of conceptualisation and the critique of traditional methodology.

Blumer's work, as Mead's, can be placed in the pragmatist tradition of Dewey, James and others. For Blumer, 'symbolic interactionism' refers to the particular and distinctive features of interaction which take place between human beings. Individuals do not react according to a simple stimulus but provide and reconsider meaning to objects in their social situation. A consideration of symbolic interaction thus involves the notion that individuals' action is constructed and not a mere release, that individuals have selves and can refer to themselves, and that group action is an outcome of the bringing together of individuals' interpretations of each other and the group. Blumer is a key figure in the 'pragmatic turn' which advocated methods focused on locating analysis in everyday experience of situations (Plummer 1998: 89). Here, he was following pragmatism's distaste for abstract theorisation and sterile 'dualistic' philosophical distinctions (e.g. subject/object) and advocating a more practical approach to the study of grounded events and experience. He argued that symbolic interactionism formed the basis of a philosophy with a 'strong humanistic cast' which was particularly appropriate for the understanding of social experience through its central focus on the 'self' as it arises in taking the roles of others (Blumer 1969: 21, fn).

Blumer's 'classic' article, 'What Is Wrong with Social Theory?' (1954), observed that traditional social theory was divorced from the empirical world (see Blumer 1969). It commonly developed by referring to itself and by an easy borrowing of theorisation from other fields. It related to the world by interpreting it in its own image. For Blumer, traditional social theory is clearly inadequate in guiding research and does not appear to benefit much from the massive collection of 'facts' that arise from empirical work. Faced with these problems, he says there are two possibilities. First, 'to develop precise and fixed procedures that will yield a stable and definitive empirical content'. The intention 'is to return to the natural social world with definitive concepts based on precisely specified procedures', and secondly, to accept 'our concepts as being intrinsically sensitizing and not definitive' (Blumer 1954: 9). It is this second response which is closer to Blumer's own approach, since it 'seeks to improve concepts by naturalistic research, that is by direct study of our natural social world, wherein empirical instances are accepted in their concrete and distinctive form'. Rather than apply 'quick statements or technical instruments' to construct 'definitive concepts' it 'depends on faithful reportorial depiction of the instances and on analytical probing into their character'. The success of the approach relies 'on patient, careful and imaginative life study' and has the 'virtue of remaining in close and continuing relations with the natural social world' (Blumer 1954: 9–10).

The core assumptions and methods of quantitative research, such as the survey, and dominant types of theorisation found within sociology – were challenged by Blumer. Such procedures and conceptualisation drew concepts away from practical contexts and the meaning given by individuals to their setting. He thus advocated that empirical study should begin with the actions of social groups rather than a conception of individuals as merely conforming to the restraint of structures; in his view, individuals take part in interaction with others according to continuing experience (Blumer 1969: 6). Blumer was critical of the adherence to a certain model of science – that drawn from the natural sciences. In 'Sociological Analysis and the "Variable"' (1956) he argues that the effort had been towards the construction of laws and the testing of hypotheses (see Blumer 1969). He argued that 'variable analysis', despite its intent, does not locate precise, fixed variables which cover varying circumstances. Its claims to be able to 'quantify' particular variables or 'measure' relationships can at best be limited and more often misguided, since they are based on a false notion of how phenomena are related.

Blumer's work, it could be argued, has been more influential in sociology than it seems because some of his critical points have become commonplace. He combined Meadian concepts, a broader pragmatic approach to research, and the Chicagoan emphasis on empirical work – a combination that is clear in Fisher and Strauss's (1979) description of 'interactionism'. One criticism has been that he concentrated more on the problems of methodology and theorisation than on actual research – he was devoted more to the intricate discussion of the nature of social interaction. However, it must be stated that he did undertake a broad range of research work yet resisted a systemisation of his approach (Plummer 1998: 87).

Blumer was responsible, as previously stated, for furthering Mead's work in some important articles. For example, in the well-known 'Sociological Implications of the Thought of George Herbert Mead' (1966) he argues that in contrast to non-symbolic interaction of animals:

> Mead's concern was predominantly with symbolic interaction. Symbolic interaction involves *interpretation*, or ascertaining the meaning of the actions or remarks of the other person, and *definition*, or conveying indications to another as to how he is to act ... Through this process the participants fit their own acts to the ongoing acts of one another and guide others in doing so. (Blumer 1969: 66)

Blumer and Mead

It is necessary to place Blumer in some intellectual context – first, as a student and interpreter of Mead and also, secondly, in terms of the relations with his colleagues and influence on his own students. Blumer, and his colleague Everett Hughes, taught a highly talented group of graduate students during the 1940s and early 1950s, including Becker, Goffman, Strauss and Turner, who were to make substantial contributions to symbolic interactionism and wider interactionism. They disseminated the work of Park and Mead and have became known as 'the Second Chicago School' (Sandstrom et al. 2003: 217–18).

Blumer says that 'symbolic interaction' refers to the 'peculiar and distinctive character of interaction as it takes place':

> human interaction is mediated by the use of symbols, by interpretation, or by ascertaining the meaning of one another's actions. This mediation is equivalent to inserting a process of interpretation between stimulus and response in the case of human behavior. (Blumer 1969: 79)

He outlines three important aspects of symbolic interaction. First: 'it is a formative process in its own right'; it is not simply a 'neutral' arena in which wider social factors operate but should be studied in itself. Secondly, the reliance on symbolic interaction makes human group life a developing process instead of a mere issue or product of psychological or social structure. Thirdly, Blumer argues that through a concentration on symbolic interaction it is possible to study the whole range of human relationships, such as conflict, competition, or even a lack of regard for each other (Blumer 1969: 67).

Blumer summarises his view as follows:

> the first premise is that human beings act toward things on the basis of the meanings that the things have for them ... the second premise is that the meaning of such things is derived from, or arises out of, the social interaction that one has with one's fellows. The third premise is that these meanings are handled in, and modified through, an interpretive process used by the person in dealing with the things he encounters. (Blumer 1969: 2)

In this argument, the view that individuals are thrust forward by inner psychological forces to act according to set instincts is challenged by the idea of the reflective actor. Similarly, the idea of individuals and groups as simply acting according to external social constraints is also not accepted. Blumer's account of action also differs from Parsons's theory which, he says, like some other such approaches which put forward a general schema of social interaction or society, rest on a particular model of social relationships, in Parsons's case the 'complementarity of expectations' (Blumer 1969: 67-8).

For Blumer, Mead's general approach conceives society not as a given structural entity. Social action derives not from such a structure but from the activities of individuals in the particular setting. This view of social actors does not see their lives as merely a reflection or reaction to structure but as due to a process of joint actions upon which society is built. The emphasis here is not on the requirements of the society or 'system' but instead on individuals' interpretations as 'mediating' between differing parts of the society. This emphasis has led to the charge that Blumerian symbolic interactionism is a particular reading of Mead that focuses on the individualistic, subjectivist side of his work.

Blumer offers the idea of 'joint action' in place of Mead's term 'social act' (Blumer 1969: 70). The combining together of various types of joint actions

(e.g. a party, a marriage ceremony, a debate or shopping expedition) constitutes the relationships which make the larger society. Individuals anticipate the
joint actions they are about to take part in to shape their future actions with
others in particular situations. They may even decide not to go ahead, or the
situation may be new in that previous meanings may not be a good guide –
leading to additional interpretive and communicative work to allow for
the alignment between individuals.

In arguing that sociological concepts should be 'sensitising', Blumer was
saying that they should focus on the intricacies of social interaction rather than
attempting to use the technical concepts of the traditional sciences. Thus, concern should be with the study of the given social situation rather than the
imposition of abstract theorising or the seeking of the rigidities of law-like regularities, 'stimulus-response' variables and pre-given procedures. Blumer's
intention was to enable an openness of approach to gain clear knowledge of
social contexts rather than depending on set techniques and procedures. He
lays down various principles to inform practice rather than a detailed methodological programme. For Blumer the search for regularities in the relations
between variables depends on a limited notion that one variable alters the next.
A 'stimulus-response' model of behaviour does not adequately account for
human action in the social situation since individuals have interpretive
understandings, creativity in defining and shaping their actions, and self-
consciousness. The central aspect of Blumer's work is the individual as an
active, creative being and society as encompassing the interpretations of acting
individuals. In his view, any methodological approach must include the analysis of meaningful action and avoid any attempt to develop abstract theoretical
structures or sophisticated methodological procedures divorced from actual
social situations (Plummer 1998: 84–5).

Blumer, in outlining contemporary approaches to social psychology (1937),
identified one view as emphasising the active, plastic nature of the child and
the 'importance of the unformed impulse' (Blumer 1937; see Blumer 1969: 1).
He says it is largely the view of a group of social psychologists who could be
termed 'symbolic interactionists' due to the importance they gave to common
symbols, common understandings and definition of the situations in the group
of individuals and the process of interaction. Here was the insertion of
'meaning' or interpretation into social interaction rather than a model that saw
a stimulus as simply producing a concomitant response.

Critique of Blumer

Blumer advocated a 'naturalistic' approach to enable the study of individual
action and meanings attributed to the social situation. Thus, individual action
within the group was to be understood directly and 'sensitizing concepts' were
essential to this endeavour (Blumer 1969: 147). The attraction of Mead was

his focus on the interconnection between individual and group which was part of a pragmatic attempt to overcome the dualism between subject and object. But Blumer's reading of Mead is considered by some critics to be oriented too far towards the individual creation of subjective meanings dissociated from practices within structure (May 1996: 81).

While Blumer points out that Mead did not provide the methodological detail of his approach, a similar point could be made against his own form of study. In seeking to avoid 'reification' of human interaction it could be said (at least in his more theoretical symbolic interactionist writings) that he 'flattens out both "society" and the "individual" ' (Zeitlin 1973: 216). The result, for Zeitlin, is that Blumer's notion of society loses 'structure' since its components have to be immediately and empirically observable as acting; hence how, for instance, can social classes be said to exist if we cannot observe them acting? Similarly, he appears to exclude motives and drives so he can retain an idea of a 'self' referring to itself – the result seems to be, ironically, an opening for a 'crude positivism or empiricism' in which concepts cannot be utilised without a 'direct empirical referent' (Zeitlin 1973: 216–17). While Blumer did undertake the study of a range of organisations and other work, his approach has been criticised for its relative inattention to structure. However, one defence is that it 'neither ignores nor minimises the importance of wider social forces, power, history or the economic' – rather he is against 'grand theory in the abstract' (Plummer 1998: 88). In Blumer's view the 'empirical world must forever be the central point of concern' as 'the point of departure and the point of return in the case of empirical science' (Blumer 1969: 22).

Finally, there has been a great deal of debate on the degree of convergence between Mead's ideas and Blumer's interpretation. One view is that Mead is a 'realist' – that social reality can be studied as not simply a construction of the mind, while Blumer is nominalist – emphasising interpretation and communication (May 1996: 75). This debate centres on how far Blumer has interpreted Mead in a particular manner and a wider discussion of whether there are two strands of pragmatism (see Lewis and Smith 1980; Denzin 1984). For instance, Zeitlin argues that while language is essential, later interpretations took one-sided, non-dialectical view of Mead 'treating social interaction and socialization as if these processes were nothing more than symbolic communication. Society is dissolved into discourse' (Zeitlin 1973: 218).

Although Blumer wrote relatively little across his long career, he did publish several seminal articles and was influential through his teaching – a legacy which became more 'formalised' as symbolic interactionism was developed by the founding of associations, journals and textbooks in the area. Plummer says that Blumer influenced a 'great many studies' 'from illness and dying to occupations and classroom interaction; from social movements and collective behaviour to the patterning and organisation of social problems; from crime and deviance to labour and industrial relations; from media studies to life history research; from self theory to race relations' (Plummer 1998: 93). Blumer's general objective was to retain closeness to the subject of study; rather than be impeded by technical procedures, he was intent to elaborate various principles that should inform research and theorisation.

Varieties of Symbolic Interactionism

A number of 'varieties' of symbolic interactionism have been identified which to some extent reflect differences surrounding the initial and continuing influences and the broadening of the body of theory and research. A starting point for some writers are the writings of James, Dewey, Cooley and Mead, with perhaps the addition of the pre-war work of Royce and Baldwin (see Denzin 1992). According to others, considering 'interactionism' generally, the influence of Simmel's formalism should be added, alongside the pragmatist emphasis on meaning within grounded activity (as opposed to philosophical abstraction), as in Robert Park's sociology. Simmel and Park shared an 'emphasis on the dialectical union between the observer, the process of observation and the phenomena observed'. They also shared a 'formalism' with the notion of 'social forms' enabling individuals and groups to give a patterning to social life; the identification of such forms (e.g. 'conflict', 'competition' in Park) 'permitted a level of abstraction and generalization which transcended the particularities of anchored experience' (Rock 1991: 234). Yet wider sources of influence on interactionism can be discerned. For example, Plummer adds that there 'is also a metatheoretical foundation less clearly articulated in which humanism, romanticism and a mild libertarianism play important roles' (Plummer 1991a: xv).

Obviously, interactionism (and symbolic interactionism) have changed over time and include a wide range of individuals and ideas. 'Historically', commentators have described a 'second generation' of interactionists following Park, Mead and Thomas, including Herbert Blumer and Everett Hughes, with a 'third' including Howard Becker, Erving Goffman, Barney Glaser, and Anselm Strauss and Barney Glaser, with further 'modification' by Denzin, Lofland, Lyman and others (May 1996: 68). Another variation was the development of the so-called 'Iowa School', which attempted to show that the central notions of symbolic interactionism could be operationalised, applied and verified within empirical research rather than pursuing abstract philosophical issues, for example, surrounding the nature of social beings.

Qualitative Research and 'Interactionism'

Blumer's three 'premises' provided a starting point for symbolic interactionism and for wider interactionism, but perhaps, as Sandstrom et al. (2003) point out, there are other assumptions which inform its philosophical basis. Despite variations and debates on origins and developments, they say, perhaps it is still possible to elucidate some 'guiding premises' of symbolic interactionism: for instance, human beings as 'unique' due to their use of 'symbols'; individuals are 'human through their interaction'; we are 'conscious and self-reflexive' and 'purposive' in forming our behaviour and acting within social contexts; society is composed of symbolic interactions between individuals; and, finally, as investigators, to understand individuals' actions 'we need to use methods that enable us to discern the meanings they attribute to these acts' (Sandstrom et al. 2003: 218–19). Sandstrom et al. rightly point to major areas of growth in 'interactionists' work, such as the 'self and identity theory; emotions and emotion work; social coordination; social constructionism; culture and art, and macro-analysis' (Sandstrom et al. 2003: 219). But, it seems here, again, we have moved between 'symbolic interactionism' and 'interactionism'.

The pragmatist influence of Dewey and Mead also brought an antipathy to the idea of 'the passive observer' in relation to knowledge and to the 'misleading separation between mind and body, subject and object' (Rock 1991: 229). The pragmatists also drew on evolutionary theory to give what they regarded as 'a firmer, less metaphysical and more scientific theory of knowledge' as 'the outcome of a process of purposive questioning which can render features of the environment problematic, interrogate them, learn, and return to the environment with new questions' (Rock 1991: 229). Pragmatism:

> gave a persistent stress to the dialectical and situated character of knowledge ... It is a person's interests and quest for meaning that stabilize situations and give them shape. Conversely, situations will give order and direction to interests: motives and understandings flow from the practical and symbolic organization of an environment. (Rock, 1991: 230)

In the wider tradition of 'interactionism', in which symbolic interactionism and Chicagoan sociology are related, a number of methods, such as the life history and participant observation or ethnography, and variety of approaches, under the heading of fieldwork, have been pioneered (see Denzin and Lincoln 2000). Much of interactionist research has focused on deviance, the workplace and schools and, more theoretically, on the self, self-identity and social interaction. But it has developed beyond its original areas; for some, 'it has become the harbinger of postmodern social theory' while also making a contribution to 'feminism', 'gay activist theory' and the 'politics of race' (Plummer 1998: 95).

In summary, Fisher and Strauss give a list of the 'concepts and ideas associated with the tradition':

> Thomas's 'definition of the situation,' 'the four wishes,' and the social organization-social disorganization scheme; Park's 'race-relations cycle,' 'the marginal man,' processes like conflict, accommodation, and assimilation, and the idea of the formation of institutions through collective behavior and social movements; Mead's

concepts of 'significant other,' 'generalized other,' 'role-taking,' and the I–me phases of the self; Hughes's 'careers,' 'dirty work,' and other ways of looking sociologically at occupations, work, and professions; Blumer's methodological idea of 'sensitizing concepts'; Goffman's innumerable and influential ideas and concepts about interaction; Strauss and his associates'... formulations of identity; Shibutani's about social control and 'reference group,' Becker's about deviancy; and Lindesmith's about addiction. Edwin Sutherland's theories ('differential association') of criminality also belong to this tradition. (Fisher and Strauss 1979: 460)

Fisher and Strauss argued in the late 1970s that 'some of the major problems that still plague the interactionist tradition derive from the Thomas–Park side of interactionism' and that some of the criticism of symbolic interactionism is a result of how interactionists have themselves "construed Mead" ' (Fisher and Strauss 1979: 460). In their view, Thomas and Park tried to find 'a mode of explaining and promoting social change that would avoid both the image of unimpeded individual action and the idea of a totally constraining society'. Broadly, in relation to sociological research and social intervention, the interactionist endeavour rested on finding the possible means of action leading to lasting change in the face of restraining forces. Change would be brought about by incremental, consistent action through greater social knowledge and reflection (Fisher and Strauss 1979: 463–4).

It can be argued, following Fisher and Strauss, that there are a number of 'problematic areas' of the Park and Thomas (and 'Meadian, as interpreted by the sociologists') interactionist legacy – including progress, process (the characteristics of change), consent (active participation), limitations on social activity, power and equity, and the intellectual's (democratic) role. They conclude that these problems have 'common features' reflecting a 'liberal–conservative bind' which stresses 'the virtues of both active, creative individuality and of secure, stable association' (Fisher and Strauss 1979: 488). While interactionism has, in fact, had a number of theoretical divergent trends, still (according to Plummer) it is said to retain a shared 'naturalistic – humanistic' approach that regards much abstract philosophical debate as decidedly unhelpful for the study of daily contexts and experiences: 'It is a fully dialectical theory where subject and object, creativity and restraint, pattern and chaos, structure and meaning, knowledge and action are ceaselessly emergently intertwined' (Plummer 1991a: xv).

Case Study: Deviancy Theory and Careers

During the 1960s interactionism underwent a very rapid theoretical and methodological development. One major area of focus was the study of crime and 'deviance'. Various names were used (often interchangeably) for this study – including deviancy theory, social reaction theory, labelling theory, social control theory, interactionism, symbolic interactionism, and neo-Chicagoanism. For some, this body of work is a perspective, rather than a theory as such, concerned with the nature, types and effects of the application of social rules. 'Deviancy theory' drew upon a combination of symbolic interactionism (and ethnomethodology, phenomenology, functionalism, Marxism and other theoretical currents); the Parkian–Thomas fieldwork tradition; and attention to social process, life history analysis and social group study (see Rock 1991: 228, 1973). 'Deviance' was conceived as 'made' rather than 'given' by biological or psychological factors or the force of circumstance. Instead, deviance 'unfolds little by little, building up motives, perspectives and actions in a series of transformations that are sometimes gradual, sometimes abrupt' (Rock 1991: 235). Key terms in the study of deviance were those of career, drift or becoming – the individual learns to become deviant in a social process containing social reaction or social control. There is a dialectical relation between the definitions of deviance or labels given by an audience and the voluntarism or choice exercised by self (Becker 1963; Goffman 1968; Lemert 1967; Matza 1964, 1969; Douglas 1984). Deviancy theory, drawing on interactionism, provided a critique against 'positivism' in criminology – the alleged 'deterministic' and 'pathological' conceptions of criminals and their criminal actions; rather it offered the study of deviance in a plurality of situational contexts or deviant worlds. Interactionists, in the study of deviance and other fields, engage in 'participant observation' or collect 'life history materials' to gain the meanings that individuals give their situation, career or identity and in responding to change over time. They study the 'social processes' in which their active, 'meaning-giving' 'subjects' are part – in schools, work, family or other situation – and the formation of a career in a profession or deviance (or some other status). Identities are taken as constructed, as learned and made by the actor, in relation to social control and may go through various transformations and turning points (Rock 1991: 236; see Becker 1963; Goffman 1968; Matza 1969).

A further example of the application of deviancy theory is in the study of youth (see Atkinson and Housley 2003: 75–9). In Britain, the influential work of the Birmingham Centre for Contemporary Cultural Studies applied the ideas of 'label' and 'social reaction' to the study of youth groups since the Second World War and the formation of a media-led 'mugging panic' in 1972–3 (Hall and Jefferson 1976; Hall et al. 1978; see also Cohen 1972; Young 1971).

Although drawing on other theoretical approaches (e.g. Marxist theory), a central focus of this work was the interactionist injunction to study the interrelation between deviance and control – how the process of reaction and counteraction results in an 'escalation' of meanings arising from the nature of 'deviant' activity and operation of control agencies. The origins of deviancy research can be found in the work of Clifford Shaw (*The Jack Roller*, 1930; *The Natural History of the Delinquent Career*, 1931; *Brothers in Crime*, 1938) at Chicago on juvenile delinquency and Meadian ideas of 'generalised other' and 'symbolic' communication.

Interactionism, and more specifically symbolic interactionism, has made an important contribution to a very wide number of areas in sociology:

> In the study of occupations, Park's student, Everett Hughes, directed attention to 'work and self', the functioning of 'institutional office', and the historical concept of 'career'. In medical sociology, research has highlighted the social definition of disease, doctor–patient interactions, negotiations and bargainings in health settings, the 'careers' of both the ill and their carers, and the organization of professional knowledge. In the sociology of education there have been studies of classroom interaction, student cultures, teacher strategies and the production of educational knowledge. The sociology of sexuality has been most influentially shaped by Gagnon and Simon's seminal idea that sexuality should be approached as scripted conduct. And in many other areas such as social movements, media, and city life, interactionist research has carved out important approaches and findings ... Indeed, it has quite possibly been the single most fruitful theoretical stance within sociology for examining the lived worlds of everyday life. (Plummer 1991b: x; see also Atkinson and Housley 2003)

Critique

A main line of criticism of symbolic interactionism is its lack of systematisation – pointing to its diverse background in various, not always fully compatible, theoretical positions and philosophical currents and differing recent influences. For some, its pluralistic view of society, its notion of reality as shifting or multi-defined, and its attempted avoidance of 'dualisms' in philosophy and sociology means it lacks consistency and precision and relies on certain insufficiently examined assumptions concerning social life. For others, the symbolic interactionist (and wider interactionist) theory and methods must be judged according to its extensive ethnographical studies of daily settings – the classroom, the workplace, deviancy, and so on – and not by its philosophical ruminations (see Rock 1991: 233–4).

By the mid-1970s a range of assessments of symbolic interactionism by practitioners and opponents were being published. For critics, it was alleged that a concentration on everyday, mundane activities or a concern with the detailed cultural variety of social situations led to over-concern with deviant or inconsequential aspects of social life. Meltzer et al. (1975) usefully outlined a number of 'in-house' criticisms by writers favourable to symbolic interactionism. For example, the view that symbolic interactionism 'suffered' a lack of clarity due to its key ideas being passed down and disseminated orally for a long time; while the later period of very active research and theoretical development merely further confused the basic ideas. For some, Mead's writings were ambiguous regarding the 'determined' or 'determining' basis of human behaviour, including vagueness on the basis of the self, which also reoccurred in later work. Another charge was that it tended to be 'asociological' since it used an 'individual' rather than a sociological model of the act, coupled with insufficient theoretical and empirical attention to the processes involved in changes in self-conception. It failed to have adequate concepts to deal with varieties of 'functional relations that regularly occur between self and other'. Meltzer et al. added that there was an inadequate examination of the questions of wider social structure and power, while, on the other hand, work on the emotional aspects of the individual remained underdeveloped (Meltzer et al. 1975: 87–8).

Meltzer et al. (1975) also described a range of 'outsider' criticisms of symbolic interactionism: 'it is non-economic, ahistorical, culturally limited, and ideologically biased, has a limited view of social power, and paints an odd picture of social reality' (Meltzer et al. 1975: 99). In part, these criticisms amount to an assertion of a traditional structuralist orientation to the importance of constraint upon individual action. Symbolic interactionists can respond that it is being accused of neglecting areas which were not part of its intended focus and are the province of other theorisation. But they also have responded to some of the criticisms by pointing to contributions in areas of perceived theoretical and substantive oversight – to provide a more comprehensive theory.

Writers committed to a more traditional 'scientific' or 'positivistic' approach reject the symbolic interactionist criticisms of its practice; they counter-charge that symbolic interactionists have unsound procedures of verification and theory formation and ambiguous conceptualisation. On the other hand, some commentators say that the critique of traditional sociological positions on research procedure and theorisation by Blumer and others has been widely accepted. Indeed, since generally 'lessons' have been taken on board, for instance on the nature of conceptualisation, there is little left to discover from the founding texts of symbolic interactionist writing. The emphasis on the meanings participants give to social situations and associated methodological and interpretive approaches, it is said, are now merely part of the sociological mainstream alongside more traditional procedures and methods (Cuff et al. 1990: 163; Atkinson and Housley 2003).

Finally, the general pragmatist legacy, including symbolic interactionism and Chicagoan sociology, has been criticised for its limited critical approach to the ravages of capitalism in America (and elsewhere). For example, Smith's discussion of the Chicago School as 'a liberal critique of capitalism' echoes Mills's examination of pragmatism (including Mead) as 'a liberal reform of the situation' (Mills 1964, 1970a: 87–112, 1970b). However, Plummer finds an affinity between interactionism and 'socialist libertarianism' with an emphasis on decentralisation and democratic involvement (Plummer 1991a: xvii).

New Developments

In the 1980s a further stage in the development of symbolic interactionism occurred, with reappraisals of its origins and the degree of consistency between its leading writers. One intellectual history, by Lewis and Smith, created a particular controversy (Lewis and Smith 1980; Denzin 1984; Mills 1982). They argued that a close reading of Mead and Blumer shows that the two are quite different in basic orientation, with Blumer having a more 'individualistic' view and representing a different strand of pragmatism. There ensued argument and counter-argument, much of it depending on rather different readings of key figures. The safest conclusion to make is to say that pragmatist philosophy is now recognised to be more varied than previously and has a number of direct and indirect influences on sociology through Mead, Blumer and Chicago Sociology and pragmatist writers such as James and Dewey. While Mead has been a central figure, alongside Blumer, there is an increasing recognition of the work and influence of other pragmatists.

Since the mid-1980s, commentators have been at pains to show the vitality of symbolic interactionism – as a lively, developing body of work with new interests reflecting the surrounding changing social environment in which it is placed. There is even the view that its influence is so pervasive that we are often not aware of (or reflect on) its presence (see Plummer 1991b: xi; Atkinson and Housley 2003). Atkinson and Housley point to the continued relevance of 'interactionism', despite the changes in theorisation brought by cultural and linguistic 'turns' and postmodern theory which have challenged, for example, the very notion of the 'subject' (Atkinson and Housley 2003: 145–75). Some of these developments may be said to be responses to criticisms of the perspective or other theorisation drawing upon it, for example, in the areas of history, social structure, power and gender (see Plummer 1991b: xi–xvii; Deegan and Hill 1987).

A further interesting development is the examination of some of the over-looked aspects of the 'founders'' of interactionism. For example, one criticism of Mead (and symbolic interactionism) was the lack of historical perspective – however, it is now clear that he placed the development of the self (and philosophical movements) within an historical view – a fact neglected by both symbolic interactionists and their critics. A similar point could be made in rela-tion to Blumer's alleged lack of attention to structure or wider groups without seeing his work more broadly than social psychological interests (Plummer 1991b: xii). Other important developments have taken place. Plummer points to the developments in terms of methodology – the use of qualitative pro-grammes on computers, more 'subjective methods' or material sources once ruled out (for instance, the analysis and use of 'fiction', new visual sources and presentation, and new forms of writing) – including the centrality of the researcher's own experiences of the research process (Plummer 1991b: xiii). Progress has also been made in the area of interpretive procedures, such as the widely influential 'grounded theory' and 'analytic induction' in ethnographic study and biographical work. Sandstrom et al. note 'emerging voices' in sym-bolic interactionism (Sandstrom et al. 2003: 225). They point out that, like other approaches, it has been influenced by feminism (or the 'feminist turn') in the cultural construction and reproduction of gender. Also, a 'critical interactionism' has emerged with a concern for areas such as 'inequality', 'ideology' and 'agency and consciousness' and fields associated with 'political economy'. Postmodernist writings have also affected interpretive work, via notions of 'multivocality', 'discourse', the process of writing in research, and shifts in the self under 'late capitalism' (see Sandstrom et al. 2003: 226–7). While the 'ethnographic' and 'career' focus on small arenas in health, education and work has continued, other concerns have been added, such as the expression or management of emotions and the semiological dimensions of interaction (Plummer 1991b: xv). There has also been substantial development in symbolic interactionist work within cultural studies – extending the early interest in the media by Dewey and Park (e.g. Denzin 1992).

Conclusion

Symbolic interactionism has made a major contribution to micro social theory – although many of its protagonists would not necessarily uphold the macro–micro distinction. It arose from the current of American pragmatist thought, particularly through the work of G. H. Mead, and his interpreter, Herbert Blumer. Much of the traditional focus was been on the nature of the self, which was often taken from a limited view of Mead's idea – downplaying its biological 'side' and ignoring its historical social development. In more recent years the heritage of symbolic interactionism, in a range of pragmatist writers, has been reassessed and it has developed into areas which critics have alleged it has not shown an interest.

Symbolic interactionism (and, more widely, interactionism) has continued to develop new conceptualisation and areas for investigation, and collaboration with new (or revived) methodological procedures. Its contribution to the investigation of micro social theory as a 'level' of analysis is very considerable. Less clear is the degree and nature of its 'reaching out' to more macro concerns, although (as Plummer argues) it has made some contribution to understanding connections of micro settings in certain wider social and historical arenas. It is here where further development could take place. Still relevant is Joas's conclusion that, while symbolic interactionist views on action and consciousness can resist the assault of structuralism and poststructuralism, it has yet to realise its full analytical potential:

> the tradition of symbolic interactionism offers important material in the categories of collective behaviour and social movement, of the determination of social structures by negotiation, and of democracy as a type of social order. Often, though, these notions have been elaborated, in the manner of a 'qualitative empiricism', in the investigation of objects of slight macrosociological relevance. The analytical richness of symbolic interactionism thus remains unutilized for a diagnosis of the

present time that is politically oriented and that takes the era's historical development and context into consideration. (Joas 1987: 111)

Further Reading

For the work of Blumer see H. Blumer, *Symbolic Interactionism* (Chicago, University of Chicago Press, 1969); M. Hammersley, *The Dilemma of Qualitative Method: Herbert Blumer and the Chicago Tradition* (London, Routledge, 1989); and K. Plummer, 'Herbert Blumer', in R. Stones (ed.), *Key Sociological Thinkers* (Basingstoke, Palgrave Macmillan, 1998).

There are many commentaries and readers on symbolic interactionism. Among the clearest older introductions are B. N. Meltzer, J. W. Petras and L. T. Reynolds, *Symbolic Interactionism: Genesis, Varieties and Criticism* (London, Routledge & Kegan Paul, 1975) and P. Rock, *The Making of Symbolic Interactionism* (Basingstoke, Macmillan, 1979).

The following 'readers' containing key articles are among the most widely used. K. Plummer (ed.), *Symbolic Interactionism: The Future of Interactionist Sociologies*, vol. 2 (London, Edward Elgar, 1991) is a very good starting point because it contains a strong editorial overview of developments and a very good selection of articles. Other texts which give a wide selection of material are: J. Charon (ed.), *Symbolic Interactionism* (4th ed., Englewood Cliffs, NJ, Prentice-Hall, 1992); N. J. Herman and L. T. Reynolds (eds.), *Symbolic Interaction: An Introduction to Social Psychology* (Walnut Creek, CA, AltaMira, 1994); J. G. Manis and B. N. Meltzer (eds.), *Symbolic Interaction: A Reader in Social Psychology* (London, Allyn & Bacon, 1967); L. T. Reynolds and N. J. Herman-Kinney (eds.), *Handbook of Symbolic Interactionism* (Walnut Creek, CA, AltaMira, 2003); and G. P. Stone and H. A. Farberman (eds.), *Social Psychology Through Symbolic Interaction* (Lexington, Xerox College, 1970). The following texts can be used to survey recent developments, for instance, in cultural studies: P. Atkinson and W. Housley, *Interactionism* (London, Sage, 2003); H. S. Becker and M. M. McCall (eds.), *Symbolic Interaction and Cultural Studies* (Chicago, University of Chicago Press, 1990); N. K. Denzin, *Interpretive Interactionism* (2nd ed., London, Sage, 2001); K. Plummer, K., 'Symbolic Interactionism in the Twentieth Century', in B. S. Turner (ed.), *The Blackwell Companion to Social Theory* (Oxford, Blackwell, 2000); and K. Plummer, *Documents of Life 2: An Invitation to a Critical Humanism* (London, Sage, 2001); L. T. Reynolds, *Interactionism: Exposition and Critique* (New York, General Hall, 1993) and the journal *Symbolic Interaction*.

5

Erving Goffman

Introduction

The work of Erving Goffman has produced various responses within sociology. He is recognised as having a particular approach to social life, often associated by commentators with symbolic interactionism, although it would be more accurate to place his work within general interactionism. While his use of a 'dramaturgical' perspective on social life is usually commented upon, he also employs other metaphorical devices (ritual and game) which together produce a sophisticated view of self, interaction and society and have inspired much later micro social theory discussion. More specifically, his 'micro theory' approach on interaction and self has attracted renewed attention due to the 'structural' aspects of his work, and more specifically his identification of the 'interaction order'. It is this 'interaction order' which various writers have taken as both as a distinctive area of study 'on its own' as well as the basis for understanding the interpenetration of the 'micro' and 'macro' – or, very simply, self and society relations.

The Origins of Goffman's Work

Erving Goffman (1922–82) was born in Canada and became a student at the University of Toronto. He did doctoral fieldwork research in the Shetland Islands and also studied psychiatric hospitals. He was invited to join the sociology department at Berkeley by Blumer and later moved to the University of Pennsylvania. His work as a sociologist is unusual in several ways; for instance, he does not quite fit any particular 'school' or approach although his work is often seen as closest to (and sometimes placed within) symbolic interactionism. Goffman is also a 'popular' author and his many books sell in their thousands. His originality has been regarded with a certain suspicion by some other sociologists, who have questioned the basis of his ideas since he draws on a varied range of disciplines, observations and reading matter to support his analyses. Goffman could perhaps best be understood as an interpreter or social critic on everyday life with concerns with the self, face-to-face interaction and social order (see Branaman 2001: 102–3). His first publication in the early

1950s was followed by a continuous stream of conceptual work and 'empirical' study. His most publicly known works are *The Presentation of Self in Everyday Life* (1971), *Asylums* (1968) and *Stigma* (1963). He could be described as a sociologist concerned with the ordinary, daily activities which we routinely take part in but which he shows anew, using unusual angles and stimulating insights and observations. In this way, the participation in daily life, merely taken for granted by us, is revealed to be the skilled way in which routines are enacted and knowledge applied. While his work in this regard has some similarities with ethnomethodology and he shares concerns found in symbolic interactionism (e.g. with the self and social interaction), he cannot be simply placed in either category. An important contribution to micro social theorisation is the differentiation and connections made between 'interaction order' and the 'institutional order' – hence his interest to various writers (e.g. Giddens, Layder) concerned with the macro–micro theory relation.

A key difference between Goffman and symbolic interactionism is in the treatment of social structure – Goffman is concerned with the interrelation between the characteristics of the interaction order and social structures. He attempts to avoid structural determinism by arguing that culture does not reflect structure, rather that structures are involved in selecting from a range of cultural phenomena. On the other hand, Goffman shares a 'cognitive-rational' conception of the individual with symbolic interactionist theory, as responding to and taking the attitudes of others in social situations. But it seems that in Goffman's view the individual takes a further step as more 'knowing' and 'manipulative', as using acting skills of presentation to influence others.

A difficulty in describing Goffman's work is that it appears to lack systematic theorisation or a clear general statement. This has led him to be dismissed as a serious sociologist. But often his work is seen in a rather superficial manner, as holding a cynical view of individuals presenting themselves favourably to obtain a desirable outcome. In short, he is said to give interesting insights into social life but demonstrates a more literary or 'pop' treatment of social interaction. Also, in his focus on the 'trivialities' of social life he is charged with paying little attention to testing his ideas. While his work is rich in terms of conceptualisation there is a lack of clarity, in part due to the shift in his notions, and his 'evidence' seems to vary between anecdote, literary works, anthropology, ethology, magazines and other assorted sources. Yet his ideas have undergone a recent re-evaluation. His focus on face-to-face social interaction and the interaction order was been taken up by Giddens and others. He is now often considered a major sociological theorist, primarily because of his attempt to link interaction with a notion of structure. It can also be said that he set himself a most difficult and crucial task – to make sense of the jumble of daily experiences in which we live, while convincing the reader of the social importance of seemingly inconsequential activities. Since his work appears unsystematic, while also being extensive and conceptually shifting over time, various attempts have been made to find its key themes – usually self, social interaction, social order and the general metaphor of drama are identified.

Goffman's work can be said to focus on the 'interaction order' – the situations of 'co-presence' where face-to-face communication and mutual observation take place. Individuals in this view may appear manipulative, but can also be seen rather as engaging in social activities that involve communication and impression in a self-conscious mutual interaction. It is this interactional order which Goffman's methodological approach attempts to render apparent. Goffman says, in *The Presentation of Self in Everyday Life* (1971), that the 'dramaturgical' perspective offered 'may constitute a fifth perspective, to be added to the technical, political, structural, and cultural perspectives'. It is focused on the techniques and problems of impression management and the identity and interrelationships of various 'performance teams' (Goffman 1971a: 233). Various writers have pointed out that Goffman's actor is no mere cynical individual seeking advantage over others; rather, in fact taking part in action which has a moral basis. Goffman, then, is interested in the nature of trust in face-to-face interaction; a concern derived from Durkheim's central issue of the moral bonds between the individual and society. Numerous other influences have also been traced from the pragmatist or interactionist tradition of James, Blumer, Hughes, Mead and Thomas; Cooley's ideas on the self; Schutz's phenomenology in understanding experience; Kenneth Burke's notions of the 'rhetoric' or 'grammar' of motives; Simmel's approach to social forms; a broad reading of literary fiction and biography; newspapers and magazines; anthropological studies; to deviancy and work studies. This eclectic range of sources was used for a central purpose, as Goffman says in introducing *Strategic Interaction* (1970):

> My ultimate interest is to develop the study of face-to-face interaction as a naturally bounded, analytically coherent field – a sub-area of sociology. To do this one must come to terms with the fact that the central concepts in the area are ambiguous, and the bordering fields marked off badly. (Goffman 1970: ix)

There is much difficulty in summarising Goffman's work, leading some authors to emphasise one aspect, e.g. 'dramaturgy', rather than another. But, more satisfactorily, following Branaman it is possible to identify four organizing ideas in Goffman's career (Branaman 1997: xlv). First, 'the production of the self' – including the 'self – society relation' and the 'self as social product'. Secondly, 'the confined self' where he links status, power, performance and self, e.g. as shown in *Asylums* (1968), *Relations in Public* (1971) and *Stigma* (1963). Thirdly, 'the nature of social life' – where Branaman argues that Goffman's analysis moves between the metaphors of drama, ritual and game. These draw attention to both the manipulative and the moral aspects of social life, including the attachment (e.g. to maintain face) to the moral and ritual orders. Finally, 'frames and the organization of experience' or identity – 'frames' are given some autonomy at the interactional level from organisations and social structure which they may support or weaken, but some social experiences are more framed than others – such as the social construction of gender (Branaman 1997: xlv–xlvii).

Drama

Goffman's work is very abundant in conceptual insights, analogy and other devices; for example, he gives as one influence Kenneth Burke's work on performance (e.g. Goffman 1971a: 35). More specifically, it is clear that there are three central metaphors to be found – ritual (order and morality), game (manipulation and advantage) and drama (Branaman 1997: lxiii–lxiv). For instance, Goffman says his study *Strategic Interaction* (1970) 'deals with the calculative, game-like aspects of mutual dealings – what will be called *strategic interaction*' (Goffman 1970: x). Each metaphor gives a somewhat different slant to his work, although it is possible to see the three as connected in a given situation. As we have noted, 'drama' is the metaphor most associated with Goffman – life as (if) a theatre – and his work is often called 'dramaturgy' or an interest in how individuals 'manage impressions' or give a 'performance' to others. In ordinary life contexts the individual 'presents' themselves to others and tries to control the impression that others gain of him or her in acting in their presence (Goffman 1971a: Preface).

As actors on a stage, individuals give a performance (lover, gardener, politician) according to a 'script' which can be edited and delivered to portray a particular self-image they wish to be accepted while recognising that an audience may have certain expectations of the actor. The actor or 'team' of actors 'perform' their parts using the set and its props. They are on stage in a 'front region' – or backstage in 'back regions' unseen by the audience as the actors perform their routines. The audience is given a performance that produces an image through tactics and strategy or 'impression management', to allay embarrassment, but it also has to grasp the actors' delivery of their performance. The actor may seek to show a seemingly 'essential' self to others rather than certain other aspects, while he or she also realises that a particular part may have to be given to different groups who may respond in different ways to the performance. In the stage setting the actor is judged according to the appropriateness and acceptability of the impressions given. Teamwork is also involved in giving an impression to others (e.g. of professional competence, honesty and trust); the actor front of stage depends on a variety of others in completing the performance. So, a great deal depends on the combination of work with others (e.g. as in legal, medical, commercial, educational and other settings). Various reasons may inform an actor's specific performance, and while the audience may be sceptical it has to comply with the meanings that are being conveyed while actors, by a number of means, attempt to maintain an expressive control.

Of course, in the performance or encounter the actors may not realise completely their motives while they might also mislead others; also a cynicism can be mixed with belief in what is being performed. A performance is a subtle and precarious thing, which may be disrupted, and hence actors employ defensive and protective practices to safeguard the impressions (or definition of the situation for the audience or 'front') given by him/her and colleagues. Again, we can see Goffman's emphasis on the interplay of both manipulation and morality in social performance (Branaman 1997: lxiv). The notion of drama indicates the 'expressive' features of interaction rather than its instrumental aspects. Goffman's emphasis is on the 'performance' in action rather than a preceding cause or realisation of an end.

Important methodological issues are raised here in relation to Goffman's approach to sociological knowledge and understanding, i.e. the 'advocacy of "naturalistic observations" as the preferred source of basic sociological knowledge' and the 'use of metaphor for the development of theoretical understanding' (Williams 1998: 157). A number of points can be noted in regard to Goffman's 'method'. First, according to Williams, Goffman's powers of observation were extremely sharp, as shown in his 'traditional ethnographic studies of social settings' (e.g. hospital wards and the Shetland Islands). Secondly, he used his 'systematic naturalistic observations' to compile examples of a particular empirical category (e.g. speech faults in radio broadcasts). Finally, his 'secondary observations' were based on an impressive array of fictional and factual action in numerous settings (such as detective and spy fiction). Goffman was not a mere collector of 'facts', but a hoarder of the 'inconsequential' detail of everyday life for a purpose. As Williams argues, in Goffman's methodology 'he never produced traditional ethnographic descriptions aimed at descriptive fidelity in their reportage of the full detail of life in the setting under study'. Rather, 'he produced collections, categorisations and interpretations of a large range of recurrent events and sequences in social life' (Williams 1998: 157). We can see a Simmelian formalism or the classification of social phenomena akin to botanic and biological method as opposed to grand theorisation or ready abstraction. Like writers such as Giddens (1987b) and Collins (1994), Williams recognises that there is a broader import in Goffman's writings in the use of general metaphors. First, to use metaphor in a literal sense, to understand a setting (life as theatre or game), and secondly, to find the limitations of each metaphor in a reflexive manner as a sociological tool:

> By asking 'what is it about games that makes them real as games', and 'what is the nature of theatre as a social achievement' his investigations are given an additional reflexive turn ... [and] can be profitably read as an extended methodological self-commentary. (Williams 1998: 158)

Goffman was influenced by E. C. Hughes and W. L Warner at Chicago and, through them, the ideas of Mead, Durkheim and Simmel. From these sources he gained a view of human behaviour as 'reality-constructing', 'the persuasive significance of ceremony and ritual in human social life, and the utility of a 'formal' orientation that overlooks historical specificities in a quest for universal generalizations' (Meltzer et al. 1975: 68). Goffman's dramaturgy shares with the Chicagoan sociological tradition a challenge to the assumption that given structural forces determine the roles that individuals perform. Instead the 'calculative and situational behavior of actors' is stressed and 'norms, positions, and roles are simply the frameworks within which human interaction occurs' (Meltzer et al. 1975: 70).

The Self

The Presentation of Self in Everyday Life (1971) is one of Goffman's most influential books. At its heart lies the idea of the 'expressiveness' of the individual which, he says, is of two very different types of 'sign activity' – in terms of the expression 'given' (e.g. valid symbols/information) and 'given off' (presented). But, he adds, the difference has only 'initial validity' since 'misinformation' can be given by both forms of communication, by consciously utilising 'deceit' or 'feigning' (Goffman 1971a: 14). Individuals' activities when in the 'immediate presence of others' has a 'promissory' nature since others must accept these activities through faith, giving a return whose 'true value' will only be realised later (Goffman 1971a: 14). Usually, the various definitions of the situation are compatible – a kind of 'consensus' when individuals give their feelings honestly and agree with those of others – individuals are expected to 'suppress' deeper feelings and give a view which it is felt others will find 'temporarily acceptable'. Goffman says the 'maintenance of this surface of agreement, this veneer of consensus, is facilitated by each participant concealing his own wants behind statements which assert values to which everyone present feels obliged to give lip service' (Goffman 1971a: 20–1). Individuals, when relating to others, can have various motives in controlling impressions. Goffman is interested in the 'common techniques' that individuals (and 'teams') use to maintain impressions and some of the 'common contingencies associated with the employment of these techniques' (Goffman 1971a: 26). In *The Presentation of Self in Everyday Life*, he defines a number of the key terms in his work, for example:

> interaction (that is, face-to-face interaction) [is] the reciprocal influence of individuals upon one another's actions when in one another's immediate physical presence ...
>
> A 'performance' [is] all the activity of a given participant on a given occasion which serves to influence in any way any of the other participants ...
>
> A region [is] any place that is bounded to some degree by barriers to perception. Regions vary ... in the degree to which they are bounded and according to the media of communication in which the barriers to perception occur. (Goffman 1971a: 26–7, 109)

Goffman says that for an effective performance commonly the extent of co-operation required will be concealed and secrecy maintained. A performance 'team' he likens to a secret society; members co-operate to maintain a specific 'definition of the situation'. As team members, he says, we all carry 'something of the sweet guilt of conspirators'. Here, we can see the influence of Simmel on the nature of secrecy and secret societies (see Simmel 1906; Ritzer and Goodman 2004: 175–81). Performances in the front region can be regarded as an attempt to meet certain moral and instrumental requirements or standard in the activity – in this personal front, 'manner' or 'decorum' (politeness, appearance) will be important. Meanwhile, in the 'back region, a place where the impression given in the performance is "knowingly contradicted", a number of activities take place, including: the storage of equipment and costume, the use of "private" facilities, and the checking and adjustment of the "personal front" ' (Goffman 1971a: 114–15).

The existence of front and back regions is repeated in institutions across society: some regional separations are rigorously upheld, while others are weak or the front region eroded. In his discussion of 'personal front' and 'presentation' of self Goffman is allowing for an individual's conscious action and the expression of self-identity in a way that structuralist accounts of the individual cannot. Thus, individuals may give one of a number of elements of themselves in a particular context to an audience through the management of impressions. Also, rather than merely acting out prescribed roles according to the requirements set (teacher, social worker, mother, father, etc.), the individual consciously gives an impression of themselves in a manner that is intended to display competence and other expected characteristics.

There are various types of 'communication of character' in teams, as outlined in *The Presentation of Self in Everyday Life* (1971), that may be different from the one given to an audience. The 'treatment of the absent' is where the team assesses the performance and may derogate (or praise) the audience, while 'staging talk' refers to the discussion of problems of staging the performance – such talk may raise morale for the next staging. 'Team collusion' includes signs by a performer to the team, which may convey a definition of the situation different from the one being given to the audience, e.g. a request for assistance. Finally, 'realigning actions' is where performers make clear their chafing against restrictions, by innuendo, significant pauses or jokes, but without jeopardising the smooth continuity of the performance and connection between the team and the audience. Where two teams are involved the 'official consensus' of co-operation may also have such 'unofficial communication' (Goffman 1971a: 166–87). These types of team communication again show the front–back stage model. Goffman concludes that the forms of communication of character show that a team performance is not a spontaneous response to a situation that takes all its energies of all its members, neither is it their only social reality. Instead, members can separate themselves from the performance and imagine or play out other realities

(Goffman 1971a: 202). Here it seems that the notions of front and back region are extended to make a deeper point regarding reality – as multiple realities – and experience (cf. Cohen and Taylor 1978).

Goffman returns to the 'presentation of self' in *Stigma* (1963) – in terms of physical deformity; character, e.g. addict, patient; and group, e.g. religion, and in *Strategic Interaction* (1970), where it is associated with 'expression games' (play, moves). Again, a view of individual action as involving 'presentation', i.e. deceit, reappears. Here, we seem to move from the discussion of face-to-face interaction as such, to everyday life as a murky world of double-dealing, spying and suspicion where there is 'no obviously innocent expression' (Zeitlin 1973: 213–14). This tendency can already be seen in *The Presentation of Self in Everyday Life* (1971) where 'backstage' collusion is contrasted 'front-stage' 'impression management' in establishing a 'definition of the situation' for the audience.

While Goffman examines impression management by individuals, his idea of the self is more a public than a private reality – a social production or institution (Collins 1994: 73). Thus, he was not primarily interested in 'human motivation, feeling, intention, unconscious'. While it is incorrect to state he ignored their importance, 'their significance was to be treated as "virtual", as available for use rather than unavoidably used' within personal histories and 'the framework of normative understanding' (Williams 1998: 154–5). In fact, various accounts of the self can be found in Goffman's work. Williams (1998), for instance, finds three differing versions. The first version is found in *The Presentation of Self in Everyday Life* (Goffman 1971a) and essays such as 'Where the Action Is' and 'On Face-Work' in *Interaction Ritual* (Goffman 1972). Here the self has two parts – 'character' and 'performer' – which are brought together as the self as a 'performed character'. The concern is for the 'organisation and management of the roles (or characters) assumed by the self-as-performer' – a view obviously compatible with the idea of life as drama (Williams 1998: 155). A second version is found in *Asylums* (1968) and *Stigma* (1963), where the self is not only a result of 'its possessor's interactions with significant others, but also [a result] of the arrangements that are evolved in an organisation for its members'. In this view, the self is portrayed as an outcome of social setting and seems determined by social circumstance, but is tempered by the way 'individuals resist, transgress and contest definitions of themselves embedded and enacted through such organisational arrangements'. The third version is a 'flexible notion of self as a social process' rather than as a phenomenon partly hidden behind events. Thus, the self is more than a collection of given roles; it is an organising 'formula' that creates a means of managing the relation between desires and the expectations of specific roles. A final aspect is the self as 'embodied' within interaction as we draw on our physical capabilities as a resource rather than a constraint (cf. *Gender Advertisements*, 1979) (Williams 1998: 155–6).

Another way of seeing Goffman's treatment of the self, as Branaman (1997) argues, is according to two contrasting (perhaps incompatible) definitions. First, the self is a 'dualistic' idea. It is a social product rather than having a 'personal core', while also there is an 'unsocialized component to the self' which may lead the individual to behave in contravention of norms (Branaman 1997: xlvii). Secondly, the individual is not completely formed by society but does engage in strategic actions in a social setting to create impressions to an audience (like a drama). But even so, the individual's images of the self are subject to the definitions credited from the roles and statuses of the social order (Branaman 1997: xlvii). Goffman, in fact, recognises he uses 'a double definition of self'. For instance, in discussing 'The Ritual Roles of the Self', he regards the self:

> as an image pieced together from the expressive implications of the full flow of events in an undertaking; and self as a kind of player in a ritual game who copes honorably or dishonorably, diplomatically or undiplomatically, with the judgmental contingencies of the situation. A double mandate is involved. (Goffman 1972: 31; see Branaman 1997: xlviii)

It appears, for Goffman, that what is important is not what a person 'really is', but the sense portrayed to others in interaction of the kind of person behind the role according to different settings. In summary, as Branaman argues, Goffman's views on the self are to be found in his discussions of drama, ritual and game, in which the self is 'performed', or the focus of social ritual or part of 'strategy' making (Branaman 1997: lxiii). These Goffmanian notions of the self are regarded, by some, as an advance on Mead's conception of the self. For instance, Branaman regards the former as 'less abstract' and 'more radical', since 'Goffman's idea is that the self does nor merely *arise* in social experience, but it is a *product* of the social scene or a dramatic effect of performances in social life' (Branaman 2001: 96).

Interaction Order

At its most rudimentary the 'interaction order' is that area where 'two or more individuals are in one another's response presence'. It is a vital part of Goffman's work since it alludes to the interrelation between the workings of social encounters and their relation with wider social structurings. While he is attempting to show the specific features of face-to-face interaction and the part they play in social ordering he also is aware (as in *Frame Analysis*, 1974) of the pre-'framing' of social situations by society. Even so, he has been accused of paying insufficient attention to the social structural issues of power. His main intention is to establish the interaction order as an independent arena for study while recognising its relation with 'institutional order' (see Branaman 1997: lxxxi). Indeed, the former may influence the latter, since individuals are part of various organisational and non-organisational settings. Personal encounters in the institution can have a bearing on the interaction order, and the daily encounters in organisations include the processing of people and the reproduction (including possible weakening) of social structurings such as social class (see Branaman 1997 lxxxi-ii). Rather than one order 'determining' the other, it would seem that the relation between the 'interactional order' and the 'institutional order' varies depending upon the substantive instance. Again, there are implications here for an understanding of the self. As Layder says:

> For Goffman, the interaction order protects itself from the self-interests of those involved by placing moral obligations on them to adhere to the ground rules of the interaction. However, the interaction order itself provides a protective membrane for the self. Since interaction and the social self are by nature fragile, the individual is never completely secure in an encounter. (Layder 1994: 173)

Thus, for Goffman there is 'not so much a real agreement as to what exists but rather a real agreement as to whose claims concerning what issues will be temporarily honoured' and 'the desirability of avoiding an open conflict of definitions of the situation' – or a 'working consensus' (Goffman 1971a: 21).

Co-presence

For Giddens, Goffman is a significant sociological thinker, who 'developed a systematic approach to the study of human life' and whose writings have suffered from a number of misconceptions (Giddens 1987b: 109–10). He is an important analyst of day-to-day social interaction – above all, of interaction in circumstances of physical 'co-presence' rather than small groups:

> His work therefore cross-cuts the distinction between primary and secondary group and other similar distinctions well entrenched in the sociological literature. For one thing, many small groups (for example, the family or kinship groups) endure over time. Goffman is not really interested in the mechanisms of such endurance. Moreover, co-present gatherings can be quite large, as in the case of theatre audiences or crowds ... Goffman's concern is therefore with 'situated activity systems'. (Giddens 1987b: 115–16)

'Encounters' may be either focused – where individuals directly communicate – or unfocused – where there is an awareness of others in the same situation, such as in the lecture hall, in a park, shop, or on a train.

In interaction in everyday life we take much for granted according to certain rules which allow for continuity although, in Goffman, this is not a conception of the production of social order as rule following. Instead, social order implies co-operation through routine 'repairing' in interchange: through apologies, and forms of supportive interchange using collaboration and trust. Goffman's interest is not only with ritual, game and drama in relation to physical space in co-presence; in his later writings he is concerned with both verbal and non-verbal interaction, forms of talk and the body (Goffman 1979, 1981). Goffman shows the great intricacy of the features of social interaction in every-day life, including the display and manner of the body in communication, and the importance of space and time (see Giddens 1987b: 120).

Ritual – Regions and Frames

The depth and complexity in Goffman's work in part stems from the influ-ence of Durkheim's notion of social reality – more specifically, at its core an idea of moral reality (e.g. *Elementary Forms of Religious Life*, 1954) (see Collins 1994: 74–5). This influence can be seen, for example, in Goffman's *Interaction Ritual* (1972) and *Frame Analysis* (1974). Goffman's work can be described as a study of the taken-for-granted rituals in everyday life in analysing social reality. As Collins (1994) describes, in Goffman's work, rit-ualistic behaviour has a number of levels in face-to-face presence, i.e. the mutual awareness of two people, the sharing and intensification of an emo-tional mood, and the interactions involved as shaping future feelings, thought and behaviour. Even conversation has a ritual and sharing of mood – a 'sym-bolic world' or 'a little social system' with its own rules and boundaries (Collins 1994: 72). Conversation is ritualistic and also part of a broader frame that we do not usually recognise. Goffman's conception of society is one that is covered in rituals. It is here that Goffman differs from a 'radical' symbolic interactionist view that the self is simply produced by interaction or exchange of meanings as such. Instead, as Collins points out, there is a 'region-alisation' of the self (e.g. front and back regions – as in rooms in the home) which bears upon the nature of social relationships. The greater the intimacy in personal relations the more they take place backstage (e.g. between hus-band and wife). Thus, rather than being private, the self is as much a 'public reality' drawn from the social constructions of people adjusting to each other in social interaction – our selves are ritually enacted as each defers to each other to uphold demeanour (Collins 1994: 73). For Collins, Goffman is arguing that there is a 'cult of the self' (cf. Durkheim on the 'cult of the individual') in modern society:

> If the self is the central sacred object of modern society, it is correspondingly unreal. The self in Goffman is not something that individuals negotiate out of social inter-actions: it is, rather, the archetypal modern myth. We are *compelled* to have an indi-vidual self, not because we actually have one but because social interaction requires us to act as if we do. (Collins 1994: 74–5)

At base, Collins says the 'self is real only as a symbol, a linguistic concept', so we can account for what we, and others, do: it is 'an ideology of everyday life, used to attribute causality and moral responsibility in our society' (Collins 1994: 75).

A development of the notions of 'front' and 'back' regions is the idea of 'frames' (and frame space). According to Collins, Goffman offers several layers of analysis of 'frames': the physical world – where communication is placed; the social ecology – where we share an awareness of each other; and the institutional frame – that takes place within the other two. While communication can occur in various ways in different places (e.g. church, theatre, casual conversation), and may be 'informal', it cannot avoid the 'institutional model' (Collins 1994: 78). The social experience of individuals for Goffman, he says, is saturated with the application of frames and frame transformation.

In the study of interaction, Goffman lays stress on the 'expressive' (conversation, bodily disposition, clothing, and facial looks, etc.) alongside the 'instrumental' aspect of ritual and the self as given through interaction between participants in interaction. Ritual, then, has two aspects in this kind of analysis, both routinised and expressive (Cuff et al. 1990: 161–2). Finally, again, it can be argued, that in everyday life 'deceitful' and 'moral' behaviour are not simply opposed in Goffman's analyses of everyday life according to the metaphors of ritual, game and drama:

> Trust and tact are more fundamental and binding features of social interaction than is the cynical manipulation of appearances. Thus people routinely shore up or 'repair' the moral fabric of interaction, by displaying tact in what they say and do, by engaging in 'remedial practices', and helping others to save face. If day-to-day social life is a game which may be on occasion turned to one's own advantage, it is a game into which we are all thrust and in which collaboration is essential. (Giddens 1987b: 113)

Case Study: E. Goffman (1972) *Interaction Ritual: Essays on Face-to-Face Behaviour*

While Goffman utilises the metaphors of drama and game, ritual is the more central conceptualisation of social life and how social order is upheld (Branaman 2001: 97). Goffman begins *Interaction Ritual* (1972) by saying that there is no 'adequate name' for the study of face-to-face interaction and that its 'analytical boundaries' are rather unclear – however, 'a brief time span is involved, a limited extension in space, and a restriction to those events that must go on to completion once they have begun'. He adds that there 'is a close meshing with the ritual properties of persons and with the egocentric forms of territoriality' (Goffman 1972: 1). He defines the 'subject matter' as follows:

> It is that class of events which occurs during co-presence and by virtue of co-presence. The ultimate behavioral materials are the glances, gestures, positionings,

and verbal statements that people continuously feed into the situation, whether intended or not. These are the external signs of orientation and involvement – states of mind and body not ordinarily examined with respect to their social organization. (Goffman 1972: 1)

Goffman gives two main objectives. First, 'to describe the natural units of interaction' which are constructed from 'ultimate behavioural materials' such as gestures and glances or verbal statements. These can range from the 'fleeting facial move an individual can make' to 'affairs such as week-long conferences'. Secondly, 'to uncover the normative order prevailing within and between these units, that is, the behavioral order found in all peopled places, whether public, semi-public, or private, and whether under the auspices of an organized social occasion or the flatter constraints of merely a routinized social setting' (Goffman 1972: 1–2). He argues that these objectives can be tackled through 'serious ethnography' to 'identify the countless patterns and natural sequences of behavior occurring whenever persons come into one another's immediate presence' and by making 'these events as a subject matter in their own right'. He states that he is advocating a 'sociology of occasions' in which social organisation is the 'central theme' or 'the co-mingling of persons and the temporary interactional enterprises that can arise therefrom'. His interest, then, is in the 'normatively stabilized structure', but nevertheless a changing 'social gathering' due to individuals leaving and arriving (Goffman 1972: 1–2).

Interaction Ritual (1972) provides a number of areas of discussion: 'On Face-Work' describes how the individual upholds their own 'face' and that of others. 'The Nature of Deference and Demeanor' outlines how mutual regard is given and image is formed and relayed to other participants. 'Embarrassment and Social Organization' examines how situations may undermine an actor's own portrayal of self. 'Alienation from Interaction' shows how the actor may contradict the imperative in conversation to give focused attention to a particular individual, e.g. due to distraction from others. 'Mental Symptoms and Public Order' explores how particular behaviour may break the social guidelines concerning demeanour and decorum. Finally, 'Where the Action Is' uses gambling terms to examine how actors participate in risky behaviour.

In the opening chapter, 'On Face-Work', Goffman defines 'face' as 'an image of self delineated in terms of approved social attributes – albeit an image others may share, as when a person makes a good showing for his profession or religion by making a good showing for himself' (Goffman 1972: 5). Goffman argues that everyone exists in a 'world of social encounters, involving him either in face-to-face or mediated contact with other participants'. The individual acts out a 'line' or 'pattern of verbal or nonverbal acts' through which the individual evaluates himself/herself and others, and the impression also given by others of himself/herself (Goffman 1972: 5). Goffman outlines a number of kinds of basic 'face-work' – the avoidance and corrective processes, how points can be made by the 'aggressive' use of face-work, the 'choice of appropriate face-work' and also, 'cooperation in face-work'. On the latter, for example, Goffman says, when: 'a minor mishap occurs, momentarily revealing a person in wrong face or out of face, the others are often more willing and able to act blind to the discrepancy than is the threatened person himself' (Goffman 1972: 26). In the section 'The Nature of the Ritual Order', Goffman adds that the ritual order appears to be organised on an accommodative basis so that the individual and society are in an arrangement that is easiest but this is not without its dangers (Goffman 1972: 42–3): 'Some situations and acts and persons will have to be avoided; others, less threatening, must not be pressed too far' (Goffman 1972: 43).

The individual 'adjusts' to his or her place in society through rationalisations and other devices, and the 'tactful' help of the surrounding group, so that all can gain their ends. Meanwhile, the individual is put under the 'informal social controls', which show his or her place, but in return the individual has a degree of 'discretion' to make it his or her own own. So, according to Goffman, to protect this position the individual does not have to make great efforts, become a fully 'committed' group member, or compete hard, but 'only be careful about the expressed judgments he places himself in a position to witness' (Goffman 1972: 43).

Critique

Goffman has been criticised for an emphasis on the cynical, deceitful or exploitative aspects of individuals' interaction – the attempt to 'con' and discredit' coupled with the fear of exposure – and the focus on expression or appearance in 'vulgar exchange-theory terms' (Zeitlin 1973: 214). Thus, individuals hide their intentions and inner thoughts by the use of a performance for an audience, they seek to manage impressions or show a 'front'. As Meltzer et al. (1975) point out, there is much that seems to be shared on the nature of roles in Goffman and the Chicago School – that roles are contextually enacted, rather than simply determining of individual behaviour. But in the former's discussion of 'role distance' (the difference between roles as given and as performed) there seems to be a cynicism, with actors giving little in the way of emotions in their role activities (Meltzer et al. 1975: 70).

Others have argued that there is, in fact, a strong moral element, e.g. regarding trust, in Goffman's work and that he is concerned with the points where self, interaction and morality meet. Some critical writers say that he is concerned with interesting trivia which may lead later to more scientific investigation; for others primarily he demonstrates an individualistic slant which has ultimately a subjectivist focus or, alternatively, that his individual is merely a 'social production' and ignores the 'biological individual'. For example, Zeitlin argues that Goffman does not 'consider seriously the constraining and oppressive character of social roles and relationships, not only from the standpoint of certain ethical and cultural values but also from the standpoint of the expressive needs of the biologic individual we call a human being' (Zeitlin 1973: 208).

Some writers see Goffman's identification of the interaction order as a distinctive area for study as of major importance for a sociology intent on integrating macro and micro features of society and everyday life (Layder 1994; Giddens 1987b). However, there are difficulties here regarding the degree of separation of this domain from the institutional order (as a 'loose coupling') or wider socio-historical factors (Layder 1994: 178–180, 217). To say that the nature of interactional–institutional linkage depends on the empirical context seems insufficient as a statement. Also, returning to the 'self', it is unclear how the interaction order relates to the lives of individuals and groups which 'live' through it since he provides differing accounts (e.g. ritual, game and drama (Williams 1998: 161). It could be argued that Goffman is, at least, giving a counterweight to (some) classical and functionalist theorists who emphasised the structural formation of individual action and subjectivity. But it can be concluded that Goffman's attention to the properties of interaction has rather overlooked the issues of social structure – the fuller analyses of domination and power, institutions and socio-historical contexts:

> Goffman is quite brilliant at demonstrating that what appear to be quite trivial and uninteresting aspects of day-to-day behaviour turn out to be fraught with implications for interaction. Yet many of the traits he identifies have more to do with the reproduction of institutions than he acknowledges. (Giddens 1987b: 134–5)

Giddens finds it 'striking' that Goffman's discussion of interaction seems rather 'flat' with the examples of activities given the same 'significance' – a fact, he says, that is related to the attempt to define the 'interaction order' as a distinctive area of study (Giddens 1987b: 133). Indicating a difference in social orders would at least give some possible idea of the levels or stratification of social life, rather than leaving society as a smooth plateau, as found, it is often alleged, in those who wish to avoid 'dualism', e.g. Giddens's structuration, Foucault's 'discourse', and ethnomethodologists' 'local practices' (Layder 1994: 219). Williams is 'more persuaded' by Goffman's own orientation of 'loose coupling' as guiding research. Goffman, he says, was 'suspicious' of grand theorisation and recognised the 'arbitrariness' of concept formation (Williams 1998: 162). Again, the focus of Goffman was on the intimacies of daily social interaction and, as Williams says, his work has been taken up by 'conversational analysis' or 'the analysis of talk in inter-action' in discourse analysis and other work (Williams 1998: 160).

For Meltzer et al. (1975) Goffman 'relied upon sympathetic introspection' as a 'method of observation' and a literary, stylistic approach. He can be criticised on theoretical, methodological and ideological grounds:

> no explicit theory, but a plausible and loosely-organized frame of reference; little interest in explanatory schemes, but masterful descriptive analysis; virtually no

accumulated evidence, but illuminating allusions, impressions, anecdotes, and illustrations; few formulations of empirically testable propositions, but innumerable provocative insights. In addition, we find an insufficiency of qualifications and reservations, so that the limits of generalization are not indicated. (Meltzer et al. 1975: 70–1)

While the symbolic interactionist 'predecessors' of Goffman (including Dewey, Cooley and Thomas) did not give 'extensive consideration to impression management, insincerity, hypocrisy, or inauthentic self-presentations',

> Goffman's social actor, like Machiavelli's prince, lives externally. He engages in a daily round of impression management, presenting himself to advantage when he is able, rescuing what he can from a bad show. (Scott and Lyman in Meltzer et al. 1975: 71)

It could be argued that Goffman's emphasis on ritual – stability and maintenance – provides something of a conservative view of society, under-emphasising disruption, change or flexibility, and conflict in social interaction while assuming conformity between social institutions. In addition, it can be suggested that his 'dramaturgy' reflects middle-class (and American) experiences, particularly of work in large organisations. Individuals whose beliefs are undermined, and lacking in ability to change their situation, attempt to resolve their problems through the management of appearances (Meltzer et al. 1975: 74).

Finally, as Giddens (1987b) argues, Goffman was reluctant to address questions on the various motivation of actors in his discussion of the self while recognising that the person plays differing roles in many social situations (Giddens 1987b: 138). Giddens also raises the important issue of social change and the relevance of Goffman's work to significant transformations in institutions and the utility of the study of co-presence to understanding of the deep, dramatic or violent shifts which affect daily social practices. Although Goffman studies the circumstances of the interaction order 'he does not examine how shifting institutional alignments condition, and are conditioned by, transformations of the settings in which social life is lived' (Giddens 1987b: 139). Giddens adds that Goffman could be used, nevertheless, in helping to examine these important areas, i.e. 'mechanisms of social reproduction across extended spans of time and space' (Giddens 1987b: 138).

Conclusion

Goffman outlines a notion of the individual self and an account of social interaction that contrasts sharply with structuralist theories, that tend to view action as responding to the imperatives of the social system or society. Though there is some recognition of differentials in power, access to information, the operation of rules and rule making, and production of meaning, unfortunately the analysis and content of the social organisation and effects of structure are limited. The reason for much of the current interest in Goffman is that his notion of interaction order has the potential to link micro and macro concerns and, in so doing, examine differentials in power and relations between and within levels. But his discussion of the production of social structure (in ritual), though important in connecting it to everyday life, lacks sufficient attention to the determination of structure and structural differentiation.

Goffman, as Branaman argues, has contributed to micro social theory in a number of key areas (Branaman 1997). First, in his analysis of many aspects of the 'self–society relation' and the view of self as a 'social product'. Secondly, 'he exposes the link between power, status, performance, and self'. Thirdly, in 'oscillating' between three metaphors of ritual, game and drama he shows the 'the inherent interplay between manipulation and morality in social life'. Finally, his idea of frames shows their 'powerful role in guiding the interpretation of experience, determining the meaning of social events, and defining the personal identities of individuals'. While they often derive from 'social structure and social organization, he also thinks that situationally based interpretive patterns can actively influence social structural arrangements' (Branaman 1997: lxxxii). The general importance of Goffman to micro social theory is in resisting a theorisation reduced to discussion of individuals and their interactions as if these were divorced from a wider social arena. His view of the societal context can be seen as inadequate, but he has a notion that social interaction can be studied 'in itself' as well as connected to the broader 'social' realm.

Goffman can, perhaps, be seen as a 'transitional figure' – a successor to Park and Hughes and a 'bridge between generations of Chicago sociology and some of the varied concerns of contemporary sociology'. He is also 'transitional' in terms of European sociology with connections to the work of Giddens, Habermas and Bourdieu (Fine and Manning 2000: 465–6). Finally, historically Goffman's work can also be placed within a range of cultural critiques of American society of the 1950s and early 1960s (e.g. Riesman, Packard, and Boorstin), concerned that social relations were increasingly influenced by 'appearance' rather than 'content' (Lemert 1997: xxxii).

Further Reading

Essential reading for Goffman's idea of the self is his *The Presentation of Self in Everyday Life* (Harmondsworth, Penguin, 1971), while one of his other most popularly known books is *Asylums* (Harmondsworth, Penguin, 1968). These two books are key starting points for understanding his work. For Goffman's important discussions of his ideas on ritual and game see *Interaction Ritual: Essays on Face-to-Face Behaviour* (Harmondsworth, Penguin, 1972) and *Strategic Interaction* (Oxford, Basil Blackwell, 1970).

There is a wide range of readers and commentaries on Goffman's work. C. Lemert and A. Branaman (eds.), *The Goffman Reader* (Oxford, Blackwell, 1997) is particularly useful due to the comprehensive overviews provided by the editors. Concise and very useful introductions to Goffman are: A. Branaman, 'Erving Goffman', in A. Elliott and B. S. Turner (eds.), *Profiles in Contemporary Social Theory* (London, Sage, 2001) and R. Williams, 'Erving Goffman', in R. Stones (ed.), *Key Sociological Thinkers* (Basingstoke, Palgrave Macmillan, 1998). A major compendium is G. A. Fine and G. W. H. Smith (eds.), *Erving Goffman* (4 vols., London, Sage, 2001). Commentaries that review and assess his work are: T. Burns, *Erving Goffman* (London, Routledge, 1992); J. Ditton (ed.), *The View from Goffman* (London, Macmillan, 1980); P. Drew and A. Wootton (eds.), *Erving Goffman: Exploring the Interaction Order* (Cambridge, Polity, 1988); P. Manning, *Erving Goffman and Modern Sociology* (Cambridge, Polity, 1992) and G. W. H. Smith (ed.), *Goffman and Social Organization: Studies of a Sociological Legacy* (London, Routledge, 1999).

6

Phenomenology and Ethnomethodology

Introduction

'Phenomenological sociology' is a micro social theory 'tradition' deriving from the philosophy of Edmund Husserl, whose work was greatly modified and brought into sociology by Alfred Schutz. The latter influenced the work of Harold Garfinkel, whose resulting 'ethnomethodology' contained further influences and concerns (see Lassman 1974; Attewell 1974). As it developed, ethnomethodology refined its strong critique of traditional sociology while focusing on the 'shared knowledge' and 'accountability' of 'actors' in given situations. Its stress on the contextualisation of knowledge and the separation of 'life-worlds' brought difficulties and criticisms, but it is also possible to see it as having some compatibility with wider structural theory (e.g. Parsons's structural functionalism). Rather differently, Berger and Luckmann's widely discussed 'sociology of knowledge' represented both a phenomenological influence and some traditional sociological concerns derived from Weber, Marx and Durkheim. Their very influential account of society as both a 'subjective' and 'objective' reality attempted to see the interrelation of micro and macro levels, at the same time retaining some analytical independence for both.

Phenomenological Sociology – Origins: Husserl and Schutz

The origins of phenomenology in sociology lay in the philosophy of Edmund Husserl (1859–1938) and the writings of Alfred Schutz (1899–1959). Husserl sought to lay bare the character of experience, free from the assumptions of science or other sources. His objective was to investigate the broad features of the subjective view of reality rather than outline its objective features. Husserl's method can be summarised as follows:

> The phenomenological method consists in the analysis of experience to discriminate within it its various properties. It involves an eventual reduction of experience to

pure consciousness and its correlates. The method assumes that every experience has essences accessible to intuitive apprehension. Husserl's ultimate objective was the investigation of pure consciousness and its correlative realm of eidetic being [essences forming pure consciousness]. To arrive at this, it is necessary that the world of objects and the 'I' as a psychophysical organism be 'put aside' or 'bracketed' for the purpose of gaining an intuitive vision of the pure sphere of transcendental subjectivity. (Martindale 1961: 227; see also Wolff 1979: 500; Pivcevic 1970: 71–3)

Alfred Schutz studied law and social sciences at the University of Vienna. Following the rise of Nazism he stayed briefly in Paris before emigrating to the United States in 1939. Schutz was influenced by Bergson, Weber and later came into contact with Mead's work. He adapted Husserl's ideas and introduced them into sociological theory. Schutz's position began with the examination of the basis of social science thinking and the view that the positivistic tradition in social science had not begun with the issue of the basis of social reality (see Schutz 1972). In this regard, he was concerned with questions of intersubjectivity or the interpretation of action by individuals. A second important starting point of Schutz's work is his critique of Weber's version of interpretive sociology as a science, which attempts an interpretive understanding of social action so that a causal explanation can be produced of its direction and consequences. A problem in Weber's use of the notion of subjective understanding, or *Verstehen*, is that, for Schutz, it is used in a number of senses, including those of a method and knowledge in daily life (see Schutz 1972: 15; Walsh 1972: xvii). In Schutz's view, individuals experience their surroundings as a socially meaningful reality and the scientific role of the investigator is to make clear how the meanings are given to action. The difficulty in Weber's discussion was that he did not analyse the basic issue of how individuals have an intersubjective experience of social reality – not just their own specific understanding but one which is held in common with others (see Schutz 1972: ch. 1). The taken-for-granted meanings of the social world result from intersubjective agreement; unless these are part of study then they may well become uncritically part of sociological thinking. This is an issue at the basis of social science knowledge; for Schutz, the intricacies of subjective meanings and common-sense concepts should be themselves studied by phenomenological investigation.

In this enterprise, therefore, Schutz departs markedly from Husserl's approach. Instead of 'bracketing' out the life-world he is concerned with the actual formation of meaning or intersubjectivity. In so doing, he advances Weber's discussion of subjective meaning further by investigating the 'common-sense' notions of individuals – their intersubjective understanding of the world around them. Ordinarily, individuals do not question or analyse that world, rather it is taken for granted, as ordered or fact outside analysis. Here, Schutz attempts to redefine Husserl's idea of 'epoché' or the 'bracketing' out of doubts related to daily reality to expose the structure of consciousness; what had been bracketed out becomes the prime focus for the phenomenological approach to society. In Schutz, epoché is used to indicate how we in our natural attitude suspend doubt that the world may be more different than it seems. For Schutz the concepts produced and used in social science are of the 'second degree' but, even so, are connected to the common-sense actions and meanings (e.g. typifications) that are constructions of a first order. Social scientists must relate these two levels; otherwise, formal scientific knowledge will have no reference in the taken-for-granted intersubjective world of individuals. In short, 'in neglecting the productive processes which members use to sustain reality, standard sociologists accept the categories, language and perspective of members, namely that society is already accomplished. They can therefore never understand how it becomes accomplished' (Attewell 1974: 197). Instead, for Schutz, by bracketing the social scientist can investigate the interpretations of the first order to render them according to second-order social-scientific understanding (Ferguson 2003: 243).

Of course, a problem here is that the social scientist is also a participant in the social world that is to be explained. The 'solution' to this difficulty is that the social scientist takes up the attitude of a 'disinterested observer', an orientation that is aimed at making clear what the ordinary person takes without question in the social world. Thus, the social scientist consciously reflects on his or her own life situation, brackets out these influences, and adopts the position of the 'disinterested observer' in carrying out scientific study.

Schutz offers the idea of 'typifications' as part of the 'natural attitude' to describe how we understand the experience of the surrounding social world. Each person acquires a 'stock of knowledge' composed of perceptions and beliefs which guide our actions and views on life and are subject to new experiences. These sets of knowledge are related to communication with other individuals and comparison with new, similar events; our knowledge is drawn from the experiences of our contemporaries and our predecessors. According to Schutz our common-sense knowledge of the world is a system of constructs of 'typicality' in which 'typical' ends are met in 'typical' ways. Common-sense knowledge in simple terms is the actors' system of constructs through which they gain a vision of the typicality of the social world. It is shaped in three ways: the reciprocity of perspectives, the social origins of knowledge, and the social distribution of knowledge. What is meant here is that there is a common knowledge or shared 'system of relevances' of what is deemed to be natural or appropriate by the group members (while varying between groups) which has an historical aspect passed down to 'contemporaries'. Thus, while individually separable, we share language and concepts that allow us to go further than our own personal world. We can interchange our standpoints but can also transcend everyday life symbolically. Finally, the individual's common-sense knowledge of the social world is due to a social distribution, although its particular use is connected to a system of individual relevances.

Schutz outlined three principles or 'postulates' as a procedure for scientific practice which stemmed from his analysis of Weber's use of *Verstehen*. First, 'the postulate of logical consistency' is concerned with the clarity of the logic of theoretical constructions. Secondly, the 'postulate of subjective interpretation' is associated with scientists laying bare the subjective meanings for the actions of individuals in the models or types they study. Thirdly, 'the postulate of adequacy' relates to the need for consistency between theoretical constructs and those found in common-sense experiences (see Lassman 1974: 129–30; Zeitlin 1973: 180–1). Schutz (and Weber) were not calling for a method of subjective understanding that revealed simply inner aspects (as far as is possible) of the individual. Instead, the immediate attempt was to explore the meanings given for behaviour by the individual rather than that of their colleagues (or the investigating detached social scientist).

Schutz allows for many different social orders or 'multiple realities'. There is the reality of everyday life and other realities, such as second-order scientific conceptualisation, and fantasies or dreams – as well as the past as a dimension of the social world. Generally, individuals focus on the working practicalities of daily life – our 'natural attitude' is to attempt to change or shape the world according to our purposes; it is our 'paramount reality'. We apply aspects of the social world, which help towards the achievement of our interests (Zeitlin 1973: 173). An interesting aspect of Schutz's work is the outlining (again in response to Weber) of the motives for action. He gives two major types: 'in-order-to motives', or the intentions informing action towards a future outcome, and 'because motives', or the reasons we give (for past action) following later reflection or observing ourselves as having acted. Through the provision of motives to actions undertaken by others, and ourselves, we are able to take part in shared action as we map out, share and communicate actions (Schutz 1972: 86–96).

Schutz's ideas became prominent in the 1960s and 1970s with the emergence of micro sociologies. In particular, it had a specific influence on the rise of the 'ethnomethodology' of Harold Garfinkel and associated writers, the work of Berger and Luckmann on the 'social construction' reality and, more broadly, in the sociology of deviance, e.g. Rock (1973), Matza (1969). For some, Schutz's writings can be seen as bridge between Weberian and other discussions on social science in Germany and the pragmatist tradition in America. The focus of social science on the examination of subjective experience had a contemporary appeal in social theory and fitted in with an associated critique of existing methodological practice.

Critique

There have been a number of common criticisms of Schutz's ideas or 'phenomenological sociology'. One charge is that since it focuses on 'experience' or 'consciousness' it is not really sociology at all but a psychological field or a form of philosophy, since these concerns are insufficiently attached to the empirical realities of social life. In response it can be argued that sociological studies and methodological practice have very much benefited from this strand of thought – and social theory itself has gained from its attention to 'experience' and other themes (e.g. time) (see Ferguson 2003: 243).

The postulates of subjective interpretation and adequacy in Schutz's programme for scientific procedure have been questioned. Sociological study, it is argued, will have 'a highly limited significance if their results are unable to modify or correct common-sense definitions of social situations'; and further, 'common-sense beliefs may not only be false but incorrigible within their own terms' (Lassman 1974: 130). Lassman adds that the interrelation between sociological theorisation and common sense is insufficiently outlined – a tension that reappears in some later phenomenological sociology where the outcome seems to be a 'descriptive anti-theoretical stance'. An associated difficulty is that Schutz is 'constrained by a consensual and static image of social relations' which militates against an understanding of shifts in the 'content of common-sense knowledge'. Further, it restricts 'conceptual innovations' in sociology and an investigation of their 'possible mutual interrelations with the "stock of common-sense knowledge" ' (Lassman 1974: 130). Criticisms have also pointed to Schutz's" ideas and subsequent research work being 'mainly programmatic' and (at least by the early 1970s) showing 'little development or application' of the method. It both 'abstracts the everyday world' and 'idealises' it since nothing is garnered about how the individual's daily living is formed in relation to the institutional and societal context 'by focusing consistently on relatively unproblematic transactions' (Zeitlin 1973: 182). Zeitlin concludes: 'The real problem with Schutz's scheme is that it provides us with no independent means of assessing the validity of Everyman's judgments about his existential conditions and his interpretations of his relations with his fellow men' (Zeitlin 1973: 182).

Hindess (1972) questioned whether Schutz's social science was a science and argued it was a complex product of his humanism, a theoretical ideology affirming in its 'results' its own necessary and unquestioned premise: that 'the world of objective mind' can be reduced to the behaviour of individuals'. It also:

> leads to a theory of science in which the determining element is the attitude of the scientist ... Schutz ... presents as scientific a humanistic social science and history which are nothing but special kinds of story-telling. The cost of his humanism is a world in which there can be no science of history and no rational politics. (Hindess 1972: 1)

While Schutz's approach to the investigation of everyday life was rather unclear, Garfinkel and others took up his work to construct a critique of traditional sociological theorisation and to form an alternative methodological basis for substantive research work but, in general,

> Schutz's legacy seems to be that of diffuse impact. He launched no identifiable school of thought, and he gathered around him no clear-cut band of disciplines. Yet his work gets cited time and time again as social theorists grapple anew with the stubborn question of what it means to share a world while living a life that no one else can have. (Rogers 2000: 386)

Case Study: P. L. Berger and T. Luckmann (1971) *The Social Construction of Reality: A Treatise in the Sociology of Knowledge*

Berger and Luckmann were intent to form a social theory that showed the social construction of the social world through the meanings and objectives people have in interaction. At the centre of their book *The Social Construction of Reality* (1971) is the idea of society as both a subjective and objective phenomenon. In giving this emphasis they were attempting to correct the structuralist (functionalist and Marxist) accounts in which individual intention was smothered by the determination of social forces. In their view the individual is a creative being with at least some choice – a voluntaristic, humanistic vision of individuals and social life is offered, in contrast to the idea of the constrained individual and deterministic accounts of society derived from many traditional approaches. Such a view attempts to provide a 'dynamic view of social realities' which shows 'social life as produced and reproduced in individual interaction' (Seidman 2004: 81).

Berger and Luckmann draw on Husserl and Schutz in detailing a series of ideas concerned with subjectivity, multiple realities and symbolic communication to allow an understanding of the subjective, uncertain, shifting side of social life, and at the same time detail the rise and continuity of social institutions. To a large extent the book, as indicated by its subtitle, is also concerned with the role of knowledge or rather the knowledge individuals have of their social world. Through social interaction social institutions arise over time, such as family, work and other organisations. The process of 'objectivation' establishes traditions or customs through the means of rules, rituals, language and symbols. Finally, by 'internalisation' the individual takes these 'external' aspects of social life into consciousness and they become part of identity formation. The result is a complex theoretical mix, which includes 'traditional' sociological theorists such as Weber, Marx and Durkheim, but also Mead, Sartre and a wide range of other writers. These diverse sources are used to inform a discussion, on the one side, of society as 'objective reality' – as constraining and shaping while, on the other, of individuals seeking to establish human meaning and order 'in the face of an awareness of the ultimate meaninglessness of existence' (Seidman 2004: 82).

Berger and Luckmann's approach is impressive in dealing with the 'subjective reality' experienced by individuals while rather weak on social interaction. Conversely, their view of society is interesting on the accumulation and distribution of knowledge and symbolic processes yet it is deficient on the structural aspects of material inequalities and social stratification. The outcome is both a rather restrictive notion of the individual as a socially interactive being and a limited view of institutions and society. The 'inclusive' nature of their enterprise has led to the observation that any 'essential phenomenological component' seems to disappear and the result is not so different from Parsons's structural functionalist concerns with moral collective integration and the importance of socialisation for social cohesion (Lassman 1974: 130–1). There is a lack of detail on organisational contexts, and the effort to place a 'micro sociology of knowledge' (from Schutz) within a wider societal conception 'remains at the level of general assertions about the "dialectical" relationship between society as "objective" and as "subjective reality"' (Lassman 1974: 131). The formulation, for Lassman, relies in part on Schutz, and has certain basic assumptions. First, from their stance that the 'paramount reality' is the reality of everyday life, they seem to argue that the 'objectivity' of institutions and social interaction 'is nothing more than the operation of taken-for-granted definitions of reality'. Secondly, that there is a 'precariousness' of social reality which is only met by the meanings of an institutional order protecting society from 'chaos'. Thirdly, 'face-to-face interaction is taken as the paradigm case for all forms of interaction and social relations'. The general outcome is a 'highly static image of social change that seems to be a process of "existential leaps" and mass conversions' (Lassman 1974: 131). At the level of objectivation, where the 'externalised products of human activity attain the character of objectivity' – and are then, 'internalized' by the individual (Berger and Luckmann 1971: 78) – there are further issues. For one critic, the whole perspective 'is curiously abstract and ahistorical' (Lichtman 1970: 87). However, Berger and Luckmann's approach did mark an attempt to bring together classical sociological approaches with phenomenology and other micro sociologies – the degree of critique which it produced was a mark of the interest in its impressive endeavour to link micro and macro sociological concerns.

Ethnomethodology – Origins

The notion of 'ethnomethodology' arose from the research of Harold Garfinkel (1917–) and the work of number of subsequent researchers. Usually discussed alongside Garfinkel is the work of Sacks (1992), Cicourel (1968, 1973), and Pollner (1987). His influences included Husserl, Schutz, Parsons and 'ordinary language' philosophy in his investigation of everyday activities and the problem of social order and its 'solutions'. There are also parallels with Goffman's emphasis on communication, 'how things take place' in action and the 'interaction order'. In his early studies of jurors, Garfinkel discovered that they exhibited a 'methodology' in relation to the evidence given in court and drew upon their available 'common-sense knowledge'. He states: 'I use the term "ethnomethodology" to refer to the investigation of the rational properties of indexical expressions and other practical actions as contingent ongoing accomplishments of organized artful practices of everyday life' (Garfinkel 1994: 62).

Initially, there seem to be some similarities between ethnomethodology and symbolic interactionism in that they share a general 'micro' orientation towards small-scale situations and, during the 1960s, offered critiques of traditional sociological theory and methodological approaches (see Denzin 1970; Meltzer et al. 1975). There was some sharing of interest in areas such as deviancy and organisational behaviour which showed the complexity of everyday life and an interest in the nature of theorisation and concept formation, in situated meanings, and in 'meaningful action'. There was also some common influence from phenomenological sociology as symbolic interactionism and interactionism began drawing on a range of approaches. For instance, ethnomethodology explained that rather than being 'cultural dopes' individuals were to be seen as 'knowledgeable actors'. Traditional causal approaches were charged with creating 'passive producers of actions' according to pre-given available general structural or cultural models. At its simplest, the difference between ethnomethodology and symbolic interactionism lies in former's concern with activities which render meanings rather than with the interest in actors' (and group) meanings as such. There are also differences in interpretive style, with ethnomethodology being more 'technical and precise' while symbolic interactionism can be considered to be 'more impressionistic and "loose"' in approach (Cuff et al. 1990: 192). Lastly, whereas symbolic interactionism, and interactionism more generally, took its place inside sociological theory and practice, ethnomethodology has sought to have a detached position.

Garfinkel's empirical research and conceptualisation influenced a broad range of others to investigate daily life in organisations and other areas. There are two main sources of influence on Garfinkel's work: Schutz's phenomenological writings and also Talcott Parsons's discussion of the 'problem of order' or how society (or a social system) is possible while the voluntarism in social life is evident (see Heritage 1984: chs. 1–2): how could individuals be conceived as having choices while at the same time recognising the social structural forces that impinge on the actions in which individuals take part? In simple terms, the explanation offered by Parsons was to conceive of a normative order – individuals are committed to conformity by the limitation of choice and a shared belief in the societal norms. Thus, he emphasised the part played by culture, socialisation, the family and the formation of the personality. The ethnomethodological charge is made that Parsons and many other sociological theorists have made a fundamental error in accepting the 'common-sense' categories rather than taking these as being the very areas for scrutiny.

Such approaches veered away from actual individual (and group) practice and specific situations and gave action a rationality from outside – by the theorist. Thus, ethnomethodology opposed conventional sociologies 'in that they leave unexamined the ways in which status, role, norm, etc. are perceived by members to be appropriate to a given situation'. Traditional sociologies 'ignore the fact that a member has first to *interpret* a given situation and the given norms (if they exist), and then make a decision as to which norms, etc., "fit" the situation' (Attewell 1974: 207).

As a graduate student of Parsons, Garfinkel was influenced by his attempt to understand the character of action but wanted to challenge his analytical approach and assumptions depicting the nature of everyday life and to question the basis of sociological theorisation further. His critique of Parsons was influenced by Schutz's approach to social science and 'common-sense knowledge'. Instead of a view, which started with the general social order or system and notions of equilibrium, continuity, regularity, and normative consensus, Schutz's approach began with daily life or experiences of the acting individual, action as it were from below rather than from above. He held up the Parsonian assumption that actors 'must possess shared understanding', and the basis for social order as resting on shared values for scrutiny, as a starting point for investigation. He set out a programme of empirical research as follows:

> An indefinitely large domain of appropriate settings can be located if one uses a search policy that *any occasion whatsoever* be examined for the feature that 'choice' among alternatives of sense, of facticity, of objectivity, of cause, of explanation, of communality *of practical actions* is a project of members' actions. (Garfinkel 1994: 68)

So, inquiry should be conducted into 'socially organized, artful practices', whether engaged in by lay or professional personnel; importantly, such investigation would include the practice of sociology itself.

Members' Methods

To investigate the 'common-sense knowledge' or 'methods' of actors ethnomethodology developed an impressive array of concepts. Ethnomethodological writings are 'replete with words such as procedures, processes, methods, practices, etc. which express this process model that becomes an underlying assumption of *all* ethnomethodologists' (Attewell 1974: 203). The starting point for Garfinkel in his *Studies in Ethnomethodology* (1967) is the study of how 'members' ordinary activities include 'methods' which inform practical actions and common-sense knowledge. This has led to some immediate criticisms. Ethnomethodology:

> became totally involved in the question: how is interaction done? and wholly unconcerned in questions like: why it gets done, how its being done results in institutions,

ideas, societies, etc. and how societies, institutions, and power modify how interaction itself gets done. (Attewell 1974: 181)

Attewell (1974) argues that for Garfinkel 'making sense out of a situation, and giving ordinary language accounts of that sense, are inextricably connected'. It is a Goffmanian emphasis: 'as actors announce to one another the situation as they see it, so the meaning of the situation becomes clear, concrete, and shared'. A 'large part of ethnomethodology becomes the study of how members build accounts of social action, while doing that action' (Attewell 1974:182). The emphasis becomes not one of individual intention in action but rather the following (or not) of rules (of action) within a situation and the description of the rationalities (or method of understanding) in everyday action. Garfinkel explains:

> That practical actions are problematic in ways not so far seen; how they are problematical; how to make them accessible to study; what we might learn about them – these are proposed tasks. (Garfinkel 1994: 68)

Thus, ethnomethodology studies 'members' methods' – their practical reasoning in giving accounts or interpreting meaningfully the particular context. Garfinkel examined such activity as the construction of suicide statistics by agencies as an illustration of ethnomethodological work. Through a 'documentary method' members select aspects of the setting to formulate a rational account:

> Garfinkel's sociology is based on the idea that common-sense reasoning is *methodical*, that is, based on methods. The methods must be social and shared, otherwise actors would not be able to reason towards the same conclusions, understand one another and act in a co-ordinated fashion. (Heritage 1998: 178)

In *Studies in Ethnomethodology* (1967) Garfinkel outlines the notion of 'indexicality' or contextuality. He is referring to ethnomethodology as the examination of the rational properties of 'indexical expressions' and other practical actions as part of the accomplishment of 'organised artful practices' within everyday life. Meanings or accounts are very much tied to the nature of the specific situation. By this he argued that social interaction is crucially 'situated' – as understandable according to its given context. There is an immediate problem here if interaction can only be understood or merely described 'indexically' as linked to context. Such a view appears to prevent an understanding of the continuity of meanings from context to context. We can argue that individuals do at least say that they can give accounts and act according to their comparative knowledge of different situations; they transfer and share meanings between settings and thereby, over time (see Attewell 1974: 185).

Accountability

Apart from attention to rules guiding and as involved in understanding action, another central idea in Garfinkel's writing is the concept of 'accountability'. It is used in two ways:

first, as a synonym for intelligible. In this usage an accountable action is an intelligible action and one which we can therefore name, or describe or, more generally, 'give an account of'. The second sense is the more usual moral one in which we speak of someone being 'accountable for their actions'. (Heritage 1998: 180)

Through accountability members are not only involved in practical reasoning in a situation but also in holding each other to account. As Heritage asks: 'the question now becomes: what are these rules like, how do they work, what are their properties, how extensive are they?' (Heritage 1998: 180). Of relevance here is Garfinkel's notion of the 'documentary method of interpretation' from which the individual obtains an underlying pattern from the actual appearances. The knowledge about the social world is used to make sense of 'what we see' in terms of 'what we know' (Heritage 1998: 183):

But, Garfinkel added, there is an element of circularity in this process of fitting appearances to a pattern ... this process is continually used in every waking moment to make sense of the world: we recognize dogs, postmen, greetings, social class, bureaucratic red tape, and 'introverted people' using this method. Most of the time, the results of the method are so 'obvious' that we do not notice how we use background knowledge to recognize things. But we become aware of the process when we are faced with ambiguous things. (Heritage 1998: 183)

As Garfinkel concludes, any social setting should be seen as 'self-organising':

All 'logical' and 'methodological' properties of action, every feature of an activity's sense, facticity, objectivity, accountability, communality is to be treated as a contingent accomplishment of socially organized common practices ... Any setting organizes its activities to make its properties as an organized environment of practical activities detectable, countable, recordable, reportable, tell-a-story-aboutable, analyzable – in short, *accountable*. (Garfinkel 1994: 70)

Conventional Sociology

Ethnomethodology has claimed that it is an approach that 'does not appropriately fit within the conventional sociological categories of either theory or method'. It is not bent on making '*discoveries*' but rather the '*recovery* of what is already known', conducting affairs competently to achieve clarification in the relationship between common-sense and analytical concepts

(Sharrock 2003: 258). A 'basic proposition' of ethnomethodology is that the activities involved in 'settings of organised everyday affairs' are the same as the actor's rendering them 'accountable' (Lassman 1974: 132–3). The result of this view is that an account is linked to the organised context of its use. It is held that the notion of 'indexicality' within ethnomethodology is directly against the positivistic approach to facts or knowledge; the accounts that members have of their settings are to be used in the researcher's descriptions of the setting.

An important ambiguity here is that social phenomena are part of the reflexive accounts of actors while also part of the methods sociologists use. 'Sociological' practice, therefore, is merely the same as everyday reflexive practice – both lay and professionals 'make use of or assume this reflexivity as a basic condition for the persistence of concerted action' and to be subject to ethnomethodological study. However, if the sociologist 'must attempt to treat the rational properties of practical activities as being 'anthropologically strange' there is a 'danger of infinite regress' since (in Garfinkel's words) there is 'no concept of context-in-general … [i.e. for actors], but every use of "context" without exception is itself essentially indexical' (Lassman 1974: 133–4). In the end, there seems (in the view of ethnomethology) little separation between sociological explanations and common-sense descriptions. The aim of sociological theory appears to be a 'literal description' of its subject matter – 'an essential part of such a description is a description of the descriptions that actors have of their own actions', while both sociologist and subject may use the same 'natural language' (Lassman 1974: 134).

Differences can be seen between ethnomethodological writers – including some who reject the term 'ethnomethodology' itself – with regard to their relationship with sociological theory and practice and the extent sociology can be 'reformed'. The basic view is that the social sciences expect to generalise from specific instances. This can only be achieved, for Garfinkel, if they ignore the irrevocable indexical properties of accounts and destroy the connection with the context. But, we can say, this seems a severely limited study even of the settings themselves – perhaps, at base, merely an attempt to collate, in an accurate manner, the rationalities given by actors. If so, a significant issue arises concerning how such a study of situated (indexical) accounts and action can be regarded as 'scientific', or to some extent 'verifiable'. Ethnomethodologists run the risk of being subject to their own critique of conventional sociology as merely another 'account'.

In fact, there are various ways in which ethnomethodologists have approached the problem of indexicality or the link between meaningful accounts and context. These have included examining the features of language and how the social world is provided through language use; by the study of cognitive processes (e.g. memory) to gain social science material (see Cicourel 1973); and by arguing that knowledge itself involves generalisation beyond the situation. Another tack, by ethnomethodologists, is to deny the relevance of the issue, carry out analysis without making claims regarding the 'validity' of analysis – and focus on the content of what is being said. Or they can also argue that there is something that is cross-situational and 'invariant' in time and setting and examine the patterns or order of conversation rather than its content. The latter position appears to contradict the commitment to indexicality or the situatedness of knowledge while also risking the traditional 'positivistic' generalisations it sought to replace (see Attewell 1974: 200).

One large body of work associated with ethnomethodology is conversational analysis associated with writers such as Sacks (1992). The intention of participants is not the object of study but an analysis of their transcribed speech, for example, the 'categorization devices' that individuals use to understand their setting. In this way the features of the situation are omitted in favour of how individuals use the rules of language. Thus, the reference is to the vital, general structures of language, which are, for example, applied in particular ways according to the occasion, producing specific results via analysis of the taped transcripts. A key point in conversational analysis is the need to distinguish between 'resource' and 'topic' in the study of conversation. Again, mirroring the previous critique of conventional sociology the argument is that through the use of language sociologists are using member's categories – what they take as a resource should also be taken as their topic. One consequence of the development of conversational analysis is the further loss of the phenomenological aspect or the conception of the experience of individuals – their motives and intentions within situations. Much of this work appears increasingly 'esoteric' as an area for committed adherents with concerns that are becoming fenced off from the sociological interest in embodied, interacting individuals within social situations.

Ethnomethodology and 'Misconceptions'?

Some ethnomethodologists have been quite sensitive to critiques of their work and have alleged a misreading of the nature of their study while being very resistant to perceived attempts (e.g. Giddens) to incorporate it within conventional sociology, or more specifically in social action theory. Sharrock argues that ethnomethodology is not a particular methodology, neither does it aspire to theory, rather it attempts to show parts of social life we 'overlook' in theorisation (Sharrock 2003: 249). Ethnomethodology is held to be very different from conventional sociology with a specific recognition that sociologists and lay individuals both use 'common-sense' understandings of what is taking place in their social situations. Its concern is with the variety and tracing of 'reasoning' or 'sociological reasoning'; since ordinary members of society can be seen as just as much engaged in sociological reasoning as professional sociologists, there should be no privileging of the latter (Sharrock 2003: 251–2). There are two immediate issues here; first, why should anyone engage in the practice of sociology at all (in departments where ethnomethodologists themselves are commonly located)? In addition, is ethnomethodological work itself just another practice of reasoning in describing the reasoning of others? In claiming to be 'dissident' or 'outsiders' to sociological work, are they not really seeking some privileged position which then is open to their own critique? Sharrock admits that there is some continuity between sociological theorisation and ethnomethodology due to the latter's central concern with social order (Sharrock 2003: 252). But rather than the social system maintaining social order via integration, he says, now the emphasis is on the 'production of the local social order'. The problem is said to be resolved in practice through the orderliness of everyday activities; the practical sociological reasoning of individuals identifies the orderliness of the setting or the 'self-organising' of the setting. While Sharrock maintains that the problem of order is not resolvable through sociological theory and method but in practice by knowledgeable actors – there does seem to be some drift here back to one of ethnomethodology's roots – Parsonian functionalism on social integration (see Lassman 1974: 141).

Critique

The response of sociology to ethnomethodology has varied from puzzlement and exasperation to outright hostility. Some have recognised its critique of sociological materials and practice, although often with the qualification that sociology has been more reflexive on the nature of its work than ethnomethodology recognised. Criticisms have tended to fall into a number of categories:

Ethnomethodology deals with the inconsequential aspects of daily life. The response to this charge is that the production of a local social order is a fundamental social activity allowing for the continuity of society. Even so, the emphasis on the local production of the 'social order' leads to the criticism that at base it has a conservative societal view lacking in an understanding of interaction, e.g. ignores processes of social change, and the origins and consequences of dissension and conflict.

Ethnomethodology has ignored social structure, domination and material inequalities – and is not concerned with the pressing social issues confronting society as a whole. One response to this charge is that such considerations are not part of its remit, that is, to investigate 'practical reasoning' – just as, in a similar way, various sociological theories have different considerations. Such criticism is said to reflect a 'perspectival bias'. Another response has been that ethnomethodologists, in fact, have carried out intensive studies of institutional settings (courts, welfare and the police) which could be used to investigate the linkages between practical reasoning and social contexts to span the 'micro–macro divide' (Ritzer and Goodman 2004: 396).

Ethnomethodology has ignored some of its basic principles. For instance, there is the charge – particularly aimed at the conversational analysis of the structural properties of language – that the phenomenological concern with the motives or experience of action has been neglected. The 'judgemental dope' as the model of the actor, which it sought to replace by a knowledgeable actor, is said to reappear within an empiricist and behaviouristic approach (Ritzer and Goodman 2004: 396). A certain 'structuralism' also arises in which the 'self' is forgotten: interaction is mere 'turn taking' in conversation, without motives or intention, embodiment, and the contexts of time and place. Ironically, given its original intentions, ethnomethodology – at least with regard to conversational analysis – becomes, it can be argued, 'scientistic' and 'empiricist' by being especially concerned with the technical investigation of the transcript. It moves away from the phenomenological legacy of intentionality and experience, and reference to context and interaction (May 1996: 97).

Ethnomethodology is in a methodological dilemma, which is also found in sociology, between treating each situation as unique, only understandable with reference to the practical reasoning in that setting, and the establishment of invariant features (e.g. perceptual, cognitive procedures) of social life. Very simply, it is caught between a relativistic and a positivistic approach to common-sense understanding and the social production of the local social order. Where its focus is on invariant features these are clearly to be found in all social contexts, whether the classroom, beauty salon or the police station. But, in this orientation the distinctiveness of particular contexts is merely seen as the backdrop for invariant features of situations rather than the start of substantial interest in broader social theory and important social issues and problems (see Attewell 1974: 208).

Ethnomethodology has lost its 'original radical reflexivity'. Some ethnomethodologists (e. g. Pollner) alleged that ethnomethodology had forgotten the need to be 'self-analytical' and have a 'critical edge' (Ritzer and Goodman 2004: 397). The charge here is that the notion that 'all social activity is accomplished, including the activities of ethnomethodologists', has lessened as ethnomethodologists have joined the mainstream of sociology and some of their ideas have become commonplace in the discipline (Ritzer and Goodman 2004: 397).

Ethnomethodology and the status of the researcher. Critics point out (following the above) that ethnomethodology itself as an accomplished, organised activity involving common-sense, practical reasoning must demonstrate how its own accounts are formed – both in relation to ethnomethodologists' own situations and in relation to lay and professional sociological practices. Otherwise, ethnomethodological researchers, by not engaging in a radical reflexivity in relation to context, will 'appear to believe themselves capable of floating freely across language games without being fettered by the constraints of their own' (May 1996: 94–5).

Conclusion

A number of shared features can be identified in phenomenological sociology from Schutz through to ethnomethodology (see Lassman 1974; Attewell 1974). For Lassman (1974) there is a 'pervasive influence' of Parsonian theory present in phenomenological sociology. But it also shows in 'interactional fundamentalism' – as shared knowledge and accountability attached to a situation appear unable to connect to wider 'interactional patterns' and social structural contexts. Lassman adds that the phenomenological perspective in sociology is to some extent compatible with structural-functional theory, and seems unable to outline the various types of interaction. Finally, when ethnomethodologists go further than 'technical, social or socio-linguistic description of isolated "life-worlds" ', they meet the 'traditional problems of sociological analysis whether they are aware of it or not' (Lassman 1974: 142). As ethnomethodology 'progressed from a critique into a sociology in its own right, it too had to grapple with that elusively objective social world' (Attewell 1974: 179).

The reception to Garfinkel's ideas were very mixed. However, defenders of the approach argue that ethnomethodological conceptualisation has entered the discipline:

> Most theories that make reference to such things as background understandings, taken-for-granted knowledge, practical reasoning, social practices, the production and reproduction of social institutions bear the marks of Garfinkel's influence. (Heritage 1998: 187)

Further, Heritage claims that ethnomethodology has been very influential in studying areas where traditional sociological investigation has been lacking, such as science (and computing), law and the arts. These, he says, are 'all areas of society whose members do use specific "methodologies" to do their work'; in particular, conversational analysis is 'now one of the pre-eminent ways of studying social interaction and language use in the world' (Heritage 1998: 188). Thus, for micro social theory, ethnomethodology brought attention to background knowledges and 'accountability' of actors and a necessary detailed focus on the analysis of conversation (despite its more rarefied technical developments). In Berger and Luckmann's (1971) distinctive phenomenological approach the accumulation and distribution of knowledges and symbolic processes allowed for an explicit attempt to connect the experience of society as a subjective and objective 'reality' (although one open to criticism from a macro structuralist viewpoint). A lasting legacy, perhaps, of phenomenological sociology, particularly ethnomethodology – for a micro social theory approach (and sociological work as a whole) – is that it pointed strongly to the uncertainties of sociological material and practice:

> it is this caution about the status of sociological data which, after all the flag-waving and trumpet-blowing has died down, will stand as the ethnomethodologists' contribution to sociological knowledge. (Gidlow 1972: 404).

Further Reading

Schutz's key ideas can be found in A. Schutz, *On Phenomenology and Social Relations*, ed. H. Wagner (Chicago, University of Chicago Press, 1970), A. Schutz, *Collected Papers 1* (The Hague, Martinus Nijhoff, 1971) and A. Schutz, *The Phenomenology of the Social World* (London, Heinemann, 1972). A useful, concise introduction to his work is M. Rogers, 'Alfred Schutz', in G. Ritzer (ed.), *The Blackwell Companion to Major Social Theorists* (Oxford, Blackwell, 2002).

Essential reading for the origin and basis of ethnomethodology is H. Garfinkel, *Studies in Ethnomethodology* (Englewood Cliffs, NJ, Prentice-Hall, 1967). Good introductions to Garfinkel's work are J. C. Heritage, 'Ethnomethodology', in A. Giddens and J. Turner (eds.), *Social Theory Today* (Stanford, CA, Stanford University Press, 1987) and J. Heritage, 'Harold Garfinkel', in R. Stones (ed.), *Key Sociological Thinkers* (Basingstoke, Palgrave Macmillan, 1998), while a more extensive treatment is J. Heritage, *Garfinkel and Ethnomethodology* (Cambridge, Polity, 1984). A good introduction to ethnomethodology more generally is W. Sharrock and R. J. Anderson, *The Ethnomethodologists* (Chichester, Ellis Horwood, 1986). For further discussion see D. Boden and D. H. Zimmerman (eds.), *Talk and Social Structure: Studies in Ethnomethodology and Conversation Analysis* (Cambridge, Polity, 1991); D. Benson and J. A. Hughes, *The Perspective of Ethnomethodology* (London, Longman, 1983); J. Coulter (ed.), *Ethnomethodological Sociology* (Aldershot, Edward Elgar, 1990); and G. Psathas (ed.), *Phenomenological Sociology* (New York, Wiley, 1973).

For studies on conversation and reasoning: for the work of Sacks, D. Silverman, *Harvey Sacks* (Cambridge, Polity, 1998); H. Sacks, *Lectures on Conversation* (Oxford, Blackwell, 1992); for further more detailed discussion, G. Button and J. R. E. Lee (eds.), *Talk and Social Organisation* (Clevedon, Multilingual Matters, 1987); P. Drew and J. Heritage (eds.), *Talk at Work* (Cambridge, Cambridge University Press, 1992); M. Pollner, *Mundane Reason* (Cambridge, Cambridge University Press, 1987); and R. Turner (ed.), *Ethnomethodology: Selected Readings* (Harmondsworth, Penguin, 1974).

7

Subjective Experience, Feminism and Sociology

Introduction

In this chapter the feminist contribution to the examination of the relationships between research, theory and experience is outlined. Different feminist perspectives are discussed and, more particularly, issues associated with feminist methods – 'experience' and 'the personal', reflexivity, gender – are overviewed and assessed.

Feminist theory, broadly, in providing a critique of existing sociology for a neglect of the dimension of gender, also brought a fundamental shift in sociological theorisation. It proposed that the disjunction between micro and macro theoretical concerns had prevented an understanding of how the daily experience of women related to various contexts (family, work, and leisure). Feminist writers were keen to argue that the wider structures of gender inequality were also felt and lived at the level of daily life and experience. These micro situations are an important site for the reproduction of structures and symbolic meanings of dominance and power and the social distribution of opportunities and resources. Again, a general feature of feminist writing, also important for micro sociology, is the question of agency and 'voice' (e.g. who defines the situation, and has that definition confirmed) in everyday practice – and whose interests are served by existing micro and macro social arrangements. Implicated here is the gendering of social relations, and access to resources and space. Finally, feminist writing has raised considerable methodological questions concerning how sociological knowledge is produced, relations between the sociologist and those who are researched, the nature of sociological writing, issues of cross-disciplinary research and theory, and problems related to the nature of experience and the definition of social categories, including 'woman'. All these areas have a direct bearing on micro social research and theory.

Feminist writing is shaped by a number of fundamental questions: *'And what about women? Why is women's situation as it is? How can we change and improve the social world?' and 'What about differences among women?'* (Lengermann and Niebrugge-Brantley 2004: 479). In exploring the position of women in society there have been numerous varieties of 'feminism', including 'liberal feminism', 'radical feminism', 'socialist feminism', 'Marxist feminism', 'lesbian feminism', 'postmodern feminism' and 'post-structural feminism', among others. As Tong says:

> I understand each of these to be a partial and provisional answer to the 'woman question(s),' providing a unique perspective with its own methodological strengths and weaknesses ... these partial and provisional answers intersect, joining together both to lament the ways in which women have been oppressed, repressed, and suppressed and to celebrate the ways in which so many women have 'beaten the system,' taken charge of their own destinies, and encouraged each other to live, love, laugh, and be happy *as women.* (Tong 1989: 1–2)

Probably the term 'feminisms' should be used, since there have been various expressions with different sets of ideas and actions associated with the term rather than a single, continuous notion (Freedman 2001: 1). It is even difficult to settle on any central list of elements across feminist theorisation. However, for Freedman, in general, 'feminisms' may be said to 'concern themselves with women's inferior position in society and with discrimination encountered by women because of their sex'. She adds: 'one could argue that all feminists call for changes in the social, economic, political or cultural order, to reduce and eventually overcome this discrimination against women' (Freedman 2001: 1). For Ramazanoglu and Holland 'feminism' is 'diverse and decentred', *'exclusionary'* (has definitional boundaries), *'implies a unified subject'* (women as in a gendered social position), *'entails some claim to common interests between women'* and *'implies a case for emancipation'* (Ramazanoglu with Holland 2002: 7). Leaving aside, for the moment, what constitutes feminism in detail, how male/female and female/female (and other differences) are theoretically defined can have important consequences for how social organisations operate; for instance, for those charged with the provision of welfare and other services.

There are problems concerning the theoretical, political and practical content of feminism, what may regarded as primarily a 'women's issue', and the self-identification of individuals and groups as 'feminist'. A pragmatic stance can be taken that 'feminism can claim to be a field with its own ideas, history and practice ...[although] ... these ideas, history and practice are far from unified, and are indeed subject to continuing debate' (Freedman 2001: 4). A further way of understanding feminism has been to see it as a 'series of waves'. These waves can include the late nineteenth- and early twentieth-century campaigns for women's voting rights and the later feminist movement of the 1960s and 1970s which fought for women's equality, in terms of both political rights and issues in the areas of family, work and sexuality. However, perhaps it would be more accurate to see feminism as rather a 'continuum of thought and action' than a series of relatively discrete waves (Freedman 2001: 5).

Varieties of Feminist Theory

Feminist theories have been influenced by a number of intellectual currents. The liberal, rational individualism of the Enlightenment period was of importance as it inspired demands for women's equality. Patriarchal theorisation pointed to the subordination of women in their everyday lives in the family, work and other spheres – and attempted to create new arenas for women and fight against dominating structures (see Tong 1989). Approaches derived from Marxian theorisation (e.g. ideas on the origin of the family and the reserve army of labour) were developed into a 'standpoint' from which research, theory and practice could take a political route and challenge existing sociological work. Finally, postmodern and some other views confronted Enlightenment liberal assumptions by interrogating the category of 'woman' as an 'essential' phenomenon. It also pointed to the complexities of 'difference' and the varied representations of women. Such a view led to the response that it rendered feminism unable to take a political stance and ignored the daily experiences of women in the family, health, work and other areas. Challenges to liberal feminist theory have also been undertaken by 'postcolonial' and 'multicultural' theorists stressing ethnic, racial and other divisions and also lesbian (e.g. Adrienne Rich; see Seidman 2004: 246–9) and psychoanalytic (e.g. Chodorow 1978) perspectives (see Rogers 2003: 289; Gershenson and Williams 2001). The complexities in liberal feminist theory can be seen according to a continuum ranging from radical liberal feminists, who also take class and sexual orientation into their accounts, through to status quo liberal feminists, 'where "postfeminism" is the order of the day now that equality of opportunity is supposedly in place' (Rogers 2003: 286).

Often contemporary feminist writing draws on a range of influences. For instance, at the centre of Smith's influential analyses is reference to women's actual, active lives, while 'gender' is involved in structuring the self and the operation of the institutions and social life of society (see Smith 1987, 1990). Importantly, she argues, knowledge and scientific practice are constructed with a specific 'standpoint' or social position and interest. While there are differences among women, they also have shared gender experiences in their routine activities and relations in home, locality, work and other areas. However, these experiences and outlook, she argues, have not been taken into account within the dominant knowledges, for example within social sciences; instead, methods and theories have reflected male perspectives and position in terms of their activities within institutions (Seidman 2004: 214). In short, the domestic labour, child-rearing and affective relations of women have been ignored or undervalued. Smith again places emphasis on knowledge and its creation, and the possibilities for activism, while also pointing to dominant capitalist economic, political and cultural structures that are implicated in social ruling. She also recognises that feminist knowledge, like any other knowledge, is temporally and spatially situated but nevertheless can be 'valid' since we also play a part in constructing society (Seidman 2004: 213–14).

The reliance on a Marxist 'realism' in 'standpoint' theory was a target for critique by postmodern (and poststructuralist) feminism and some other views which raised issues of representation and difference – including a challenge to the 'category' of 'woman' itself. Postmodern feminism (e.g. Butler 1990; see Brooks 1997) was in part a response to the myriad new feminist identities that were becoming apparent on the basis of ethnicity, sexuality, class and post-colonial experience and the criticism of a feminist–foundational outlook. For many, these shifts required a new response in feminist politics which could recognise diversity while positing a new complex politics based on creating forms of alliance. Butler (in *Gender Trouble* 1990) sees gender as 'performative', neither essential internally to the individual or societally given; she argues that a notion of a definitive, unchanging identity is both illusory and a limitation on the potentialities of gender and sexual politics. In general, postmodern theory argues that 'some time during the twentieth century modernist values and dreams began losing their grip on people's consciousness. In their wake came an appetite for ambiguity, irony and paradox and a feel for how localized and situated our knowledge is in the end and for all practical purposes' (Rogers 2003: 289). In terms of conceptions of masculinity and femininity these are deemed to be changeable and constructed in discourses – shifting and multiple conceptions – through which individuals as subjects are formed. Thus, there are no fixed meanings or singular truths. A problem immediately arises here for feminism, and hence, the wariness of many feminists relating to an unreadiness to give up 'stable' identities and an emphasis on women's actual experiences. The deconstruction of meanings of 'stable categories', alongside a postmodern or poststructuralist view of power, leaves society as rather 'flat' conception – a plain of competing discourses. Therefore,

> the post-modernist claim that there is no valid (or verifiable) knowledge and the death of the subject (that knowledge is about control not liberation) is problematic for feminists who are concerned to uncover the systematic disadvantage of women and to produce the knowledge that will enable them to liberate themselves. (Abbott 2000: 62)

In 'postmodernist feminism' it is difficult to have fixed goals, or even a relatively consistent definition of problems and definitions concerning feminism and 'woman'. It appears to lack an institutional or economic view on the one hand and the notion of a reality of women's problems, as in health, work and welfare, on the other.

A parallel movement to feminism in the 1970s was the rise of interest in 'masculinity'. This new concern, in part, was due to the neglect of the issue of how definitions of 'maleness' or male identities are formed – its cultural specific nature within differing conceptions socially and societally (see Gardiner

2002; Connell 1987, 1995; Tolson 1977; Whitehead 2002; Whitehead and Barrett 2001). The study of masculinity pointed out that feminist and other writings saw men in 'ahistorical', 'essentialist' (i.e. sharing basic, given characteristics) and 'stereotypical' terms. Instead, it was pointed out that what it is to be male undergoes change, while masculinity is also 'performative' – and men are also hierarchically divided (Seidman 2004: 227–8).

As part of a re-emergence of interest in social class, it is possible that the discussion and investigation of the links between social class and gender will undergo a revival. A renewed attention to the class–gender relation may result from some frustration with the abstract nature of much postmodernist or poststructuralist theory, including associated feminist theorisation. For example, Rogers (2003) expresses sympathy with 'materialist feminism' and 'feminist state theory'. She sees the lack of a detailed focus on complex connections between gender and social class, a link as important (she says) as between gender and race or disability. It is the most important 'consequential gap' in feminist theory, having had a diminishing role in First World (as opposed to elsewhere) feminist theorising (Rogers 2003: 292). Further, she argues that a great deal of feminist debate and theory implicitly recognises economic subordination and restriction. Yet there is the need for a theoretical focus on poverty, the family 'wage' and the nature of 'work', and sexual harassment: in short, the economic 'prospects and outcomes' – the class position – of individuals are 'profoundly gendered' (Rogers 2003: 293).

In the end, the attempt to separate out 'schools' of feminism has some important limitations. It often seeks to make greater contrasts between writers than are sometimes perhaps justified and, of course, particular theorists are influenced by a range of sociological and broader social thought. For instance, Dorothy Smith, one of the most influential feminist thinkers, and other well-known feminist writers such as Wise and Stanley, are influenced by radical feminism, Marxist or socialist ideas, phenomenology and ethnomethodology (Wise and Stanley 2003: 1.13).

Critique of Sociology

The central criticism of ('malestream') sociology is that it has been carried out largely by men, has reflected male perspectives on life and has assumed that male interests are those of everyone. So, traditionally, it has ignored the experience of half the population – women – and gender issues of discrimination, subordination, identity and the societal contribution of women, including their input into the practice of sociology. Sociology, in a feminist view, is a 'political practice' which 'masks its gendered character by speaking abstractly of humanity, the individual, society, and moral agency, rather than of gendered selves, behaviors, and experiences' (Seidman 2004: 213).

Even more recent sociology – including work by major sociological theorists and textbook overviews of contributions to major subdisciplinary fields – despite the several decades of feminist work in sociology, may be criticised for not sufficiently addressing (or again often ignoring) questions relating to the interrelations between gender, structure and power (Delamont 2003a, 2003b). There has also been a feminist questioning of dominant notions of scientific practice. But a simple feminist view that science was a 'wholly masculine enterprise' has been questioned by growing awareness of the major contribution of women in the natural sciences, while their early intellectual achievements in the social sciences and applied fields are increasingly recognised (see Lengermann and Niebrugge-Brantley 2003). In fact, the impact of feminist thought and research since the 1950s on the range of social sciences has been considerable, including an important challenge to disciplinary boundaries. For instance, feminist writers have been prominent in the critique of traditional social science methodology, particularly on issues relating to the nature of 'data' and the ethical and power issues within research relations. The challenge of 'radical sociology' in the 1960s to the 'institutional' basis of sociology, its funding relations (with government and corporations), its selected topics of study, political conservatism, and hierarchical power relations, was joined by a feminist critique of the discipline allied to its broader view of society's gendered hierarchy and practices.

Experience, Reflexivity, Interdisciplinarity

The questioning of the basis and orientation of the discipline of sociology (and other social sciences) has raised some fundamental epistemological questions regarding the construction and nature of meaning, including the methodological procedures appropriate for recovering 'women's experience' and a critique of notions of science and objectivity:

> this transformation of the discipline has posed questions of method, of the relation of knowledge to its subject-matter – questions about the nature of the discipline itself. For some feminist writers this has posed the *philosophical* question: may knowledge itself be a matter of gender? Can there be a distinctively female, or feminist, understanding of what knowledge is – a feminist epistemology? (Benton and Craib 2001: 145)

Implicated here is the nature of (women's) 'experience', which can be described as 'a loose, commonsense term referring to people's consciousness of their social existence' (Ramazanoglu with Holland 2002: 124). Issues arise concerning how 'experience' is to be represented – the extent that it is to be seen as grounded in 'reality', 'materiality' and 'embodiments' while also generalisable across time, space and the experience of others (Wise and Stanley 2003: 1.30).

Does 'experience' stand as good quality knowledge without being subjected to rigorous methodological analysis? Do accounts of women's experiences make for 'better knowledge' than accounts of others' experiences in the sense that they may offer 'uniquely valid insights'? ... We cannot assume that black/white, young/old, and so on, experience life in the same way ... we choose standpoints and standpoints may change over time; they are transitional, not 'fixed' points. (Gelsthorpe 1992: 215)

Importantly, for Gelsthorpe, an opposition to an idea of 'objectivity' in favour of an *'experience in method'* does not mean that critical standards of rigour and accuracy are abandoned. '[R]ather, it can mean making interpretive schemes explicit in the concern to produce good quality knowledge.' Women are seen as having 'uniquely valid insights' not simply as women but also according to the multiple relations they have according to age, family, work, and so on (Gelsthorpe 1992: 214–15).

In assessing the 'case against taking experience as a source of knowledge', Ramazanoglu and Holland say that feminists 'have been criticized for having simplistic beliefs in experience as a direct source of general knowledge of material social realities'. In particular, postmodernists have argued that experiences should not be seen as factual in the sense of connecting knowledge with a basis in reality; instead 'facts' are 'socially constituted' (Ramazanoglou with Holland 2002: 124–5). In addition, for postmodernists, 'any one person's experience will be limited, partial and socially located, and so cannot be taken as general knowledge of how social phenomena are organized as social relations' and, of course, people may be 'deluded and yet experience the evidence of their senses as real' (Ramazanoglu with Holland 2002: 125–6). If feminists accept, Ramazanoglu and Holland argue, that 'accounts of experience' may not be 'simply' factual, then the argument becomes more complex. But if it is taken that 'Gendered social relations and decentred subjects may be discursively constituted' it does not follow that they do not exist: 'Embodiment, violence, institutionalized dominance, material resources, for example, produce experiences that are more than discourse or performativity' (Ramazanoglou with Holland 2002: 126).

Various approaches to the issue of the relation between feminism and epistemology have been proffered: for example, 'feminist empiricism', 'feminist standpoint epistemology', and 'feminist postmodernism'. Those feminists holding an 'empiricist position' point out that women have been poorly dealt with by science, but that this need not be so – the 'problem' is 'bad science'. Even so, whether the term 'feminist empiricism' 'really captures the depth of the challenge to mainstream approaches which has been mounted by feminists' in a variety of disciplines can be questioned (Benton and Craib 2001: 146). A 'feminist standpoint epistemology' (Harding, Hartsock, Smith and others) arose in the late 1970s, inspired by the women's movement and drawing on various Marxist and psychoanalytic theory. It was 'concerned with the "masculinism" of the natural sciences, and especially with biology, the science most intimately connected with defining women as a "natural" category'; and 'the revaluation of women's experience as a resource for critically addressing orthodox biomedical knowledge' (Benton and Craib 2001: 146). A leading figure here is Nancy Hartsock. There are three parts to her argument: women occupy a different position in society – there is a sexual division of labour and difference brought by different embodiment; their 'way of knowing' and 'experiencing' is distinctive; and an epistemological claim is made, even allowing for differences between women, that it is 'also superior, better grounded, or more reliable as knowledge' (Benton and Craib 2001: 147–8). Whatever the separations between versions of standpoint theory, there is a strong convergence on the 'character of the alternative feminist forms of knowledge':

> They favour concreteness, sensitivity to qualititative difference and complexity as against abstract concern with merely quantitative relations; they anticipate the overcoming of the abstract dualisms of Western, masculine thought (nature and culture, subject and object, reason and emotion, body and mind) in favour of contextualized, holistic understandings of the relatedness of things; and they propose the reintegration of knowledge with everyday life-experience. Finally, they emphasize the relationship between these alternative forms of knowledge and the struggles of subaltern social groups (primarily, but not exclusively, women) against social domination, exclusion and devaluing. (Benton and Craib 2001: 151–2)

Thus, a feminist standpoint generally 'requires some theory of gender and power, a conception of feminist knowledge and conceptions of experience and reality', and also the notion that 'women speaking their truth' produces 'new knowledge of gendered social lives, grounded in women's experience' (Ramazanoglu with Holland 2002: 64).

Since feminist standpoint theorists see epistemological, theoretical and political concerns as interlinked, there is a view of knowledge as socially formed, but one in which certain groups who have very different experiences in society have been largely marginalised in taking part. For Benton and Craib (2001) there remains a question of verification, the 'matter of *evaluation* and *testing* of rival knowledge-claims once they have been produced'. They argue that feminist standpoint epistemology is not 'justified' simply because the arguments are delivered by feminists and contain the perspectives of women. Rather, it 'compares very well with traditional epistemologies' in viewing the processes of knowledge creation and does provide 'testable explanations' (Benton and Craib 2001: 156–7). The point is that something more than merely adding a gender dimension is necessary in correcting a factual bias in existing science. There is a more fundamental 'challenge to prevailing research programmes, conceptions of what counts as "good evidence", methodological procedures, social relations and institutional forms, the relationship of scientific work to popular social movements, and also access on equal terms to scientific work on the part of previously excluded or marginalized groups' (Benton and Craib 2001: 158).

Finally, as previously stated, feminists who have been influenced by postmodern thought argue that theories based on 'essential categorical differences' or 'universal' accounts, for example, patriarchy, are ill-judged. Thus, categorisations seeking to account for general gender and other differentiation are, in fact, situational, shifting and subject to dissolution and recombination:

> There is no intrinsic unity to being a 'woman' apart from the anatomical similarity of sex. This sort of standpoint has a substantive as well as theoretical thrust. For in postmodern conditions, it is held, social life itself has become fragmented and decentred. (*Polity Reader in Social Theory* 1994: 186)

Feminist, standpoint theorists, however, while differing somewhat in their responses to the rise of postmodern theory (and poststructuralism), gave recognition to the idea of the situated, material differences in the experience, position or identities of women – a view also strongly argued by postcolonial and other forms of feminism. In doing so, they recognised the force of the postmodern opposition to a singular notion of 'truth' based on a given or discoverable 'reality', while holding that the view of the ultimate 'deconstruction' of the category 'woman' had to be confronted.

Feminist theorists have replied to the charge of 'essentialism' (a basic, given gender category) in postmodern feminism in various ways, at the same time often accepting that a caution in conceptualisation is needed. For example, the idea of 'patriarchy' has been defended by writers such as Walby, who argues that the term is still useful in indicating continuing important structural features, and issues of differential power, across societies, affecting women (*Polity Reader in Social Theory* 1994: 186). Secondly, the idea that the 'individual' should be abandoned in favour of 'discourse' or the analysis of 'representation (as in relation to gender) is seen as misguided'. Individuals may be in some sense 'constructed' in discourse and representation and have a multiplicity of identifications and, admittedly, there are issues of 'truth' and objectivity. But this 'construction' cannot disguise the fact that women suffer oppression and have 'real' 'factual' health and other practical needs, and sociopolitical activism is necessary to meet these issues (see *Polity Reader in Social Theory* 1994: 186–7; Cooper 1994; Rogers 2003: 292–3).

Feminist Methodology

Feminist writers have added to the growing diverse critique of 'positivism' in the application of natural science principles and procedures in the social sciences. For some the critique ruled out quantitative methods in general as holding a 'masculinist' view of the individual and an 'objectivist' portrayal of the social world which contradicts women's experience. However, many feminists have questioned such a simplistic methodological dualism and argued that it is not quantitative methods per se but the use of 'insensitive' quantitative procedures, which can be overcome. They argue that unless quantitative data is collected, the experience and position of women will not be fully understood:

> The case against quantitative ways of knowing is based on a rejection of reason and science as masculine and an embracing of experience as feminine; but this is essentialist thinking which buys into the very paradox that it protests about … The construction of 'quantitative' and 'qualitative' methods as opposed impedes critical thinking about developing and using ways of knowing capable of respecting the autonomy and subjectivity of the researched, at the same time as minimising bias, in creating an appropriate knowledge for women … [and an] emancipatory (social) science. (Oakley 1998: 725)

Broadly, feminist theory and research have emphasised the importance of 'experience' in daily life, and the experience of research for both researchers and participants. Critics have raised questions concerning how and on what basis 'experience' is to be included in research – are all 'experiences' (views, feelings, outlook, and so on) to be treated as equally 'valid', and will 'experience', when gathered, 'automatically increase the validity of that knowledge' (Gelsthorpe 1992: 214)? In Gelsthorpe's view, recent feminist discussion has been about the 'role of experience *in* method rather than versus method' (Gelsthorpe 1992: 214; see also Fonow and Cook 1991). More generally, she says, the emphasis on 'experience' perhaps reflects a recognition of the importance of personal reflexivity in doing research, including feminist researchers also placing themselves within the research process. The issue of whose viewpoint is 'privileged' in relation to others has encouraged feminists to investigate 'new ways of knowing' through what can be called a 'feminist methodology' (Ramazanoglu 1992: 209; Gelsthorpe 1992: 214–15). For Ramazanoglu:

> What feminist thought and practice have done is both to empower women and to problematise yet again what we mean by knowledge, reason, objectivity and validity in divided societies … Feminist methodologies are not privileged ways of accessing 'reality' but they are varied explorations (some more adequate than others) of how we can validate knowledge which is produced from different standpoints. (Ramazanoglu 1992: 209–10)

It can be asked here whether feminist methods and practice are any different from other methodologies. Ramazanoglu and Holland argue that:

> If feminist methodology is not distinctive in terms of women studying women, or in its methods/techniques, or in its epistemologies and ontologies, or in its conceptions of rationality and validity, then any distinctiveness must come from the relations between epistemology and politics in feminist research. (Ramazanoglu with Holland 2002: 15).

Meanwhile, for Reinharz (1992), 'feminist methodology is the sum of feminist research methods'. She offers a meta-induction, i.e. an 'inductive definition' that is based upon her extensive survey of research across a wide span of research methods. She says that feminism is 'a perspective, not a research method', since feminists are interested in women 'as individuals and as a social category'. In using a variety of methods, feminist research is 'guided by feminist theory', 'involves an ongoing criticism of nonfeminist scholarship', 'may be transdisciplinary', 'aims to create social change', and 'strives to represent human diversity'. It 'frequently includes the researcher as a person'; 'attempts to develop special relations with the people studied (in interactive research)'; and 'defines a special relation with the reader' (Reinharz 1992: 240–1; see also Roberts 1981). In short, feminists argue that before feminist theory and research gained ground, male experience and knowledge was in dominance in sociological approaches without this being recognised. But now what is needed (they argue) is not simply some 'addition of gender' to existing theorisation and methodological practice. Rather, of importance is the generation of 'new theories of power in the context of sex/gender politics' and attention to how knowledge is produced in social science procedures and research relationships (see Ramazanoglou 1992: 209).

Finally, there is the question of the general place of feminist theory and practice within sociological work. In an interesting review of recent feminist texts, Wise and Stanley (2003) argue that 'any claim that feminist sociology is "other" makes little sense to us' – due to the 'the proliferation or sub-areas, specialisms and national differences'. Therefore, they question the notion that there is now a 'mainstream' within sociology; rather there are 'centres and peripheries' in each area with different ideas and practices (journals, books, conferences, etc.). Indeed, 'in some sub-areas of sociological work' feminist theory has 'become central, and some feminist theorists have achieved canonical status in some aspects of social theory' (Wise and Stanley 2003: 2.6–2.7). The origin of many ideas in feminist debates, teaching and publication has been obscured, but:

> ideas about the work/leisure relationship and domestic divisions of labour, or concerning reflexivity and the grounded nature of sociological modes of inquiry, have gained wide currency but are not seen as particularly feminist in character. (Wise and Stanley 2003: 2.7)

Case Study: The Family

One area in particular has been re-examined by feminist writers – the contemporary experience of women in the family and the assumptions traditional perspectives have made about it. Feminist writers have focused upon women's daily life in family relationships and the 'ideologies of domesticity' or the disjunction between 'ideals' and the actual difficulties, demands and strains in the daily lives of women (Abbott and Wallace 1997).

In the examination of the family the broad feminist concern has been on the contrast between the portrayals of family life in traditional sociological approaches (and wider media and other ideological constructions) and the actual intimate, emotional aspects of face-to-face relationships in familial social relations. In the attention to individual experience and interactive relations in everyday social life, feminist writers have drawn on a range of micro theorisation, including symbolic interactionism, ethnomethodology and phenomenology, to understand the routine gendering of 'male' and 'female' worlds. There is, in this examination, a challenge to the sexual division of labour as 'natural', with women's prime responsibility in the 'private sphere' of home and separated from the public life of male dominance. Involved here is the application of the well-known phrase 'the personal is political' in that the formation of personal identity is inextricably connected to the wider structures and ideology. Thus, while in general feminist theory there is an emphasis on subjective experience, various feminist approaches also utilise patriarchal ideas, Marxist conceptualisation and notions from discourse analysis, to reshape sociological notions of 'structure' or 'structuring' to understand the formation of gender categorisation.

The psychoanalytic feminist writers, such as Chodorow, have taken a rather different approach, although again there are various viewpoints influenced by the 'psychoanalytic tradition'. As Rogers (2003) says, for instance, Chodorow sees 'a *maternal continuum* where those like Rich postulate a lesbian one'. Generally, Chodorow argues that 'the institutionalized division of childrearing labor in the hetero-normative family ensures that women's and men's *unconscious* psychic structures will differentiate them in socially and psychologically consequential ways' (Rogers 2003: 289). So, without some basic changes in the practices of parenting the inequalities between men and women will remain. The focus in Chodorow's major work, *The Reproduction of Mothering* (1978) (see Gershenson and Williams 2001), is on the particular generational connection between mother and child in the formation of gender identity. This is characterised (according to object relations psychoanalytic theory) by the development of a close relationship between mother and daughter: an identification with the mother and mothering produces a socially given gender identity (Seidman 2004: 223). But a son represses his 'desire' or love of the mother at the Oedipal stage and becomes separated and defensive. The daughter's closeness remains and her separation occurs later. Chodorow's account gives an explanation of gender differentiation and also of women's part in their own gender formation, without relying on certain key Freudian ideas such as penis-envy or some notion of inner drive. It also has a social or cultural aspect as it can help to explain the difficulties in the expression and communication of feelings by men to women, and seeks to ground the self in its sociocultural and historical setting. However, Chodorow's approach to internalisation is questioned by Butler, who argues that rather than gender being an 'inner core of the self that drives behavior' it is 'a learned, situational performance whose dramatic effect is the illusion of an inner gendered self' (Seidman 2004: 223).

In broad terms, feminists offer a number of specific criticisms of family life as it is often described in sociological work and have given an alternative view. Feminists:

1. ... claim that forms of family organisation and ideology are based on social organisations and assumptions about people's roles held by the people of a given society. For example, there is no inherent (biological) reason why men cannot do housework ...
2. ... have sought to claim the family as an area for analysis ...
3. ... argue that different members of families experience family life in different ways. They argue that women's experiences of motherhood and family life have demonstrated that families embody power relationships that can and do result in conflict, violence, and the inequitable distribution of work and resources ...
4. ... question the assumption that the family should be a private sphere. While women and children are often cut off from outside contact in the modern nuclear family, this is partly an illusion at the level of public policy. The form that the family takes is heavily influenced by economic and social policies and the family is permeable to outside intervention. (Abbott and Wallace 1997: 141)

Abbott and Wallace, following Oakley, describe four areas of 'conflict in family life'. First, there is the economic dependence of women on men due to the sexual division of labour in which they undertake domestic work and caring. Secondly, women have to perform emotional work to help partners and children and yet they in turn lack emotional support. Thirdly, there are differences in economic and physical power between partners with women restricted in the control of finances, leisure and other areas and are subjected to violence. Fourthly, there is male control of sexuality and fertility. Very important also is the general role of 'familial ideology' as portrayed through mass-media conceptions of women's lives as a restricted set of roles, particularly as wife/mother (Abbott and Wallace 1997: 146). Historically, this ideology found dominant expression in the view of 'separate but complementary spheres'.

Feminist Theorisation and Micro Social Theory

Feminist theorisation and micro social theories have a large degree of overlap but feminist writers also point to significant differences in the portrait of the actor and the nature of interaction in their approaches. Both generally share an orientation towards how individuals relate to each other and how meanings are created and shared. However, much feminist sociological theorisation takes issue with 'individualistic' assumptions, in interactionist and other micro theories, as contained in the notion of the independent, goal-seeking actor who may have advantages or disadvantages in some situations, but assumed to be largely in an equal position. The traditional model of the individual in micro theorisation, it is stated, rests on an actor with a wide range of choice in deciding which situations to participate in and the type and degree of involvement. Even where the differences in power and control are recognised between participants, feminist theorists argue that there is a limited view of the 'structuring' processes of which women are part:

> feminist research shows, first, that women's lives have a quality of incidentalism, as women find themselves caught up in agendas that shift and change with the vagaries of marriage, husbands' courses of action, children's unpredictable impact on life plans, divorce, widowhood, and the precariousness of most women's wage-sector occupations. Second, in their daily activities, women find themselves not so much pursuing goals in linear sequences but responding continuously to the needs and demands of others. (Lengermann and Niebrugge-Brantley 2004: 472)

Female subordination, therefore, has both a continuous and structural pattern – which is further 'intensified and complicated when factors of race and class are included in the feminist analytical frame'. While meanings are generated and shared in social contexts 'this assumption must be qualified by the fact that micro interactions are embedded in and permeated by the macro structures of power and ideology' (Lengermann and Niebrugge-Brantley 2004: 473). This is a point made very strongly by many feminists, for example those influenced by Marxian ideas on ideology and social structure, and those who seek to modify feminist work by taking a more micro or interactionist viewpoint. Even so, feminists hold that it is in private, informal spheres that women can find emotional support, 'confirming' their experiences. In general, the view offered, by feminist theorists, is that micro social theories exhibit an 'individualistic' bias which requires substantial modification. Certainly, like other sociological theories, micro social theorisation does rest to some degree on common assumptions, not only on the individual but also concerning society. But, commonly it does not merely see individuals floating around with unlimited choice over behaviour, even if its societal view, including of major inequalities, can be somewhat limited. At the very least, micro theorisation (broadly) sees limitations based on the expected reactions of others and the requirement to cooperate. It does allow for some 'social' element and a connection with a wider social and societal set of arrangements. In this regard, it is interesting that various feminist writers, such as Dorothy Smith and others, draw on micro social theorisation. Micro and macro dimensions of gender inequality and gendered experience (e.g. in material resources, definition of the situation, structuring of knowledge, visual and other representation, defining social categories) interconnect, and the interrelation can be shown in important ways in health, family, work and other fields. The recognition of this interconnection in shaping gender (and other experiences) is an important contribution to micro social theorisation.

Conclusion

Various criticisms have been made of feminist theorisation and there are vigorous debates between feminist viewpoints. For example, charges of essentialism are made where it appears fundamental, psychic differences between 'males' and 'females' are being proffered – a criticism supported by feminists influenced by postmodern theory. A 'determinism' or 'ahistoricity' is also alleged, by some feminists, against theories of patriarchy as seeing a 'fundamental' domination of male over female. Even so, it must be remembered that

> There has never been a shared theory of gender oppression or male dominance; a unified vision of justice and liberation; a common approach to the production of knowledge; agreed knowledge of the extent of women's differences; or a consensus on truths about gender. Any definition of feminism can, therefore, be contested. (Ramazanoglu with Holland 2002: 7)

Feminist theory, in general terms, has put forward a range of 'proposals' for the modification of sociological theory which are important in the discussion of micro social theory (Lengermann and Niebrugge-Brantley 2004: 476–9). First, the micro and macro levels of theorisation require intricate reconnection to account for both the conditions and the experience of women's lives. Structures of social and economic domination are not simply external forces but 'lived' in everyday practice. Secondly, 'micro situations' reproduce these systems of dominance, e.g. the power over resources and who has 'voice' and opportunities, including the shaping of forms of interaction and social difference. However, feminist theory (generally) also stresses the role of agency, as well as structure in relations – recognising differences according to patterns of domination according to gender, age, ethnicity and sexuality. Thirdly, the structures of domination (institutions, ideologies and major social processes) are 'gendered' in terms of their interests, construction and application. Fourthly, and this is problematic for feminist theorisation itself, is a scrutiny of the categorisations of 'female' ('male'), 'woman' ('man'), 'femininity' ('masculinity'), and so on. Theorists, of course, should all be reflexive in the use of categories in their theorisation. Finally, as Lengermann and Niebrugge-Brantley argue:

> the practice of sociological theory must be based in a sociology of knowledge that recognizes ... the function of power in effecting what becomes knowledge ... one must question the use of any categories developed by a traditionally male-dominated

discipline, most particularly the divisions between structure and agency and between micro and macro sociologies. (Lengermann and Niebrugge-Brantley 2004: 479)

In terms of micro social theory, we can see that feminist theorisation has contributed in two ways, first, by drawing attention to the micro gendering of social interaction, social identity and self, and definition of situations, and secondly, the interconnection of the micro 'level' with wider social patterning – in this case, general gendered inequalities. Nevertheless, there is still a great deal of contention surrounding what constitutes feminist social theory and political and ethical practice in research, just as there is regarding the features and objectives of the women's movement. Both feminist social theory and feminist politics have been and will be subject to change and variation – according to different social locations, leading to differing claims and renewed sources of dispute – and will have a continuing influence on micro social theorisation.

Further Reading

There are a number of recent detailed discussions of feminist theorisation and research: S. Delamont, *Feminist Sociology* (London, Sage, 2003); M. Evans, *Gender and Social Theory* (Buckingham, Open University, 2003); G. Letherby, *Feminist Research in Theory and Practice* (Buckingham, Open University, 2003); and C. Ramazanoglu with J. Holland, *Feminist Methodology: Challenges and Choices* (London, Sage, 2002) – these provide general overviews and are very good starting points. A short recent introduction to feminist theory, with further reading and relevant websites, is L. Adkins, 'Feminist Social Theory', in A. Harrington (ed.), *Modern Social Theory: An Introduction* (Oxford, Oxford University Press, 2005). A useful collection of readings is *The Polity Reader in Gender Studies* (Cambridge, Polity, 1994). For an historical account and overview of varieties of feminist thought, see R. Tong, *Feminist Thought: A Comprehensive Introduction* (London, Unwin Hyman, 1989). Some of the most important work by key feminist writers on theory and methodology are: (for Butler) J. Butler, *Gender Trouble* (London, Routledge, 1990); (for Chodorow) N. Chodorow, *The Reproduction of Mothering* (Berkeley, University of California Press, 1978); (for Harding) S. Harding (ed.), *Feminism and Methodology* (Milton Keynes, Open University Press, 1987) and S. Harding, *The Science Question in Feminism* (Milton Keynes, Open University Press, 1986); (for Smith) D. E. Smith, *The Everyday World as Problematic* (Milton Keynes, Open University Press, 1987) and D. E. Smith, *Texts, Facts, and Femininity: Exploring the Relations of Ruling* (New York, Routledge, 1990). Other influential texts are: C. Gilligan, *In a Different Voice* (Cambridge, MA, Harvard University Press, 1982); A. Lorde, *Sister Outsider: Essays and Speeches* (Freedom, CA, The Crossing Press, 1984); and L. Stanley and S. Wise,

Breaking Out: Feminist Consciousness and Feminist Research (London, Routledge, 1983). On the topic of masculinity a key writer is R. W. Connell: see *Masculinities* (Berkeley, University of California Press, 1995). Useful recent introductions to the study of masculinity(ies) are: S. Whitehead, *Men and Maculinities* (Cambridge, Polity, 2002) and S. Whitehead and F. Barrett (eds.), *The Masculinities Reader* (Cambridge, Polity, 2001).

8

Theoretical Developments in Micro Social Theory

Introduction

This chapter reviews a selective range of sociological theories that have been used at the 'micro social level', especially those which have become prominent since the early 1980s, but not necessarily commonly placed within the interpretive, subjectivist 'tradition'. Exchange theory, rational choice theory, control theory and network theory have a degree of overlap in terms of mutual influence, although there is a variation between a focus on the 'rational' actor as a decision maker and an emphasis on kinds of exchange or on social relationships involved in networks. However, in general, they share a positivistic approach towards social life and methodology. In addition, the chapter examines the work of Giddens and Foucault with reference to how they view the 'micro level' – or 'micro structure' and the 'making' of the individual. Although not usually regarded as 'micro theorists', their influential ideas – in Giddens in terms of structure as 'emergent' or 'lived', in Foucault how knowledge/power 'flows' through particular contexts or institutional settings – are relevant to the micro situation.

Exchange Theory

In general it would appear that in various types of interaction some form of exchange takes place (in services, materials, and so on) for the social and economic benefit of participants. An interchange of necessities can only be gained through contact with others, a relation which seems a basic condition to all forms of society (Molm 2003: 260).

> Exchange (attempted, aborted, or accomplished) is intrinsic to social relations in the virtually self-evident sense that social relations consist of people offering or not offering things to one another and demanding, accepting or avoiding things from one another. (Bredemeier 1979: 452–3)

114

Exchange theory developed from a number of sources. Rational choice theory was a leading influence, itself derived from utilitarian thought and associated ideas in economics resting on the notion of the 'rational actor' – the individual as endowed with purpose and able to exercise choice. Nevertheless, it had to be realised that the pursuit of an outcome was restricted owing to its access, availability and the costs that ensue in pursuing one outcome rather than another (Ritzer and Goodman 2004: 401). In economic theorisation independent actors met as a series of others and forged contracts based on their individual interests – and by this myriad, shifting set of contracts, society emerged. A second line of influence is behaviouristic psychology, although later writers have attempted to shift away from this basis, which began by examining rewards that reinforce, and costs or punishments that deter, behaviour. Thus, past patterns of reward and cost will strongly shape future conduct. Social exchange theory sees social transactions between 'actors' according to opportunities and the benefits given and received not as merely transitory relations, but according to how patterns of support are formed. Important here are the amount and type of information which an actor can draw upon in making a choice. Thus, from the bases of utilitarian philosophy and behaviourism, exchange theory broadened into a social theory in which actors have some resources (goods, skills) that are wanted by others and form relations which have costs and benefits. Institutions or 'opportunity structures' are seen as important constraints on what is rewarded (or not) for particular kinds of behaviour which seek a beneficial outcome (Molm 2003: 260).

Homans, Blau and other early 'pioneers' of exchange theory all noted the widespread nature of exchange relations in daily life (Homans 1974; Blau 1964, 1969). For Homans, social association can be considered as an 'exchange of activity, tangible or intangible, and more or less rewarding or costly, between at least two persons' (Blau 1971: 220). He argued that social theory required propositions that could be subject to research and test – more general sociological theorisation had a high degree of conceptualisation but lacked clear explanation (Ritzer and Goodman 2004: 405). By a set of propositions (e.g. involving stimulus, success, value) relating to actors' behaviour, an account of social behaviour could be established by the identification of its 'elementary forms'. This behaviouristic model is supplemented by 'rationalistic' propositions through which actors assess the degree of benefit particular actions will accrue. Left unexplained is why certain outcomes are valued more; rather the emphasis is upon the rational pursuit and attainment of highest benefits. Although it recognises differences in power, Homans's theorisation tends to underplay this important aspect of exchange relationships. Overall, his theory 'was weak on mental states ... and large-scale structures' (Ritzer and Goodman 2004: 409).

The work of Homans was extended by Blau, who attempted to understand social structure through competitive exchanges and relations between individuals and groups – how exchanges produce differences in power and lead to social organisation formation and opposition. His work becomes centred on macro-social structures and norms rather than individual or small-group exchanges. A further important development was made by Emerson, who sought to tighten the propositions of exchange theory – to make it more open to test while also emphasising power (power-dependence) as a central concern (Ritzer and Goodman 2004: 416). The latter shift in attention from actor transactions to structural relations and change was helped by using ideas on groups and exchange networks (Molm 2003: 263).

Within broader sociology the notions of exchange have appeared in various ways (see Chapter 9). For example, in what he terms of 'exchange structuralism', Wallace discusses Gouldner's work on 'reciprocity', Goode's examination of 'role strain', and Durkheim's ideas on the social basis of the 'contract', alongside Blau's social account of exchange (Wallace 1969: 28–31). A very important focus in Gouldner and Durkheim was on some exchanges in terms of a more 'objective' definition – on some relations as 'objectively' exploitative and unjust rather than using a more subjective notion of 'fairness' (Zeitlin 1973: 95–6). Recently Bauman and May have contrasted 'love' or 'gift' with 'exchange' as the ends of a continuum of human relationships, arguing that most relationships are 'impure' with a mix of these elements (Bauman and May 2001: 78–92). They also make a 'crucial distinction' between personal and impersonal relations; they particularly refer to work by Giddens, Beck and Luhmann in considering how people give 'trust' each other and consider 'risk' in relationships. Of interest here, for micro social theory, is the continued usefulness of the notion of 'exchange', in various forms, in the study of (even intimate) social relationships, and how this idea can be used as a linkage to wider social patterns or structures.

Rational Choice Theory and Control Theory

Rational choice theory, associated especially with the work of Coleman (1990), has its origins in economic theory; more specifically, in a model of the rational actor who seeks ends that maximise the rewards in the meeting of desires and needs. Rational choice theory 'is first and foremost normative' since:

> It tells us what we ought to do in order to achieve our aims as closely as possible. It does not, in the standard version, tell us what our aims ought to be. From the normative account we can derive an explanatory theory, by assuming that people are rational in the normatively appropriate sense. (Elster 1994: 121)

'Rational choice' is an idea that has perhaps had more influence on sociological theory than it first seems. As Benton and Craib point out:

> Schutz's work can also be seen as offering a foundation for rational choice theory, an approach developed out of the marginalist revolution in economics in the second

half of the nineteenth century, a development with which Weber was intimately acquainted. (Benton and Craib 2001: 85)

Notions of 'rational action' can also be found in sociology; for instance, Weber placed it alongside other forms of action (affective, traditional). Coleman (1990) is credited with being the main influence on the development of rational choice theory within the field of sociology – in applying the theory at the micro level as a means of understanding macro or societal levels. Coleman was intent to show that individuals have a degree of choice and various resources even though there were restrictions upon their actions, and that there were possibilities for change that were under-recognised by traditional emphases on the integration of the individual into the society (Ritzer and Goodman 2004: 432). Thus, on the one side, he was arguing against action as determined by society and on the other, that much of action was irrational or mere exhibition. In using a model of rational choice he was stating that actors have goals which are guided by choices and values and secondly, that by studying the small scale the way large-scale social phenomena are built can be understood. For example, as Ritzier and Goodman point out, it could be said that social norms are due to individuals' support for their benefits, or in one actor being allowed authority over another, a micro unit of the larger system is formed; alternatively, at the system level, (perhaps) economic organisations and government could be seen as 'purposive structures' as 'actors' (Ritzier and Goodman 2004: 433).

According to Ritzer and Goodman (2004), there have been a number of criticisms of Coleman's work. First, that the main causal priority is given to micro to macro rather than other directions (macro–micro, or micro–micro, and macro–macro). Also, it seeks to replace all other social theory, neglects to indicate causal mechanisms, has a misleading psychological reductionism, and includes biases deriving from a notion of rational selfishness. Finally, there is an interpretivist criticism that Coleman has an inadequate view of the self and human interaction, including issues related to the emotions and power in social relations (Ritzer and Goodman 2004: 434).

One specific and important area of criticism is that rational choice theory cannot understand social solidarity sufficiently:

> In contrast to Durkheim's emphasis on cooperation and shared values, there is in the rational choice approach much more attention paid to competing interests and social closure. The extent to which it is appropriate to posit a rational basis for social solidarity has in consequence become a crucial aspect of contemporary debates. (Crow 2002: 115)

Seemingly, it cannot account for those individuals who put group interest ahead of their own, but on the other side, it is argued that there is nothing in the approach which rules out individuals acting altruistically and 'socially' (Crow 2002: 115).

Some may argue that Weber's ideas on rational action have a degree of similarity with rational choice theory since he emphasised the importance of market relationships. But it can be seen that Weber's idea of rational action is a broader view than as a continuous individual calculation of benefits from action. Rather, he conceived a number of types of action, including action that is informed by values that may not result in a measurable benefit (Benton and Craib 2001: 85–6). Within pragmatism and its interactionist social psychology (e.g. Mead), as Benton and Craib argue, it is not Weber's conception of means–end rationality or rational choice theory that are starting points. Instead, it is the processual notion of action and the self and 'different rationalities that exist in different situations' with many 'means–end chains, varying from situation to situation' that are posited (Benton and Craib 2001: 88). There is an initial similarity between rational choice theory and interactionist social psychology to the extent that both have presupposed a rationalistic, cognitivist individual. However, the idea of the rational actor assumes more a unitary individual exercising choice in action rather than an individual attempting to integrate experiences within a disparate society – whereas, at least in Mead, some allowance is made for differing selves. We can agree with Elster who says, while individuals have an 'organizing centre', they 'often do not know what they want; or do not know what they know; or fail to do what they have decided to do' (Elster 1994: 125).

'Control Theory' could be considered as a variant of rational choice theory, and is particularly associated with criminological thought. It has risen in prominence in recent years, especially because of its connection with crime prevention policies. Control theory also originates in the work of eighteenth-century 'classicist' penal reformers, Hobbesian ideas on social order, and Durkheim's view on the moral basis of 'contracts'. In addition, there is the influence of Bentham's utilitarian notion that action should be planned to maximise pleasure and minimise pain. The development of control theory is due, in part, to criminological disenchantment with the search for individual (or even more general) causes; the rise of programmes to control criminals within the 'community'; and finally, the re-emergence of 'alternative' principles to incarceration (e.g. forms of restorative and communal justice) (see Roshier 1989; Downes and Rock 1995). The emphasis can be said to be on 'practical' theorisation, for example, a key idea in the application of control theory is the restriction of opportunities for crime.

While control theory has not been widespread until recently, its principles can be found in previous criminological studies of family relations and the 'self concept' (Downes and Rock 1995: 242). It is also implicit in Chicagoan social disorganisation theory (i.e. lack of cultural controls) and subcultural theory (i.e. lack of conformity). There are also similarities with ideas in exchange theory and Sutherland's 'differential association' (Downes and Rock 1995: 260). Hirschi's key study *Causes of Delinquency* (1969) gives the basic assumption of control theory – that 'delinquent acts result when an individual's bond to society is weak or broken'. Thus, it is the delinquent's connection with the family that is important prior to joining a delinquent subculture. By the time of delinquent activity the link with conformity has been compromised. He gives four elements to the social bond: attachment, degree of commitment, involvement and belief, and recognises that individuals will have been in 'various situations' according to these elements and according to social patterns (e.g. subcultures). Control theory does not ask the traditional criminological question 'Why do they do it?', rather 'Why don't we all do it?' Its claim is that it has empirical support for its ideas (Downes and Rock 1995: 245–7).

Box (1971) tries to overcome some of the difficulties within control theory by linking it to a notion of 'motivation' and deviancy theory, to rectify what he regards as a rather simple view of deviant forms and conformity. Drawing on Matza (1969), he argues that whether an individual deviates depends on motivation (Downes and Rock 1995: 247–9). Various dimensions are relevant here: the ability to keep activities secret, access to skills, a supply of specialist equipment, social support (relationship to conformity) and symbolic support (the justifications and values involved). Box argues that control theory tends to be rather better at understanding 'ordinary' crime rather than serious crime and crimes of the powerful, and fails to consider sufficiently the initial differences in individuals' bonding. There is also an assumption of a certain criminal type – an individual endowed with rational choice and decision making – but the theory does have the advantage of a focus on the criminal situation and practical proposals for the reduction of opportunities for crime.

In summary, rational choice theory (and control theory) has had various traditional criticisms relating to the 'non-rational' aspects of social action, and as a micro social theory, a neglect of the nature of collective action and a conception of social structure. In reply, its adherents can point to more recent theoretical and empirical work on trust, dilemmas, emotional bases of behaviour, and work on 'multiple actors' and institutional forms (Heckathorn 2003: 282–3). Rational choice theory, within sociology, has also found applications in social mobility and class analysis, voting behaviour and crime – as in control theory. However, there are other trends in rational choice theory towards more mathematical formulations, as in micro economic theory. Therefore, rational choice theory is developing work which goes some way to meet criticisms that certain areas have been avoided, as in the empirical study of emotions, religion and socialisation, or it has not reached out sufficiently to interrelate with the study of social solidarity or wider social structure. As a 'micro social theory' it can be considered as an analysis of the small-scale setting but with possibilities to show the activities in a given location connecting with broader social/societal patterning. But, according to Heckathorn, it is not yet possible to give a 'definitive assessment of its ultimate potential' (Heckathorn 2003: 283).

Network Theory

Network theory takes various forms but essentially it is concerned with the web of links between individuals and the regular patterns or structure that can be discerned (e.g. in relation to families and communities) (see Scott 1991, 2000; see also Bott 1957; Stacey 1969). There is a connection with ideas on exchange relations as the basis of such 'networks'. As Blau concluded on the 'structure of associations':

> It is essential ... to conceptualize processes of social association between individuals realistically as finding expression in networks of social relations in groups and not to abstract artificially isolated pairs from this group context. (Blau 1969: 199)

Wallace argues that Blau's exchange theory 'implies the same premises of innate (therefore imposed) psychological qualities that Homans does' but 'one can set aside his discussion of "starting mechanisms" of complex social life as a preliminary to his principal theory'. Blau's approach:

> seeks to derive simple types of associations between persons from different types of exchange of different types of rewards, and from these associations to derive social integration, differentiation, opposition, and legitimation as dimensions of complex social structures. (Wallace 1969: 30)

Here, there is a place for values and norms in social processes. In general, in network theory and analysis there is an increasing emphasis on the types and strength of relational ties or 'regularities' that link individuals in society rather than on a 'rational actor', decisions or choices, microscopic relations and shared internalized norms (Ritzer and Goodman 2004: 420–1).

By broadening the term 'actor' to include groups, and even large organisations (or perhaps society itself), connections can not only be made between the micro and macro levels but also major social differences can be demonstrated (e.g. in power, resources) between groupings. In this approach there is not so much emphasis on the rational actor choosing, as a stress upon the ties between social groups and the pattern that is set. Ritzer and Goodman note an interesting recent discussion of the importance of 'weak' ties (i.e. lesser bounded groupings or looser connections). Such ties can be important linkages, via acquaintainship, between stronger networks (e.g. of long-term friends), and ease the dependence of the individual on strong group ties (Ritzer and Goodman 2004: 421). Another interesting development is 'network exchange theory' which, as its name suggests, brings together network analysis and exchange theory in an attempt to omit the drawbacks of each view and build on their positive aspects. Thus, there is an intent to link a structural account of various kinds of 'objective' ties with a notion of types of exchange between actors to maximise rewards (Ritzer and Goodman 2004: 425).

A rather different kind of use of 'network' is in 'actor network theory', which again has a concern with micro–macro interrelations. It demonstrates the influences of structuralist and post-structuralist theory, with an emphasis on 'semiotic' conceptualisation. Phenomena are seen in relational terms and there is an attempt to overcome the 'dualistic' difference perceived between nature and culture. In this view, both society and nature should be conceived as 'constructs' which require explanation (Benton and Craib 2001: 69–70; Barnes 2003: 343). Finally, often the idea of 'social network' has been used quite descriptively in sociological study in the same sense as 'social relations'.

Michel Foucault – Discourse, the Body and Discipline

The work of Michel Foucault (1926–84) has had a significant influence across the social or human sciences, including in the analysis of welfare, prisons and education. He is generally described as a 'poststructuralist' whose analysis of 'discourse' and the body, including his particular approach to the understanding of power and knowledge, have greatly informed theory and research in philosophy, history, literary studies, sociology and other disciplines. Foucault argued against the idea that there was a universal 'truth'; rather than no truth, instead there were multiple truths. Thus, he offered a poststructuralist questioning of grand theories, including Marxist theorisation, which claimed general societal explanation. As part of the poststructuralist current he was also critical of 'humanism' and the active subjectivity of the 'centred subject'; rather the individual is always 'fragmented' with no core or fixed 'identity'. While writers such as Sartre began with a conception of the basic human freedom of the individual, Foucault opposed such 'subjectivism'.

His broad range of work, including *Madness and Civilisation* (1967), *The Order of Things* (1970), *The Archaeology of Knowledge* (1972), *The Birth of the Clinic* (1973), *Discipline and Punish* (1977), *Power/Knowledge* (1980) and *The History of Sexuality* (3 vols., 1978–86), contained historical research, not simply into specific institutions, but according to 'discourses'. A discourse, in Foucault's work, 'is the matrix of *texts*, the specialized languages and the networks of power relations operating in and defining a given field' (Sim 1998: 245).

At the centre of Foucault's historical approach is the intention to take a second look at what appears familiar and contest the traditional assumptions of continuity in historical explanation. His approach is 'archaeological' – placing elements in relation to each other as in a layer of strata rather than arranging them as a continuous, linear sequence. Such a view questions the conceptions held of phenomena such as 'mental illness', and even the notion of the 'individual' as given; rather they are 'contingent', as formed within an historical setting of discourse or power/knowledge relations. The major example of Foucault seeing areas afresh is to be found in his view of the eighteenth-century

Enlightenment. In traditional accounts, the Enlightenment brought new conceptions of individual rights. But, for Foucault, this period had another side – it also saw the rise of a 'great confinement' of individuals and a new 'gaze', the observations of those incarcerated in new institutions (e.g. the modern prison). This overseeing of subject populations generated new forms of knowledge and the development of new human 'disciplines': the knowledge and practice of social sciences.

A new 'disciplinary power', Foucault argued, had spread across society in the eighteenth century. He says disciplinary power is not located in a specific source as invested in a particular individual, group, class or institution a such, or even the state – neither is it based upon the duality of the rulers and ruled. He has in mind an array of techniques or technologies – a 'micro physics of power' that covered eighteenth-century society like a fine mesh. Disciplinary power 'makes' individuals and they are also its vessels or transmitters. In this way, it is not simply 'repressive'; in the institutional confines of the school, hospital, factory and prison there are the routines and categorisations which shape space, time and body. The eighteenth century also brought the 'exclusion' of parts of the general population. While Foucault's main concern is how practices relate, he does give some of the 'sources' of disciplinary power. For instance, the districts of the medieval town suffering from plague were separated; the military commander observed the armed camp; the segregation and daily timings of monastic life; and the regulation of the body ('docile bodies') in the newly professionalised armies were all disciplinary elements (Foucault 1977). Bentham's architectural plan of the 'panopticon' or 'all-seeing eye' for the prison was the epitome of this new kind of surveillance. Within these institutions there was the operation of 'infra law' or a whole array of micro penalties for lapses in time, incorrect behaviour and speech, and irregular bodily gestures. Regulation was more than simply an exterior control of behaviour, it was at its most effective when its imperatives became interiorised in the individual. In this manner the individual was constituted as both subject and object – as under the inspection of the gaze while also engaged in a surveillance of him/herself.

In his early work, Foucault regarded the body as a 'docile' entity – politically passive but nevertheless active – whereas in his later writings, as on the constitution of sexuality, it becomes more associated with pleasure, action and even resistance. He begins to consider the body as a 'site of bio power', still disciplined but also engaged in self-fulfilment. Here, Foucault distinguishes between an 'anatomo-politics', which involves the health rules applied to individual bodies, for instance on sexuality, and 'bio-politics' that refers to health measures governing the social–spatial movement of bodies generally. In *The History of Sexuality* (1978–86) Foucault contests the assumption that the post-Victorian era opened up the discussion of sex, in sharp contrast to a previous repression of the issue. Very differently, he asserts that the Victorian era marked an increasing range of discourses relating to the outline and control of sexual behaviour; more recent 'scientific' theorisation, including psychoanalytic perspectives, is an extension of the Victorian concerns. Again, Foucault questions previous assumptions, here regarding sexual activities as not simply 'given' but subject to discourses or guidelines and rules of behaviour.

Foucault's work has been an inspiration for a broad range of writers and perspectives. Influential ideas and investigations have, for instance, followed his account of the rise of prison and other institutions, as increasingly part of the modern state and the location for new disciplinary procedures focused on the body. As McNay describes:

> In relation to the body, power does not simply repress its unruly forces; rather it incites, instils and produces effects in the body. There is therefore no such thing as the 'natural' or 'pre-social' body; it is impossible to know the body outside of the meaning of its cultural significations. (McNay 1994: 193)

This conception of 'power' for instance, 'problematizes oversimplified notions of the "feminine" body – used by both traditionalists and some radical feminists – which tend to equate the biological capacities of women with their social capabilities' (McNay 1994: 193).

Foucault's work has generated an enormous amount of debate. Criticisms have been numerous. First, there is the question of the origin of 'disciplinary power' reaching out across eighteenth-century century society. Foucault gives two reasons for its rise – the increase in population in Western Europe and the beginnings of new industrial patterns – both requiring a new form of regulation. But, without more extensive discussion of its origins, disciplinary power appears to be an abstract, possibly deterministic process. Here, there seem to be similarities between Foucault's notion and Weber's idea of calculative rationality as a general, all-enveloping entity that reaches into every aspect of individual, political and other institutional life. In addition, the idea of discourse as an attempt to avoid both the humanistic conception of the human subject and forms of general determinism (particularly Marxian) brings problems of its own. In his later work, discussion of subjectivity appears to shift somewhat, as shown with the introduction of ideas on the 'technologies of the self', but the degree of agency or self-reflection and self-formation still seems limited. At its simplest, individuals are 'positioned' in webs of discourse rather exhibiting subjective experience, and a range of choice and variety of interaction with others. What emerges overall in Foucault's theorisation, for many critics, is a 'level' conception of society comprised of overlapping or competing discourses rather than some sense of material difference, institutional hierarchy and the structuring of power and dominance.

Feminists have argued that Foucault's analysis, like social theory generally, has not sufficiently recognised the gendered aspects of disciplinary techniques on the body. Even so, as McNay cautions, while attention has to be paid to the 'female body' such consideration should not be polarised from the history of the male body and the manner in which both are also 'inscribed by other for-mations: class, race, the system of commodity fetishism' (McNay 1994: 192). Where feminist writers have taken up Foucault's discourse theory (and other poststructuralist writing) in depth they meet the criticisms (raised in Chapter 7) that everything becomes merely 'discourse' – 'woman' becomes a category con-stituted in texts – and 'real-life' problems and feminist interventions, in research and politics, are undermined. But these criticisms have not ruled out feminist work (among much other theorisation and research), using Foucault's ideas in particular ways to examine 'power' in micro contexts (e.g. the family) as well as at other meso or macro 'levels' in relation to gender and other forms of social stratification. We can argue – and here lies something of the reason for Foucault's influence across health, welfare and other fields and in feminist, cul-tural and other theorisation – that his account of power also links individual practices with wider social institutions even if he does neglect certain dimen-sions of the 'institutional'. For example, his central example of the rise of the modern prison – although outlined in a novel, but very suggestive manner – does examine the micro social (e.g. 'the micro physics' of power) in connection with the development of its socio-historical and institutional context.

Anthony Giddens – Structuration: Legitimation, Domination and Signification

Structuration theory is not 'new' in that the idea of 'structuration' was put for-ward by Anthony Giddens (1938–) in the early 1970s – however, it has been developed and is still the subject of a great deal of controversy. 'Structuration' has become a key term within sociological discussion. For some commentators the term can be applied to a number of other writers (e.g. Bourdieu, Archer and Mouzelis) who have sought a synthesis, common ground or path between seemingly conflicting approaches (see Parker 2000). Parker explains the 'rise' of structuration theory in the 1970s as a result of the social and political change of the 1960s and the increasing turmoil within sociological theory. A particular feature of 'structuration' theorists has been an intent to popularise their ideas (Parker 2000: 5).

   Giddens's 'structuration theory' has been subject to an enormous range of comment. It is an ambitious attempt – and this accounts for at least its initial appeal – to tackle the 'dualisms' within sociological theory, particularly struc-ture vs. agency, macro vs. micro, stasis vs. change and subject vs. object. It aims to overcome some of the main deficiencies in major theoretical approaches by finding contributions from each. Therefore, Giddens is intent to take ele-ments from a wide range of interpretive sociology, hermeneutics and some branches of philosophy to join with a reformed structural or institutional approach. He is critical of traditional structural theories, taking as his target functionalism in particular and its ally positivism in social research, objecting that sociology's methodological model has been too closely aligned to that of the natural sciences. Structuralism and functionalism 'suppress' or 'discount' actors' meanings. Even so, Giddens does not want to provide a theory of society resting on a form of individualism. While trying to overcome the difficulties he sees in interpretive or action approaches to meaning and experience, he also seeks to avoid the rigidities of structuralist accounts of society. He is not attempting to offer a general theory as such, but more a kind of programmatic outline and set of sensitising concepts that will inform sociological research, opposing the 'natural science' model as applied in sociology, which strives for the construction of general laws. Giddens draws on interpretive sociological theorisation in placing emphasis on the spatial and historical variability of actors' meaning informing action. In short, he argues against an 'objectivism' that uses structures, systems or society as simply determining action and 'facts' as gathered and studied in some 'objective' manner. As Giddens's approach has developed he has addressed an exceedingly wide array of subjects including 'intimacy', modernity, the nation-state and war, 'risk', and latterly, the 'third way' in politics.

Functionalist and Marxian theories are criticised for appearing to advocate a view of society and social system which has 'needs' or 'intent', e.g. to maintain the social order, which are met by the organisation of work, the economy generally, education, family, and so on. While using ethnomethodology he recognises it as social order approach, albeit at a micro level; he seeks a rather different model of the individual and social practice. Interpretive or action approaches are seen as insightful on the production of social meanings and interaction while having difficulties in accounting for the reproduction of social relations over time, including social differences in social interests. Giddens also provides a view of a knowledgeable, reflexive, skilled subject who has a number of 'levels' of consciousness. He argues that in 'reproducing structural properties, agents also reproduce the conditions that make such action possible' (Giddens 1994: 87).

In short, structuration theory, while using a very broad range of ideas and perspectives, generally is in debate with structuralist and functionalist writing, on the one hand, and interpretive sociologies, including work inspired by hermeneutical (the investigation of interpretation and understanding) philosophy, on the other. The attempt is to provide some unifying theoretical programme by overcoming 'dualisms'. Perhaps confusingly, given his opposition to 'dualisms', he uses the term 'duality of structure'; a conception of 'duality' is to replace 'dualisms' in theorisation. Giddens, therefore, has an unusual view of structure:

> Structure, as recursively organized sets of rules and resources, is out of time and space, save in its instantiations and co-ordination as memory traces, and is marked by an 'absence of the subject'. (Giddens 1994: 86)

In this view, 'structure' is 'both the medium and the outcome' of situated action. He adds:

> Structure is not 'external' to individuals: as memory traces, and as instantiated in social practices, it is in a certain sense more 'internal' than exterior to their activities in a Durkheimian sense. Structure is not to be equated with constraint but is always both constraining and enabling. (Giddens 1994: 87)

Nevertheless, he argues that this 'does not prevent structured properties of social systems from stretching away, in time and space, beyond the control of any individual actors' or, on the other hand, actors creating their 'own theories' of social systems – which may become reified within 'dimensions of ideology in social life' (Giddens 1994: 87). In this perspective, structure 'has no existence independent of the knowledge that agents have about what they do in their day-to-day activity'. At the 'level of discursive conscious-ness' individuals 'always know what they are doing' but may be unaware of the 'ramified consequences of the activities in which they engage' (Giddens 1994: 87–8).

Comparisons have been made between Giddens's approach to 'structure' and Bourdieu's (1977) notion of 'habitus' or stock of knowledge and the dis-positions of individuals (see King 2005; Parker 2000: 39). The latter takes a more 'conventional' view of structure and appears to give the individual less 'freedom', while his view of structure appears to avoid Giddens's confusing use of the term (see Layder 1994: 143–4). Bourdieu's 'genetic structuralism' utilises ideas such as 'fields', 'habitus' and other terms as a way of 'straddling the divide between "action and structure", "macro and micro" and "objectivity and subjectivity" ' (Atkinson and Housley 2003: 173). An interesting further comparison could be made with Bernstein's (rather neglected) ideas of 'classi-fication' and 'frame', as used in his attempt to 'understand the interrelation-ships between symbolic orders, forms of social organization and the shaping of experience in terms of codes' (Bernstein 1973: 227).

Social systems, for Giddens, are '[r]eproduced relations between actors or collectivities, organised as regular social practices' (Giddens 1979: 66), or 'the situated activities of human agents, reproduced across time and space' (Giddens 1994: 86). He says that the analysis of the structuration of social sys-tems means studying the modes of such systems 'grounded in the knowledge-able activities of situated actors' who in action contexts draw upon rules and resources, are produced and reproduced within interaction' (Giddens 1994: 86). In this manner, structuration refers to the 'Conditions governing the con-tinuity or transformation of structures, and therefore the reproduction of sys-tems' (Giddens 1979: 66). By the idea of the 'duality of structure' Giddens sought to cross the divide between structure and action. His concern was not so much with philosophical or epistemological issues (which leaves him open to the charge of making important assumptions) but rather a practical approach which placed agency within action in particular settings (hence his critique of the 'structuralist' aspects of ethnomethodology).

An interesting feature of Giddens's early work in relation to micro social theory is the outline of three main aspects of 'structuration' – legitimation, domination and signification (drawn from Weber, Marx and others; Giddens 1979: 97). Here, Giddens is attempting to understand structuration by utilising theories of normative regulation, authorisation and allocation, and coding. Domination relates to 'facility' and 'power'; while implicated in autonomy and dependency it is not conceived as simply repressive, but also has more productive ends. It involves the 'resources' of 'authorisation' (use of materials and technology) and 'allocation' (control of bodily reproduction, self-improvement, interaction and organisation). The notion of domination is held to be both constraining and enabling in the use of resources. It is linked to 'transformative capacity': in the application of agency individuals change the situation, but are constrained by the actions of others and unintended consequences (and the reproduction of social systems) can result. Legitimation refers to sanctions in interaction via norms. Sanctions (coercion as well as inducement) are utilised to govern the actions of individuals in the application of resources in social practices. Signification refers to communication (signs, symbols, meanings) in interaction through the usage of interpretive schemes held by actors. If we can leave aside Giddens's broader perspective on structuration, this model containing three major dimensions of interaction – domination, legitimation and signification – is an interesting contribution to 'micro social theory'. It also seeks to retain a notion of human agency with an emphasis on 'praxis' or the link between consciousness and actual conditions in the pursuit of action. The examination of legitimation, signification and domination in interaction is a corrective to approaches that develop only one of these aspects, such as power, in understanding specific social contexts or social life in general. It can be applied, for example, in institutional settings, say to the study of forms of interaction such as the 'interview' in social work, health, employment or other agencies, or indeed, any other interaction in formal or informal social situations.

Giddens offers a theory of the individual and is critical of notions of the 'decentred' subject (see Giddens 1987a, 1979: 38). Instead, he prefers a 'stratified' model of the personality in which there is a gradation of human wants, a 'basic security system' (mainly not consciously recognised) and the operation of a 'reflexive monitoring' of action by the individual (Giddens 1979: 56). The sources of this conception of the individual are quite varied but include elements of psychoanalytic conceptualisation and an action approach. In the actor's attempts to overcome insecurity there is also a use of Garfinkel and Goffman on trust and tact in social relations and the production of social order via conformity. The result is a stratification of unconscious and conscious levels between a biological and social basis for individual agency. The unconscious includes the 'mobilisation of unconscious desire', usually involving 'unconscious cognitive elements'. Practical consciousness is described as 'tacit stocks of knowledge which actors draw upon in the constitution of social activity'. Finally, discursive consciousness includes 'knowing "how to do" or "how to be" ' or 'involving knowledge which actors are able to express on the level of discourse'. He says that 'All actors have some degree of *discursive penetration* of the social systems to whose constitution they contribute' and produce spoken reasons for their actions (Giddens 1979: 5). Giddens emphasises the importance of 'practical consciousness': human intentionality should be regarded as a routine part of human action but as only becoming apparent in discourse, and then imperfectly, 'through reflexive monitoring of conduct' (Giddens 1979: 24–5). Through self-monitoring of action the individual also monitors the actions of others in taking into account the social setting in praxis. Again, he also leaves a place for unconscious features of human action and agency. Finally, Giddens argues that the '*continuity of social reproduction involves the continual "regrooving" of established attitudes and cognitive outlooks* holding down potential sources of anxiety in the basic security system'. In his view, 'Most elements of social practices are not directly motivated', while 'motivational commitment' includes 'habitual practices' which are the outcome of interacting agents' reflective monitoring related to their individual basic security system (Giddens 1979: 128; original emphasis).

In formulating these aspects of structuration theory (the idea of the individual and components of interaction) Giddens is critical of traditional notions of socialisation as 'a passive imprinting by "society" ' on the individual. Rather, he says, the individual is active, and the notion of the 'process' of socialisation can only be used loosely. He argues that individual development is not the storage of a 'series of competences'; it is a 'social becoming' which requires an understanding of ' "dialogical" contexts' or discursive and practical knowledge of the production and reproduction of social interaction (Giddens 1979: 129–30). Giddens rejects the notion that social systems are composed of roles. Instead, social systems are 'structured "fields" ' in which 'actors occupy definite *positions vis-á-vis* one another' (Giddens 1979: 117). A 'social position' he defines as 'a social identity' that contains a specific number of 'prerogatives and obligations' that an actor may fulfil. In this conception a social identity is 'essentially a category, or a typification, made on the basis of some definite social criterion or criteria: occupation, kin relation, age-grade, etc'. For Giddens, role as thus redefined must be analysed in relation to rules and resources and in association with practices. He argues that 'role-prescriptions' – roles as 'given' – may not be consensually based or 'given' and contain conflicts which reflect 'broad structural features of society'. Roles, he says, may also contain a disconnection between what they prescribe and what actors actually carry out. Finally, since they are involved in the utilisation of resources, and are also linked to structures of domination (Giddens 1979: 117–18).

There was some shift in focus in the early 1990s in Giddens's concerns with a more extended micro examination of 'self-identity' and 'intimacy' (although within a wider societal context) (Giddens 1991, 1992). His relative neglect of the 'inner' aspects of the individual (apart from levels of consciousness and some discussion of the self), e.g. emotion, had been an area of criticism of his work. Giddens now explored identity as a fluid conception – as the traditional, set routines of daily life have become less certain. There are consequences here for his previous discussion of structure and its relation to time and space, since 'structuring' (according to rules and resources) and the social practices of agents allowed for separated but comparable social practices to take on a systematic character. At first glance there are also questions for Giddens's earlier assumption of trust as ensured by convention and the reproduction routines in the face of potential threats to 'ontological security'. But Giddens's interest in Goffman's notion of the interaction order is evident here, since recent shifts in time and spatial relations have brought changes in communication and technology which have extended the opportunities for (non-face-to-face) interaction.

In *Modernity and Self-Identity* (1991) the self is conceived in a dialectical relation to wider societal shifts: the transformation in self-identity is connected with globalisation as 'the two poles of the dialectic of the local and the global in conditions of high modernity'. Thus, the movement in the intimate features of personal life are linked to the formation of very broad sets of social relationships (Giddens 1991: 32). Here, Giddens appears to be extending the classical tradition of conceiving an historical development of the 'self' or 'individual' (e.g. Weber, Mead and Durkheim – and later Foucault). He argues that the 'self' and 'society', for the first time, are connected in a global situation. While there is the threat of 'personal meaninglessness' brought by the new situation within the transformation of the self and society there is also the potential for the significant emergence of existential and moral questions in the daily lives of individuals and at wider levels. For Giddens, 'reflexive modernity' is now at the very centre of the self – a self that reflects on itself and others, and has to be shaped and maintained. The individual self in the context of the dissolving of traditional patterns of work, family and other aspects of life has to be in charge of its own formation and continuance, including the creation of intimate connections with others. This responsibility also includes bodily appearance (through exercise, dieting and other means – alongside the rise of therapeutic help). Finally, here Giddens's ideas on the body differ from both Foucault's (as discursively constructed) and Goffman's (socially constructed in impression management) conceptions. In Giddens, the body is a crucial aspect of reflexivity since it demonstrates self-identity and its place in the life-style(s) we have decided to pursue.

In the *Transformation of Intimacy* (1992) Giddens argues that there has been the development of the 'pure relationship' in which each individual partner experiences sexual and emotional equality and, thereby, continued satisfaction (see Jamieson 1999). He argues that women have taken the lead in fostering this 'democratisation' of relationships and emotional reorganisation. Importantly, there is the potential for this process to affect the wider institutions of society. Thus, the reflexive construction of the self and the transformation of intimacy are not limited to the micro level; they may have massive implications for the rest of society. In addition, Giddens has also written on the issue of 'risk' in contemporary society – not merely the concern for external risks of nature (e.g. floods), but also the 'risk' formed by our realisation of the increasing effects of knowledge about our surroundings. The realisation of risk is not only a concern for 'macro' phenomena – risk is also part of our daily personal life.

Giddens's prolific output has stimulated very extensive debate. There has been praise for the scope of his work and the attempt to integrate theorisation from very different kinds of sociology to overcome 'dualisms' (e.g. especially agency–structure). However, criticisms have included the difficulties in understanding his conceptualisation; the insensitivity to the original theoretical context of the concepts he takes from elsewhere; and the lack of empirical referents or guide to methodology in his work (despite its intention to be practical). In addition, there is a reliance on a 'language' (i.e. rules) model for social relations; and the view of the individual is still rationalist or cognitive, even given the later emphasis on intimacy and emotion. Particular criticism has centered on his notion of 'structure': that he has not overcome 'dualism' in his structuration theory by his idea of 'duality of structure', he has merely reproduced the difficulty or veered to the 'agency' or 'subjectivist' pole of explanation. Structure, since it is based on rules and resources and is 'emergent', is too disconnected from system, while system – as the reproduction of social relations – pays insufficient attention to the institutional asymmetries of power, opportunities and distribution of material goods.

According to Barnes, Giddens's account of agency at the micro level is held by very many theorists as an alternative to previous accounts. The idea of an individual as acting according to norms and rules although not simply constrained by them has a wide acceptance. However, Barnes argues that Giddens's conception of agency is actually a rather larger notion which is independent of the individual's power to intervene in events – it is 'a metaphysical postulate', a pre-given assumption, rather than being empirically based (Barnes 2003: 346). Giddens has also been criticised for having a fundamentally voluntarist idea of action. However, Barnes points to a certain confusion here: Giddens views the patterns of action that are reproduced and persist as social systems, and explains the action of individual agents, as applying the resources of structure. While trying to avoid the 'determination' of traditional notions of structure, and allowing actors to act 'otherwise', the connection between the 'macro' and 'micro' begins to be unclear. Some account is needed of how individuals choose from resources and the extent to which wider 'structurings' can 'determine' (Barnes 2003: 345). Barnes also observes that the idea of 'ontological security' (e.g. in reducing anxieties) relies on a belief in the existing conventions of coding (signification) and regulation (norms) that reproduce daily life. The tendency in this theorisation, for Barnes, seems to lead back to the 'normative' ideas of Parsons in structural functionalism (Barnes 2003: 346). Alternatively, Atkinson and Housley, while finding it 'striking' that in Giddens (and Bourdieu) there is little direct use of interactionist thought (but phenomenology, ethnomethodology, Parsons, Marx, Weber and Durkheim all feature), structuration theory, and its success, seems to reflect the 'continued relevance of core interactionist themes' as described in the duality of structure (Atkinson and Housley 2003: 173).

Finally, detailed comparisons have been made between Giddens and a number of other writers on the issues of duality and dualisms (especially agency/structure and subjectivism/objectivism). For example, Parker examines various writers in his extensive discussion of 'structuration' according to whether they appear to uphold 'duality' (Giddens and Bourdieu) or are 'post-structurationists' who support 'dualism' (Archer and Mouzelis) (Parker 2000).

It is difficult to summarise the implications of Giddens's structuration theory for micro social theorisation. However, a number of immediate elements, although often adapted from the work of others, are certainly worth pursuing further – such as the self-monitoring of action, levels of consciousness, onto-logical security and role. These could be connected more to his very suggestive outline of three main aspects of structuration – legitimation, domination and signification – and could be used a great deal more in the study of specific situations or 'the interaction order' (as in Goffman). This conception of the three components of action could be very usefully further interlinked with his later concerns for the shifts in intimacy and self-identity as reflecting social transformation.

Conclusion

It has not been possible to outline all the developments in micro social theory in this book or review the ones selected in this chapter in as great a depth as those covered in previous chapters. The emphasis in this chapter has not been to identify 'new' theories as such but outline a number which are of continuing importance in terms of influence and likely further theoretical development.

There are a number of issues which have arisen in this chapter related to the continuation of micro social theory. First, the question of the model of the actor that is used in a particular theory: the individual as 'rational' in exercising choice; or as (also) emotional, with feelings, and as embodied; or as an 'exchanger' involved in various kinds of exchange and networks; or as positioned in discourses; or as knowledgeable and reflexive. Secondly, there is the question of 'structure': as arising from rational decisions of actors; or as a network of exchanges; or as patterns of discourses; or in terms of a 'duality of structure'. This question raises difficult problems, for instance, surrounding how the agency–structure relation; domination, legitimation and signification; and 'discourses' can be examined at the 'micro level'. Finally, these issues regarding the 'actor', 'structure' and 'agency' have a great bearing on theoretical concerns regarding identity formation, the nature and change of the 'self', affective relations and embodiment. All these issues lie at the heart of a micro social theorisation. In my view the 'micro social' can be both taken analytically at its 'own level' as well as interpenetrating with wider social ('meso' or intermediate) or societal 'levels'.

Further Reading

For overviews of exchange, network and rational choice theories, G. Ritzer and D. J. Goodman, *Sociological Theory* (6th ed., London, McGraw-Hill, 2004) provides useful introductions to key figures, ideas and criticisms. Other reviews can be found in I. Craib, *Modern Social Theory* (2nd ed., New York, St Martin's Press, 1992); B. Hindess, *Choice, Rationality and Social Theory* (London, Unwin Hyman, 1988); and D. D. Heckathorn, 'Sociological Rational Choice' and L. D. Molm, 'Theories of Social Exchange and Exchange Networks', both in G. Ritzer and B. Smart (eds.), *Handbook of Social Theory* (London, Sage, 2003). For the work of Coleman and Emerson in particular see S. Lindenberg, 'James Coleman', and for detailed biographical introductions, K. S. Cook and J. Whitmeyer, 'Richard M. Emerson', both in G. Ritzer, *The Blackwell Companion to Major Social Theorists* (Oxford, Blackwell, 2000).

Foucault's work is wide-ranging and has produced an enormous secondary literature. On the idea of 'discipline', this chapter is particularly based on M. Foucault, *Discipline and Punish* (Harmondsworth, Penguin, 1977). There are numerous readers and commentaries on Foucault's work, for example G. Cutting (ed.), *The Cambridge Companion to Foucault* (Cambridge, Cambridge University Press, 1994); G. Danaher, T. Schirato and J. Webb, *Understanding Foucault* (London, Sage, 2000); A. McHoul and W. Grace, *A Foucault Primer: Discourse, Power and the Subject* (London, Routledge, 1995); and S. Katz, 'Michel Foucault', in A. Elliott and B. S. Turner (eds.), *Profiles in Contemporary Social Theory* (London, Sage, 2001) are among the more accessible. For generally more advanced discussion and sources see: D. Hoy (ed.), *Foucault* (Oxford, Blackwell, 1986); C. Jones and R. Porter (eds.), *Reassessing Foucault: A Critical Reader* (London, Routledge, 1994); L. McNay, *Foucault: A Critical Introduction* (Cambridge, Polity, 1994); P. Rabinow (ed.), *The Foucault Reader* (Harmondsworth, Penguin, 1984); B. Smart, *Michel Foucault* (Chichester, Ellis Horwood, 1985); B. Smart, *Foucault, Marxism and Critique* (London, Routledge, 1983); and B. Smart, *Foucault, Marxism and Critique* (London, Routledge, 1983).

For Giddens's work and his notion of 'structuration' see his *Central Problems in Social Theory* (Basingstoke, Macmillan, 1979) and *The Constitution of Society* (Cambridge, Polity, 1984). Useful, concise reviews of Giddens's work: I. J. Cohen, 'Structuration Theory and Social Praxis', in A. Giddens and J. Turner (eds.), *Social Theory Today* (Stanford, CA, Stanford University Press, 1987); I. J. Cohen, *Structuration Theory* (London,

Macmillan, 1991); I. J. Cohen, 'Anthony Giddens', in R. Stones (ed.), *Key Sociological Thinkers* (Basingstoke, Palgrave Macmillan, 1998); A. Elliott, 'Anthony Giddens', in A. Elliott and B. S. Turner (eds.), *Profiles in Contemporary Social Theory* (London, Sage, 2001). A good, book-length introduction to Giddens's work is I. Craib, *Anthony Giddens* (London, Routledge, 1992); see also S. Loyal, *The Sociology of Anthony Giddens* (London, Pluto, 2002). More broadly on structuration theory, a good starting point is R. Stones, *Structuration Theory* (Basingstoke, Palgrave Macmillan, 2005); see also A. King, 'Structure and Agency', in A. Harrington (ed.), *Modern Social Theory* (Oxford, Oxford University Press, 2005) and J. Parker, *Structuration* (Buckingham, Open University, 2000). C. G. A. Bryant and D. Jary have produced a number of edited volumes on Giddens's work, which are commonly used. See their *Giddens' Theory of Structuration: A Critical Appreciation* (London, Routledge, 1991), *Anthony Giddens: Critical Assessments* (London, Routledge, 1997) and *The Contemporary Giddens: Social Theory in a Globalizing Age* (Basingstoke, Palgrave Macmillan, 2001).

9

Substantive Developments in Micro Social Theory

Introduction

In recent years a range of previously relatively neglected areas of theorisation and empirical study have emerged within sociology, for instance, place, time, friendship, body and emotion. This is not to say that these areas have not been present, or not deemed important by some previous writers, but that they have now become the focus of a re-evaluation and re-emphasis in sociology. The emergence of these concerns has important consequences for micro theorisation; in terms of providing a new sophistication in how traditional ideas concerning the individual subject, situation and interaction are to be considered. Thus, current substantive work further develops themes in micro theory, such as community and place; or themes that require further attention, such as the importance of time in social interaction; or rather overlooked aspects of theoretical areas regarding individual experience, such as emotions and body in relation to self-conception and interaction. In this chapter, therefore, we can see the interrelation between theoretical and substantive endeavour – for instance, how social changes in friendship and intimate social relations, community and place are raising micro social theoretical issues or how the increasing focus on emotions, body, time and narratives relate to more 'traditional' micro concerns with self, experience and social meaning.

Community and Place

The term 'community' has a long history in sociology. It is a basic 'concept' originally indicating a more 'conservative' brand of thought stressing the importance of order and cohesion at a time of rapid industrial and urban change and the emergence of a capitalist society (Nisbet 1967; Lee and Newby 1983). Such changes in the nineteenth century were to bring increasing interest in 'crime rates' and other social problems as moral indicators of 'social health' and 'social order'. Early sociology and social reform were concerned with

134

'social disintegration' and how society could re-establish order and cohesion. One emphasis was on how social bonds could be strengthened and a 'moral order' consolidated – in the face of the rise of the modern 'metropolis'; the appearance of new competitive social values informing daily interaction; and shifts in the 'mental life' of the individual (cf. Park, Chapter 2 in this book); and the work of Durkheim, Tonnies and Simmel).

In the late 1960s the idea of 'community', as used in the Chicagoan sociological legacy including in British studies, was subject to critique. The notion of 'human ecology' had long been abandoned but what the term implied, apart from a loose description of social life, remained vague – was it a group, an area, or both? Some writers chose to move to the 'urban' level; they argued that communities were crucially shaped by 'external forces' such as economic and political decision-making by city councils and business, the effects of the media, and increasing social and spatial mobility. Also, the opportunities of leisure industries and travel were lessening communal differences. In sum, the use of 'community' was criticised due to an imprecise definition, an inadequate theorisation of the basis of communal cohesion and solidarity and the unclear methodology used. It seemed an underlying assumption that a community was somehow hermetically sealed from the 'outside'. However, by the mid-1980s some writers began to argue that the term 'community' was still useful and saw a revival of community studies (e.g. Bulmer 1985). The term was increasingly being used to describe local services (e.g. community policing, community psychiatry, community mental health, and so on) and policies of 'community care' were identifying 'the community' as the place for 'decanting' certain groups from state institutions or as the setting for 'communal alternatives' to incarceration. Further, people clearly still had communal attachments. Some sense of community appeared to be important for identity: as a notion of 'home' it was highlighted by the 'symbolic markers' (buildings, statues, roads, and so on) which carry meanings given to one's area. Individuals, it seemed, commonly expressed a strong local feeling or 'sense of belonging' in the meanings attached to their surroundings (see Cohen 1985). The importance of 'community', in sociological and social policy fields – and in wider social discussion – despite the previous difficulties, once again emerged and was recognised as an essential aspect of civil society. Wider investigation turned to how it could be established or revived in the face of destabilising forces.

A renewed interest in the importance of 'place' and 'locality' arose as part of a broader interest in 'spatial differences' in the 1970s and 1980s, particularly in the work of cultural geographers. Issues were raised regarding the nature of symbolic meaning in relation to 'spatial' differentiation and the inclusion and exclusion of groups in terms of space and control (see Jackson and Penrose 1993; Dickens 1990; Urry and Gregory 1985). The importance of 'place' and community was further fuelled in the mid-1980s by the rise of 'new' communal politics, for example, protests around ecological and planning issues, as resistance to new road schemes and other developments grew. There were some efforts to decentralise local government services and decisions (as in Britain) and include residents more in local planning (e.g. housing development). In addition, the year-long British miners' strike of 1984–85 and the subsequent effects of the miners' defeat led to quite a number of local studies (e.g. Green 1990; Waddington et al. 1991).

While there was some 'return' to community in sociological work there was also a recognition that a much greater effort had to be made regarding the use of theory and the methodological procedures to be used in such study. For example, recently Crow has drawn from diverse empirical examples and a broad range of theory, particularly around the idea 'social solidarity' as an organising term, to study community, including the resources, circumstances and characteristics of a particular group (Crow 2002; see also Crow and Allan 1994; Crow and Mclean 2000; Crow et al. 2002). He argues that much contemporary observation and debate points to the fragmentation of familial, group, communal, work and other relations as undermining the bases for social solidarity. There is an urgent need, it seems, to establish the conditions of social solidarity, which can also allow (as Durkheim recognised) for elements of freedom and security (Crow 2002; see also Hoggett 1997). Crow draws on Durkheim's legacy and a host of contemporary writers (Bauman, Beck, Bellah, Castells, Etzioni, Giddens, Melucci and Sennett) to try to reinvigorate the theoretical (and research) basis of 'community'. He uses the examples of families, solidarity in mining communities and the Polish Solidarity movement to examine inclusion and exclusion and the conditions that bring people together or separate them in terms of class, gender and other parameters. For Crow, social solidarity is not conceived as simply natural or fixed; he says its basis has been sought both in self-interest and altruism, as well as the operation of 'inclusion' and 'exclusion' of others. Here, a recent issue (in Britain and elsewhere) has been the extent to which a given community or society should enforce 'boundaries' (e.g. in terms of asylum, immigration regulations) and whether newcomers receiving citizenship, from whatever background, should comply with an affirmation or certain other requirements to become societal 'members'. In addition, an associated concern has arisen regarding whether some commonality of values, forms of joint action and a mutual trust are required for a 'viable' community to continue rather than division, separation or hostility to ensue. Crow takes the general view that

> traditional forms of solidarity have greater durability than is suggested in some of the more despairing assessments of contemporary social relationships, and ... new forms of solidarity continue to emerge as they have done in previous generations. (Crow 2002: 132)

The traditional criticism of the notion of community was reinforced during the 1980s with the rise of postmodernist theory within urban sociology. The concern was with the effects of global processes, not merely in terms of economic restructuring but flowing from cultural shifts, with cities seen as the prime base for possible new collective identities and resistance. Smith (2001) argues that the various writings of Harvey, Zukin, James and Soja had some commonality of view on the 'postmodern city', where 'images of urban spectacle created by multinational capital replace "authentic" local cultures' with 'hyperspaces' which disintegrate local consciousness and the ability to understand and resist (Smith 2001: 124–5). He says that such a view paid little attention 'to the impact upon cities of the spatial practices of ordinary people or the politics of urban difference, save to marginalize them as part of the spectacle'. But, he adds, some postmodernism did allow some shift in focus from the 'macro urban' context to everyday 'micro political relations of power, domination, resistance, and struggle, particularly as these articulate with issues of race, ethnicity, gender, ecology, and locality' (Smith 2001: 126). Smith offers an interesting, alternative 'social constructionist' view of the processes of 'transnational urbanism' in which '*networks of power*, subsisting at every point from the most "local" to the most "global," are formed, related to each other, and transformed'. In this way culture, community and place are not seen as enclosed but constituted as 'circuits of communication'. In everyday life, people are connected in sometimes overlapping ways and the local is where reproduction of cultural meanings and resistance to 'dominant modes of power and ideology' take place (Smith 2001: 127). Kraidy (2002), in her study based in the Lebanon, also advocates terms that 'better reflect global/local encounters than the now cliché "globalization" '. The term '*glocalization*', she argues, 'is a more heuristic concept that takes into account the local, national, regional, and global contexts of intercultural communicative processes ... [and] the recognition that cultural hybridity is the rule rather than the exception'. This view of the hybridization of 'local' and 'global' 'entails re-formulating intercultural and international communication beyond buoyant models of resistance and inauspicious patterns of domination' (Kraidy 2002: 204–5).

Of particular interest in the study of 'global–local' relations is the phenomenon of migration both within and between countries. Migration is now generally seen as a lifelong process, as well as connecting to other areas of social investigation, for example, as overlapping with the study of ethnic communities (Thomson 1999: 24–5). The experience of individuals and groups can been seen within migration patterns. However, the study of groups and their continuity of experience should not simply be limited to their origins. As Thomson (1999) argues, the group may not consider origins as important compared with current difficulties or may even wish to avoid earlier associations since they may connect with stereotypes surrounding 'immigrant', 'refugee' or 'asylum seeker'. Thus, there is a need to recognise the 'complex interconnections between migration and the formation and development of migrant communities and ethnic identities' in theory and research (Thomson 1999: 25). Similarly, Benmayor and Skotnes (1994) argue that the problems of migration and the 'resulting reconfigurations of social identity are fundamental issues'. They say that in the 1990s the use of oral history in particular social settings contributed to an understanding of migration by providing 'glimpses' into the inner life of migration experiences. Oral history was able to show the processes involved in the formation and ref-ormation of identity, while also demonstrating the connection between oral tes-timony and global experiences (Benmayor and Skotnes 1994). Within sociology the study of migration, including communal or ethnic identity formation, has recently become a major area of methodological and theoretical study.

Another very important area of renewed development, related to ideas on community study, has been the study of nationalism. Ideas on inclusion/exclusion, communal symbols, traditions and conceptions of 'homeland', and the notion of the 'construction' of community have featured strongly in attempts to understand the history and current 'rise' of nationalism (see Anderson 1983; Brehony and Rassool 1999; Hutchinson and Smith 1994; Kellas 1991; Smith 1986, 1991). Similarly, the sociology of religion and reli-gious communities and experience is now returning as a main subject of socio-logical development in response to social changes and pressing social issues.

Time

Time has become another area of development in sociological study since the early 1990s (see Adam 1990, 1995, 2004). Although discussions of time can be found as important aspects of the classical sociological work of theorists such as Marx, it has only recently returned to prominence. Time can be considered to be a fundamental part of human existence – within our creation of meaning and the construction of our 'life' as we are situated, and situate ourselves within the interweaving of past, present and future (Adam 1990: 127). As Berger and Luckmann argue:

> All my existence in this world is continuously ordered by its time, is indeed enveloped by it ... I have only a certain amount of time available for the realization of my projects, and the knowledge of this affects my attitude to these projects. (Berger and Luckmann 1971: 41)

We have shifted our conceptions of time, space and speed through technologi-cal innovation and other changes, which have significant implications for how we perceive our life and its key aspects, such as health (Adam 1990: 127, 1995: 43–58). The centrality of time can be seen in the work of Mead and Schutz. Mead's writings on time have been revisited by recent theorists, for example, because of the connection he makes between change and time. Petras argues that Mead sees the past and the future as 'expansions out of the present, rather than the common conception of a sequence proceeding from the past, to the present, to the future'. Thus, the past is 'not a fixed condition of a structured time period, but will vary in accordance with any particular present' (Petras

1968: 12–13; see Mead 1932, 1964: 328–41). So even if we had all the relevant materials from a person's life in helping to produce our portrait, the 'truth' would still reside in the present, and a later present would again reconstruct it according to its 'emergent nature' (Petras 1968: 13). As Adam adds: 'reality to Mead exists in the present. The present implies a past and a future, but they are denied existence. Any reality that transcends the present, he argues, must exhibit itself in the present' (Adam, 1990: 38). Schutz's phenomenology has also been taken as a starting point for the discussion of time in sociological theory due to its relation to social consciousness, interpersonal relations and the production of meaning (Adam 1990: 34–7). For example, its importance in Schutz can be seen in his discussion of the 'reflective attitude':

> What alone I can grasp is rather my performed act (my past acting) or, if my acting still continues while I turn back, the performed initial phases (my present acting). While I lived in my acting in progress it was an element of my vivid present. Now this present has turned into past, and the vivid experience of my acting in progress has given place to my recollection of having acted or to the retention of having been acting. (Schutz 1971: 214; see Roberts 2002: 82–4)

I found in my study of south Wales (Roberts 1999) that individuals moved between various 'tenses' of time when describing the community and their reactions to social change. Some elements of life were taken as Past-past – as gone never to return; others as still here, or Present-past, and finally, others to be found once again in the future (Present-future), as previous experiences are relearnt and used again (Roberts 1999; see also Allan and Thompson 1999).

Emotions

The study of emotions has been marginalised in sociological work but is increasingly being seen as a vital area within micro (and wider) theorisation (see Barbalet 2001; Bendelow and Williams 1988; Layder 2004; Williams 2001). For Bauman and May:

> None of the many impersonal exchanges in which we are involved will suffice to supply the identity we seek because it lies beyond any of those exchanges ... Only in a personal context, with its diffuseness, particularity, emphasis on quality and the mutual affection which saturates it, can we hope to find what we are looking for and even then, we may be frustrated in our attempts. (Bauman and May: 2001: 85)

The overlooking of 'emotional' aspects of interaction has been due to a cognitive emphasis in the study of individual action; attention has broadly been on the rational or calculative motivation to act. Perhaps, more mundanely, the discussion of emotion has been conceived more as the province of the psychology of individual motivation or social psychological work on group relations.

In addition, emotions or 'feelings' were often relegated to the 'irrational' aspects of individual and social motivation and action (e.g. the crowd). Williams, in developing a sociological viewpoint, argues that there are a number of central questions in the study of emotions, including 'whether or not emotions can be isolated, defined, observed and understood as universal "things" in themselves or as "social constructs" ' (Williams 1998a: 122). Further, there is 'the relationship between emotions and embodiment, social action and self-identity', and the connection between 'emotion management' and 'broader macro-structural issues of power and status, conflict and control' (Williams 1998a: 122; see also Williams 1998b, 2001). Williams says that in general terms there is a continuum of positions on the question of emotions. At one pole, are organismic theories, which relate emotions to instinctual gestures or some libidinal base, and root them in biological and universalistic perspectives (e.g. Darwin and Freud). On the other pole, they are seen as 'social constructions' within a social context in opposition to a view based on biologistic and individualistic factors – as produced as part of social action in the group and historically and culturally variable (Williams 1998a: 122–3).

Interactionist work is credited with bringing the study of emotions to prominence within sociology, seeing them as part of 'lived experience' and the construction of meaning and identity (Sandstrom et al. 2003: 221). Particularly following Hochschild's study *The Managed Heart* (1983), 'emotionality' has figured prominently in interactionism as 'emerging in interaction and often with contrivance' or skill in expressing and verbalising 'emotion' to others (Plummer 1991b: xv). Thus, interactionists may focus on self-feeling while linking it to community; or on feelings such as anxiety and fear, perhaps stimulated by illness and leading to identity changes; or on how feelings are displayed, even by researchers. Such work may use Goffman's notion on 'the presentation of self', or Hochschild's ideas on 'surface acting' or management of emotional display, in which individuals shape their emotions according to group influences and negotiations. Thus, emotions are part of 'interpersonal control' and how individuals negotiate definitions of self and others, and their situations (Layder 2004; Sandstrom et al. 2003: 222).

Duncombe and Marsden (1993) (again in part using Hochschild's work) examine the 'ideologies' of love and intimacy in heterosexual couples with reference to gender theories relating to differences in 'emotional work'. Instead of merely focusing on 'instrumental' measures of family activities such as family finance and division of labour, they argue for attention to be given to expressive or emotional dimensions which people find important – such as love and intimacy (Duncombe and Marsden 1993: 221). Based on their research they argue that:

> despite dissatisfaction with gender inequalities in domestic tasks and finance – many women express unhappiness primarily with what they perceive as men's unwillingness or incapacity to 'do' the emotional intimacy which appears to them necessary to

sustain close heterosexual couple relationships ... raising questions about how far men's and women's emotional behaviour can and should change. (Duncombe and Marsden 1993: 221)

However, Burkitt argues that Duncombe and Marsden's distinction between 'real' and 'acted' feelings is inadequate; rather, he argues that 'techniques of the body' 'forge real emotional dispositions within the person, ones that can appear in situations that evoke particular emotions ... emotions should be regarded as performative' (Burkitt 1999: 127; see also Burkitt 1997). Also of interest here is how individuals engage in 'emotion work' with others (see Frith and Kitzinger 1998). Jackson notes that while 'the institutionalisation of love in marriage and its representation in romantic fiction' has been widely discussed in sociological and feminist writing, 'the cultural meaning of love as an emotion has been neglected' (Jackson 1993: 201). Her position is that 'emotions are culturally constructed'. She puts forward ideas on subjectivity and love employing 'narrative or discourse' to examine the common distinction between the powerful feeling of being 'in love' and love as 'longer-term affection', 'and the ways in which the ideology of romance has been associated with women's subordination' (Jackson 1993: 201). Craib, in criticising Jackson and Duncombe and Marsden, states that while sociology has a contribution to make to the study of emotions, so does psychology, biology and various other disciplines (Craib 1995). He asserts that a range of common human emotions may have some basis in our 'biological make-up' while also noting that the 'available register' of emotions can differ according to culture and historical setting. However, it could be argued (following Burkitt) that while Craib may be right here, 'his next move – to give emotions an inner existence separate from cultural norms or cognitive categories does not necessarily follow'. Instead, '[e]mbodied emotional experience' may arise from the social situations 'in which people are enmeshed, and yet still be against some more generally prescribed norms ... or people may feel a conflict of emotion stemming from a particular situation' (Burkitt 1999: 117). But Craib further argues that a social constructionist view (at least as offered by Jackson) appears to give precedence to cognition rather than hold the suggestion that there may be an interchange between cognition and feeling (Craib 1995: 153).

At times we cannot express fully the experiences we are having and make others understand, or we experience differences between our feelings and thoughts. The problem with Jackson's argument and potentially for a sociology of emotions, for Craib, is that emotions 'will be reduced to ideas' and will have 'no autonomy from the rational world' (Craib 1995: 153). Methodologically, according to Craib, it is important that sociologists are aware that asking individuals about their feelings takes them 'to the reality beneath the ideology'. Sociologists should be mindful of the 'depth of what they are studying and the comparatively abstract level at which they are studying it' (Craib 1995: 157).

For Burkitt's 'relational' view, emotions 'exist only in the context of relations and are to be conceptualized as complexes; that is, as irreducible to social structures, discourses or the body. All these elements are constitutive of emotions, which are felt only by active, embodied beings who are locked into networks of interdependence' (Burkitt 1999: 127). Rather differently, Williams develops a general argument on 'modernity and the emotions' (Williams 1998b). He argues that in Western thought and practice there is an 'irrational passion for dispassionate rationality' and examines 'current debates surrounding the *ambivalent* nature of modernity as both order and chaos, conformity and transgression'. In his account, since emotions and reason are not 'antithetical', a fundamental 'rethink of epistemological models and ontological ways of being and knowing' is needed. He says the classical writers such as Marx, Durkheim, Weber and Simmel were aware of emotional consequences, and now there is growing discussion of emotions in social life and connections with how the body is constructed in discourse. Williams points to increasing tensions within modernity; the division between emotionality and rationality has been questioned and attention drawn to the part played by symbols and meanings in the formation of the self, mind and emotion (Williams 1998b: 747). In his perspective, emotions are central to the 'effective deployment' of reason and may aid the construction of knowledge, while knowledge may also help in the formation of appropriate emotions. He sees emotions as '*emergent* properties, located at the intersection of physiological *dispositions*, material circumstances, and socio-cultural *elaboration*' and providing 'the basis for social reciprocity and exchange' – the ' "link" between personal problems and the broader public issues of social structure' (Williams 1998b: 750). Williams concludes by arguing that a recognition of emotion is necessary for the investigation of the 'expressive body', for instance, in health research. But, in such differing activities as gang aggression, New Age movements, and musical and sporting events 'spontaneous emotions' are very much present and cannot be curtailed by rational modernity (Williams 1998b: 764; emphasis added).

Emotion is now appearing as a major factor in understanding self-formation, embodiment and social interaction as diverse micro perspectives (e.g. areas of social interactionism, structuration theory and feminist work) have begun to reconsider the duality of 'emotion' and 'rationality' and connections (drawing on more macro considerations) between individuality, emotional life and modernity.

Friendship and Intimate Relations

A related subject to emotions – and also under-recognised – is the area of bonds of friendship and intimacy, now also receiving consideration (e.g. Bauman and May 2001: ch. 5; Bauman 2003; Layder 2004). Of course, marriage and the 'marriage bond' has been a traditional subject, but as feminists have argued, the experience of family relations and, in particular, the position of women has been insufficiently investigated (see Chapter 7). Discussion has traditionally been focused on the role of the family in socialisation and the maintenance of social order with a general assumption of a gendered division of labour (i.e. the affective role of women and the instrumental role of men) and its basis in romantic love. Of course, while the conception of the 'traditional family' itself was not the 'full' reality, recent changes have made it even more imperative to reassess the traditional view. A variety of 'family forms' have become more apparent together with some changes in (at least expected) roles. The rise of divorce (towards half of recent marriages in the UK) and remarriage, and also the increase of individuals under middle age living alone (up to a third of all households contain only one person in the UK), have led to changes in family structures (Abercrombie 2004: 28). Further complexities have included shifts in values related to the family, changes in the relations between parents and children, alterations in domestic and financial arrangements, declining numbers of children per family, childlessness within relationships, and the rise of cohabitation. In addition, movements in workforce composition, same gender partnerships, increasing longevity, and some changes in the familial division of labour have all led to a questioning of traditional assumptions regarding family experiences and relationships (Vincent 2000: 140–3).

Marriage may seem to be in decline but cohabitation is commonly a prelude to marriage. What may be happening is a reorientation in marriage or 'couple-dom' relationships associated with increasing career possibilities, job changes, and varying periods of unemployment among couples and increasing formal work involvement of women (Vincent 2000: 140–1). These shifts may be affecting the 'patriarchal' notions of marriage or cohabiting partnerships due to the economic power and relative independence these changes may afford. However, some commentators remain sceptical on the extent which greater female participation in the workforce has affected domestic patterns and male attitudes (see Abercrombie 2004: 27–8; Abbott 2000: 73–5). Also relevant here is the 'planning' involved in relationships, especially on decisions when, or even if, to have children, i.e. delaying having children or not having children at all due to career demands or the feeling of a need for freedom from certain responsibilities. Further factors affecting relationships include the rise of career breaks, 'downsizing' or switching to 'less demanding' careers, and planned or unplanned early retirement and, for some, greater leisure time – all can disrupt the 'traditional' occupational pattern. The growing number of younger people living alone is also another factor, which is beginning to raise concerns regarding the possible effects of social isolation on individual well-being. To some extent the phenomenon may be a deliberate strategy and may reflect greater leisure socialising with work colleagues and friends – and 'serial' intimate relationships. Finally, there is a rise in the number of years that couples (potentially) are together, and without children in the home, which may bring shifts or pressures on the marriage or partnership bond. For

Abercrombie (2004) these changes raise an important question regarding the degree to which changes in marriage degrade the ideas of intimacy and romantic love. He argues that paradoxically the rise in independence, change and equality in relationships may support partner closeness since it is not intimate personal relationships which are replaced – rather one partner is succeeded by another, while the rising independence and equality within various forms of partnership actually produce greater intimacy (Abercrombie 2004: 29). Finally, young people may be living with friends rather than their partners but there is still evidence that their expectations may include a traditional sense of 'settling down' (see Heath and Cleaver 2003).

Bauman and May (2001) argue (drawing on Sennett and others) that there is a tension between 'love' and 'exchange' in human relationships – with most actual relationships being an impure mixture of various elements and expectations. 'Love' may become devalued, as it becomes subject to various inner tensions and exchange pressures. There can also be conflicting needs – to 'belong' by seeking ties and security and 'individuality' or freedom from demands. The more one need is satisfied the 'more painful may be the neglect of the other' (Bauman and May 2001: 92). Sennett (2002) adds a further dimension by pointing to two 'tyrannies of intimacy' in social relations. First, as the 'oppression' brought by the 'claustrophobia' of restricted horizons and expectations in ordinary daily life (i.e. in domestic routines and concerns) which arouses a 'belief in one standard of truth to measure the complexities of social reality'. Secondly, the 'tyranny' brought by the 'seduction' of being 'governed by a single authority'. Setting a notion of 'community' against the 'impersonal' nature of society, he argues, is misguided, instead the 'city is the instrument of impersonal life, the mold in which diversity and complexity of persons, interests, and tastes become available as social experience … that civilized possibility is today dormant' (Sennett 2002: 338–40).

Friendship as a form of personal or intimate relationship has been surprisingly marginalised within sociology. One reason, perhaps, is due to the difficulties in defining who may regarded as a friend rather than merely say, a colleague, lover, acquaintance or neighbour, and how such relationships differ from a being a family member. Of course, someone may be several things at once to another, for instance, a colleague, a neighbour and a friend. Frequency of contact is not a sufficient criterion since, for example, one may simply share the daily task of taking children to school with another local family whereas an 'old friend' may have very irregular contact. Perhaps also the number of friends and the frequency of contact may be changing. Just as people may differ on whom they regard as 'family' (some may even include the family pet!), so the definition of whom are regarded as friends may differ between individuals, and across age group, class, cultural group and over a lifetime. There may also be differences in types of friends and what they are 'used' for – some may be friends limited to an activity, say sport; others may be friends in more than one context, e.g. home, work or leisure. Family 'ties' are usually regarded as those based upon blood and marriage (and, more recently, long-term relationship/partnership with a family member), with commonly a high degree of emotional attachment and a reliable source of support and mutual obligation. However, it is also possible to have a friend who gives a high degree of support and attachment, much more than that given by a family member.

Friendships are often seen as rather different according to gender. In adolescence, the intimate dyadic and triadic relations appear very important for girls, with frequent detailed conversations, and a high value placed on the sharing of intimate thoughts and experiences; today such interaction is daily supplemented by the use of mobile phone conversations, texting and emails. For boys a rather more truncated form of communication is often apparent with less sharing of feelings or emotions, and a more competitive, hierarchical grading is perhaps likely to be found. These patterns may be said to continue into adulthood, with women retaining friendships over many years and adding new close ones when in new contexts and separated from older friends. Men's friendships, it may be said, are more dependent on the changing circumstance – 'fit for purpose' towards a particular goal. However, there is a danger with these formulations in perpetuating stereotypical views of gender difference. It may well be the case that men in some Western cultures at least are more prepared to express affection and exchange of intimacies and bodily expression than previously. Again, historical and sociocultural generalisations can readily be made whereas empirical support is required – hence the need for research in these areas. Fortunately, a great deal of work is now being conducted into some interpersonal relationships and areas such as the construction of masculinity, although here often in regard to the body and bodily identity and on gender, 'relations' rather than emotional ties and inter- and intra-gender friendships as such (see, e.g., Connell 1987, 1995).

The study of informal relations in sociology should be recognised as important since it is in close social relationships that we receive material and emotional support; also they are very important in the generation of our personal identity and sense of belonging. As Willmott, who anticipated some recent concerns, states:

> Personal relationships with friends, relatives, neighbours and work colleagues are crucial in every society. Though largely hidden beneath the large and visible institutions, that obviously influence the opportunities and daily lives that people have, this subterranean informal order is important for many reasons. Along with the nuclear family, which is at its core, it has the responsibility for 'socialisation' – for imbuing infants with the values, rules and customs of their culture ... It accounts for most of sociable human contact which people apparently need and enjoy. And it is a major source of support and practical help. (Willmott 1986: 1)

The innovative studies by Willmott and Abrams in the 1980s on the 'social basis of care' drew on a great deal of locality research on informal relations and raised important questions, including the nature of 'social exchange' and the interplay between social identity, social relations and social structure (Willmott 1986; Bulmer 1986, 1987; see also Crow et al. 2002). In some ways both 'co-operative' and 'rational' approaches to social relations are combined in work on social exchange. Titmuss (1970) put forward three main types of exchange: economic exchange, which involves the immediate obligations of market relations; reciprocal exchange, which is reflected in the rights and obligations of family kinship arrangements; and his main interest, unilateral transfer. This latter, altruistic type is exemplified by blood donorship, where there is no particular right to something in return for the 'gift' (Titmuss 1970; see Uttley 1980).

The importance of notions of altruism and reciprocity as bases of social interaction are to be found in research on 'neighbourliness' and social provision (see Bulmer 1986; Willmott 1986; Uttley 1980). More specifically, the issue whether some communities are more likely to support members in need (in particular, the elderly) and, if so, whether their distinguishing characteristics could be identified. A key concern involved the extent to which mutual support still existed amongst the working class (a traditional assumption in sociology and popular observations) or was being superseded by a greater support enjoyed in more middle-class areas, whose members had the time, skills and other resources to help neighbours. Also discussed was whether a new form of community politics was emerging to defend the area against perceived external threats. The problem of neighbouring and informal care, for Abrams (Bulmer 1986, 1987), was how to find ways in which people could be involved in help, despite unfamiliarity of the neighbourhood, social mobility and kin-distance, but without believing that the traditional neighbourhood could be revived. His faith was placed in the network of 'modern neighbourhoodism' which was the result of social disruption of traditional patterns. The modern neighbourhood, it seemed, did not exhibit the same problems, and hence the same reciprocity and trust of previous local relations. For instance, friends can be more widely chosen and local residents are not the same source of help. Only two features of these older social patterns were seen as important in the provision of informal care – kinship relations between parents and children and the local information network, gossip (Bulmer 1986: 94). Abrams argues that the modern neighbourhood shows the features of modern industrialisation – mobility, choice, formal organisation and the increasing role of public and political life. Under these conditions, modern 'neighbourhoodism' is the 'attempt by newcomers to *create* a local social world through political or quasi-political action'. The application of skills and organisational expertise is used to great effect to bring control of the immediate area and protect its amenities from outside authority. In this situation neighbourhood care depended upon creating 'constructive relationships' between the State, neighbourhoodism and the political expression of local attachment (Bulmer 1986: 95).

Abrams's work represents a bringing together of network analysis, the notion of solidarism, and the idea of modern neighbourhoodism. In short, he describes the important value of friendship as experienced in neighbourliness, and therefore, its centrality in the study of communities and, in addition, to the formation of social policy (Bulmer 1985, 1986).

Willmott gives a number of conditions that are conducive to the formation of a 'community of attachment'. These conditions include population stability; the presence of kin, class, income or ethnic homogeneity; an isolated location; a physical layout conducive to casual neighbourliness; values and skills among many local people which facilitates getting to know others; the presence of many locally based organisations, and finally, the existence of an external threat which results in the formation of campaigning organisations. Some groups develop local attachments more often, such as those with a background, experience, or temperament that predisposes towards sociability, those with appropriate skills and values and those with a readiness to join local organisations.

The Abrams and Willmott studies represented some changes of direction in community studies by a more detailed and theoretically informed discussion of social solidarity, with an emphasis on policy implications for welfare provision. However, the theoretical basis of their work needed greater elaboration and more connections to be made with theoretical developments in related fields. The question of whether the basis of neighbouring is changing significantly (due to working-class decline and new middle-class forms) and the reasons for such changes needed more attention – both writers appeared to retain conceptions of middle-class and (traditional) working-class neighbourhoods, which were overdrawn.

Friendships and other relationships, as well as giving emotional support alongside the family and sometimes as an alternative to family relations, provide for social identity and are confirmatory of status (e.g. as established via work relations and the job we do). We tend to search for and feel more comfortable with those who share our concerns and outlook and with whom we can discuss common issues either in terms of work or more socially and politically. These relationships, groupings or networks, therefore, provide channels for views and experiences or act as points of attachment or as reference groups and sources of identity. At a wider level, the issues of intimacy are connected to the effects of the erosion of traditional patterns and expectations. For some social theorists there has been a 'loss' of self-definition and increasing insecurity brought about by the loosening of fixed or durable social bonds while the domination of bureaucratic and other authority structures is apparent. This situation has led a range of social commentators to discuss the nature and consequences of the shifting social ties in contemporary society and (for some) the possibilities of 'reestablishing community' or other 'solutions' (see Bauman 2003; Etzioni 1998; Putnam 2001: Sennett 1998, 2002; Giddens 1992). As Bauman and May conclude:

> If the personal context cannot accommodate the whole business of life, it still remains an indispensable ingredient. Our craving for 'deep and wholesome' personal

relationships grows in intensity the wider and less penetrable the network of impersonal dependencies in which we are entangled. (Bauman and May 2001: 84)

Narratives

Narrative 'theory' and analysis have become so widespread within the social sciences that some have stated that there has been a 'narrative turn' in social study (see Chamberlayne et al. 2000; Czarniawska 2004; Roberts 2002). Within sociology it has been applied in research extensively in education, health and other fields (see Hatch and Wisniewski 1995; Muller 1999). The origins of the study of narrative lie in literary studies (including myth and folklore), but its utility as a means of analysis has become apparent in other disciplines since the early 1980s (see Mitchell 1981). Its use has become commonplace, from media and popular culture through to more policy-based studies, with reference to such diverse experiences as serious illness, mental problems, career trajectories and divorce.

An initial, important difficulty in the idea of narrative is its definition. There has not been a general agreement on its meaning and the approach taken to research. As a methodology it is within the area of qualitative methods and is committed to inquiring into how stories are used to describe human action (Polkinghorne 1988, 1995). For some, stories and storytelling are central to how we understand our lives (Bruner 1986, 1990; Sarbin 1986; McAdams 1997). While definitions vary, key terms in narrative approaches are story, plot and narrative itself. In short, narrative refers both to how stories are constructed and told as well as a method of inquiry.

Clandinin and Connelly make distinctions between 'narrative inquiry', 'story' and 'narrative'. They point to narrative as a phenomenon and also a method: the former involves a story which individuals relate about their lives while the latter refers to the collection of accounts by researchers (and we can add that researchers have stories of their own, for instance, as writers of research narratives) (Clandinin and Connelly 1994: 415–16; Roberts 2002: 117). There are varieties of narrative analysis, ranging from the identification of formal or structural elements (e.g. as derived from Labov); the finding of turning points or epiphanies in the account (see Denzin 1989); showing certain themes or an overall personal world-view; uncovering the generic type of story, such as in romantic, tragic and other forms; and, finally, noting the poetic or metaphorical structure or elements. Certain writers have sought to identify types of narrative more formally. Polkinghorne distinguishes between the 'analysis of narratives' (using 'paradigmatic reasoning') which is inductive and refines conceptual categories and 'narrative analysis' which is concerned with 'emplotted narrative' ('a story, or a storied episode in an individual's life'). Thus, a distinction is made between the production of taxonomies drawing from various individual accounts and narrative analysis used to form 'explanatory stories' (Polkinghorne 1995: 13–15). Another definitional attempt is by Lieblich et al. (1998), who examine stories along two axes: holistic vs. categorical approaches – according to whether a part or a whole narrative is used, and content vs. form – relating to the motives, meanings, images or structure, coherence, style, etc., given. The result is four types of narrative study (Lieblich et al. 1998: 12–14; Roberts 2002: 122). A crucial element of narrative research is the assumption that narratives are relational and reflective, being told between individuals (and groups) and involving how experiences and events are conceived – and also informative of subsequent action (Muller 1999: 223–4). They also, therefore, raise the question of time; for Ricoeur (1981), who has been very influential in this regard, narratives are timed, and time is narrativised as individuals (and groups) describe their activities.

A complex issue is raised concerning the 'origin' of narratives as not being simply individual, but as in part drawing on a social stock of knowledge (e.g. the popular myths, stereotypes, images, sayings and metaphors). It is here where often some confusion occurs, with 'narrative' being used interchangeably with the notion of 'discourse'. Unlike discourse, narrative emphasises how individuals and groups use such social resources to generate their own accounts to understand their experiences. There is an interrelation between the given stories and wider culture myths and genres. But individuals and group are not merely the 'vessels' for or even 'composed' of these broader phenomena (as appears to be the case in some discourse theory), but have some degree of autonomy of expression. A study which shows the complex relation between private and public narratives in one location is Finnegan's research on Milton Keynes (Finnegan 1998). She outlines the intricate connections between individual experiences and more formal accounts of the establishment and growth of the city.

A number of criticisms have been made of narrative theory and analysis – and the idea of a 'narrative turn' in the social sciences:

> 'realists' can respond that, in such analyses, all becomes fiction, that a relativism intrudes, or that lives become studied for their form rather than relationships with others or 'real events'. Further, is there a prenarrative experience informing 'narrative processing' taking place in daily interaction, which may be grasped by some psychological and other analyses … ? A feminist or radical response may also include a word of caution – that narratives may appear to provide a forum for empowerment and self-definition through a recovery of 'voice' and alternative perspectives but they often reflect dominant conventions and hide ideologies, such as patriarchy. Thereby, they can restrict new possibilities of expression and alternative actions. (Roberts 2002: 124)

Body

While recently the body has become established as a vital area for understanding the interactions of individuals and groups, there has been recognition that ideas relating to embodiment were present in classical sociological and broader theory. The work of Foucault, Turner, Shilling and others have very much placed the 'body' on the theoretical 'agenda' in sociology (see Foucault 1977, 1978–86; Turner 1984, 1992; Shilling 1993; Featherstone et al. 1991). As Burkitt says:

> How could we ever have become, or how could we remain, a person with our own sense of identity if we were not a bodily presence capable of movement and sound, able to attract the attention of others who could then focus upon us as a distinct being made of flesh and blood? (Burkitt, 1999: 1)

For Shilling (2003) the relative neglect of the body was connected to a mind/body dualism in Western ideas. More specifically, in sociological theory the individual has been seen as a 'cognitive agent'. Parsons, for example, who dominated sociological theory in the 1940s and 1950s, was later alleged to be advocating an 'oversocialised', even disembodied notion of the individual 'whose internalization of norms was a predominantly cognitive process' (Shilling 2003: 440). Maybe the body 'has been excluded from the social sciences for so long because it tended to be thought of as unruly and unpredictable, the seat of the emotions and passions, things which cannot be calculated or represented in any regular way' (Burkitt 1999: 1). Shilling argues that even in interactionist, ethnmethodological and phenomenological sociology, despite various emphases on intersubjectivity, experience and reflection, action is conceived as cognitive and the omission of the body is evident. Even in the work of Goffman, where there is a focus on presentation – and his work has admittedly influenced much subsequent attention to the body – it is the 'cognitive' which is stressed. A number of reasons, for Shilling, can be given for this recent rise in interest, for example, the body as a 'site' for consumerist culture, the feminist challenge to naturalistic assumptions regarding gender and action, and advances in medical technology (Shilling 2003: 441).

Various kinds of approach have influenced recent understanding of the body. For example, some theories have stressed the variable contextual, cultural and social perceptions of the body, and there has been Foucauldian-inspired work, for instance, feminist approaches connecting gender differences, power and the body. In fact, feminist theory has done much to challenge the traditional split which conceives of men as associated with the rational embodied mind that organises, decides and governs, while women are seen as the repository of emotion and irrationality – caring and 'femininity'. The work of Judith Butler from a 'constructionist' viewpoint has contributed to the unpacking of such definitions, while (for many) overly stressing the discursive view. Other theorists on the body have argued that the body is not dependent on pregiven discourse or powerful norms, but instead that allowance should be made for counter-definitions and action – as both a site of resistance to dominance and transmission of power relations (see Burkitt 1999: 90–109). There are also those taking an eclectic interdisciplinary approach using philosophy, history, sociology and other fields. An 'integrated' view is given by Burkitt, for whom we are 'bodies of thought' rather than exhibiting a distinct divide between mind and body. So, while we can think of ourselves as separate from our bodies (at certain times or due to specific conditions), there is a more intricate relation between body, body image and sense of personhood (Burkitt 1999: 2). He argues for 'a multidimensional' approach to the body and the person which conceives of human beings as complexes of both the material and the symbolic:

> embodied persons are not simply constructs, but are *productive bodies* capable of activities that change the nature of their lives ... *communicative bodies* with the power to symbolize through gestures, metaphors and speech ... In both these ways all individuals become *powerful bodies*, with abilities and capacities that can radically alter the conditions of life ... also *thinking bodies* because the powers of agency and communication involve thinking, something that does not simply occur 'inside' the body. (Burkitt 1999: 2–3)

An interesting study of connections between changes in the body and how this is perceived is Sparkes and Smith's work on spinal cord injury (SCI) suffered by a group of men playing sport. They examine how three men responded to serious disablement through different narratives regarding the body, experience of time and constructions of the self. They reported:

> The data suggests that when they inhabited able, sporting, disciplined, and dominating bodies pre-SCI, cyclical notions of time closely associated with work routines and the social organization of sport, framed their everyday experiences. Immediately following SCI the taken-for-granted nature of cyclic time is disrupted as the men experience ruptured time during a process of rehabilitation in which attempts are made to reintegrate time with the body and the body with time. (Sparkes and Smith 2003: 315)

Sparkes and Smith say there were subsequent significant differences following SCI, as shown by three types of narrative – restitution, chaos and quest – which moulded their outlook:

> The restitution narrative ... connects the individual to notions of a restored and entrenched self that has its reference point firmly in the past ... [in] the chaos narrative ... constructing any sense of self or exploring any other identity becomes extremely problematic ... the quest narrative provides the opportunity for time to be reclaimed ... and a more communicative body to emerge that is willing to explore different identities and possible selves as the need arises and circumstances allow. (Sparkes and Smith 2003: 315–16)

They conclude that how individuals transfer from one kind of narrative to another – how the change operates, say, from restitution to quest following a 'disruptive life event' is an important question to be addressed from a number of disciplinary perspectives (Sparkes and Smith 2003: 316). This kind of approach shows an interesting complexity for sociological investigation and theory of the interconnections of body change, self-construction and 'biographical time' in an understanding of experience and action. Again, in Burkitt's terms, 'modern individuals' are conceived as 'bodies of thought – as theoretical, aesthetic, symbolic and bodily beings, whose existence is multidimensional and fundamentally related to other people and objects in the world' (Burkitt 1999: 152). Shilling (2003), in a wider view, concludes that debates surrounding biotechnologies and cyberspace are reducing the human–machine boundary – and technological advances in virtual environments and biomedical intervention are transforming how we relate to others in work and other settings. Even so, he says, the degree to which people connect via virtual environments will be restricted by the human need for sustenance and the degree to which people can (or wish to) adapt to these new social arenas. Therefore, the body 'remains irreducible' in terms of nature and society requiring the theorisation of human embodiment to conceive its societal formation and, in return, its part in social processes (Shilling 2003: 453).

Conclusion

It is clear that micro social theory faces a range of challenges in understanding these (and other) substantive fields of community and place, time, emotions, friendships and intimate relations, narratives and the body. These areas have not been entirely overlooked in micro social theory; in fact, many are to be found in older theorisation but have been left, until quite recently, rather underdeveloped. Attention to these and related areas in the study of self-formation, social motivation, and the features and types of social interaction are leading to rapid developments in micro theorisation and research study. What is apparent in the examination of these increasingly 'popular' areas for theorisation and research is how they can be studied simultaneously – as a 'level' in themselves while also in a movement from micro–meso–macro and back. In other words, we can see wider transformations as being 'inscribed' at the local social setting or situation, as experienced in daily living and given meaning, while also being lived through, changed and reflected back – produced and reproduced – in the 'micro social'.

Further Reading

The best source for general and up-to-date substantive developments in sociology are the major journals, for example, in Britain: *Sociology, The Sociological Review, Sociological Research Online, British Journal of Sociology* and journals in more specific sociological and other fields, for example, *Auto/Biography, Body and Society, Social Problems, Time and Society* and *Feminist Review*. Publishers' catalogues and websites are essential sources of information on new texts on particular research areas. A further source are the many (often basic) sociological textbooks, which attempt to link theoretical and substantive issues: for example, N. Abercrombie, *Sociology* (Cambridge, Polity, 2004) and Z. Bauman and T. May, *Thinking Sociologically* (Oxford, Blackwell, 2001). Other introductory textbooks on substantive areas often have useful up-to-date overview articles by leading researchers: see, for example (for Britain), N. Abercrombie and A. Warde, *Contemporary British Society* (3rd ed., Cambridge, Polity, 2000); N. Abercrombie and A. Warde (eds.), *The Contemporary British Society Reader* (Cambridge, Polity, 2001); A. Giddens (ed.), *Sociology: Introductory Readings* (rev. ed., Cambridge, Polity, 2000) and G. Payne (ed.), *Social Divisions* (Basingstoke, Palgrave Macmillan, 2000).

10

Conclusion

The Micro Social Theory Tradition as a 'Cluster'

It is not easy to locate and summarise what constitutes micro social theory. The notion of a 'cluster of approaches' gives some indication of commonality while also giving room for points of difference. Some flexibility in 'assignment' is required (Benton and Craib 2001: 75). While divisions into different groupings can be made in social theory, it is not always so apparent where particular theories should be placed or if such groupings are so opposed across a wide range of criteria (see Craib 1992a).

A number of issues have entered the discussion of micro social theory in this book. First, the question of structure. While micro theorisation is commonly seen as emphasising agency, process and the construction meaning, the question of structure has also been present, in various ways. In micro social theory some notion of 'structure' is evident from ethnomethology's ideas on accounts and conversational analysis of language use; Goffman's ideas on ritual, framing and the interaction order; network theory's emphasis on the patterning of relationships; through to Giddens's use of a language 'model' (rules and resources) and duality of structure in structuration theory. Secondly, micro theorisation could be seen as a 'strategy' by those, for example, who recognise the importance of macro theory and micro–macro relations, but wish to retain a sense of the 'micro' as a perspective – or way of looking or focus on the 'microscopic' rather than the 'macroscopic'. In this stance, there is an associated immediate (even more 'practical') concern with social situations, the interactions within or between smaller groups, as something like a social laboratory. As a strategy there are certain generally shared set of assumptions in this vantage point – individual agency, embodiment and interpretive or subjectivist procedure related to individual and social meanings as arising in the process of research and the place of the researcher within it. Here, then, is a sense of direction from micro to macro (but usually with little development after the micro starting point to relations with other 'levels'). There can also be a 'micro to micro' orientation where further research in another setting or generalisation to other settings of a 'similar' kind is explored, while retaining the sense that each situation is unique in time and space. Of course, macro social theory can have a concern for social action and a notion of 'agency', but as more

154

associated with organisations, major social groupings or the 'social system' (as if an organism with its own needs).

In general terms, sociology and social theory have a long conceptual concern with the basis of individual agency and social action – and indeed, an increasing interest in these matters (Barnes 2003: 344). Further, 'mainstream' or 'traditional' sociological theories, it can be argued, whether symbolic interactionism, conflict theory or even structural functionalism, 'are analytic and descriptive theories' that all 'share the same basic assumption: that the proper object of sociology is social action' (Craib 1992a: 29). The move in emphasis towards human agency from the 1960s onwards was part of a more extensive change in the balance of sociological theorisation as more interpretive, interactionist theorisation grew in strength.

Action and Structure

The micro–macro distinction has a close associate – agency–structure – and the two are often confused. The agency–structure 'problem' in some form has been at the heart of sociology since its beginnings, but has become a central issue of discussion in more recent decades (Barnes 2003: 344).

> What the classical authors tended to neglect (although Weber was something of an exception with his concern with subjective understanding) was the constructive dimension of human action itself ... Parsons and the structuralist Marxists have tended to reinforce this neglect by stressing that individual subjectivity and action were reflections of structural conditions. (Layder 1994: 217)

Questions arise here concerning the nature of individual agency and the nature of 'group agency'. Further issues include whether 'agency' is uniform or is a range of kinds, and the differing strength of individual or collective agency. From an intepretive viewpoint questions surround how individuals make sense of experience and describe it to others – and how interpretations inform action (by motives and rationalisations). There is then the problem of how sociologists interpret the reasons and actions given by actors. Obviously, actors may not be 'fully knowledgeable' regarding their circumstances and experiences or may 'wrongly' account for their actions and those of others. On the other side of the 'equation' questions arise concerning how 'social bonds' (ties, attachments) constrain or allow actions according to rules. In this concern is how social institutions and structures, or the wider 'society' 'produce' the activities and social trajectories of individuals and groups – and thereby maintain and reproduce social patterns and social order itself. For sociology the traditional issue of how to understand action and structure, and their connections, in turn relates often to the kind of methodological approach to be taken: one derived from the natural sciences or from a more interpretive or humanistic approach to procedure. The 'social structural' – macro sociological – explanation was widely accepted as the central approach to theoretical and methodological questions for some time. In this view, according to critics, 'Actions manifest pattern; the pattern is described; the pattern is taken as a separate real macro-entity; the macro-entity explains the actions' (Barnes 2003: 344). But a 'distaste for the passive role allegedly being accorded to the individual "human subject" did eventually become irresistibly strong' (Barnes 2003: 344–5).

The subsequent 'explosion' of micro social theorisation encompassed symbolic interactionism, interactionism, phenomenological and ethnomethodological approaches, Goffman's work, inductive and interpretivist methodology, and the growth in participant observation and other methods (as in the study areas such as deviancy). It led to a diversity of theorisation around issues of agency and the nature of 'everyday life'. The 'fragmentation' in sociological theory motivated Giddens and others in the 1970s and 1980s onwards to find some way through this crisis of diversity in theorisation, by addressing 'micro – macro', 'agency–structure' and other 'dualities'.

The micro–macro distinction is often shorthand for or merely confused with a number of other associated 'dualities' within social theory. For example, while the 'micro–macro' distinction is commonly discussed alongside agency and structure, there are significant divergences and overlaps between these polarities in theoretical approaches. Ritzer and Goodman (2004) locate the macro–micro debate as arising in the 1980s in the United States with some writers having taken 'extreme' positions regarding the differences between microscopic and macroscopic theories. On the macro extreme in the twentieth century were forms of Marxism and structuralism, varieties of conflict theory, exchange theory (Blau) and network theory as applied to the 'macro level'. On the 'micro extreme' were symbolic interactionism, exchange theory (Homans) and ethnomethodology (Ritzer and Goodman 2004: 484). In contrast, they argue that while it is possible to interpret classic theorists such as Marx, Weber, Durkheim and Simmel in both macro and micro terms, the more 'defensible' position is to see them as concerned with the linkage between these levels.

In the 1980s there was also a movement in American sociology, according to Ritzer and Goodman (2004), towards micro and macro integration. This shift was either made by uniting differing theories (e.g. structural functionalism and symbolic interactionism) or constructing a theory that addresses the relations between macro and micro levels of social analysis (e.g. social structure and personality) (Ritzer and Goodman 2004: 485). (Their subsequent discussion focuses on the latter approach and the work of Ritzer, Alexander, Coleman, Collins and Elias.) Interestingly, they say, at the same time in Europe sociologists were concerned with the agency–structure relation. Of course, 'agency' and 'structure' can be both micro and macro phenomena, and while 'micro' usually refers to an active creative agent it can also relate to 'a more mindless "behaver" of interest to behaviorists, exchange theorists, and rational choice theorists'. On the other hand, they argue that 'macro' can refer to both large institutions and 'cultures of collectivities' and 'micro may or may not refer to "agents" and macro may or may not refer to "structures"' (Ritzer and Goodman 2004: 509). What is apparent here, is that caution must be exercised in simply linking 'agency' and 'action' to an 'interactionist' or other micro approach – as though wider processes and institutions can be completely ruled out, and a specific method and interpretive procedure automatically preferred. In this view, both agency and structure can be associated with different levels of analysis, unlike the micro–macro distinction. More broadly, Ritzer and Goodman argue that the agency structure dichotomy is 'much more firmly embedded in a historical, dynamic framework' and has 'more powerful roots in, and a stronger orientation to, philosophy' and 'moral issues'. Conversely, 'micro–macro theory is largely indigenous to sociology and is oriented to the hard sciences as a reference group' (Ritzer and Goodman 2004: 536). *I would argue that the micro–macro distinction can be used very fruitfully in the social sciences as long as it is treated in a truly dynamic fashion, so that one is often aware of the need to move from micro through meso to macro and back again, with a sense of structure and agency there at every step.* I have been keen to stress throughout, for example, that there are both structural and agentic features at the micro level. Both of these dimensions within the micro have connections, spatially (near and far) and temporally (past and present), with macro and meso levels. Thus, for instance, very powerful political or military agents drawing on their structural resources within a micro situation may well have strong connections to events on the other side of the globe (macro) or the other side of the city (meso). Likewise, events that could be treated to a micro sociological analysis, such as the joyous claiming of mementoes from the Berlin Wall by ordinary people in 1989, also clearly had deep connections to events and power structures in the medium and longer terms.

A degree of consensus perhaps is necessary for a basis of discussion in the discipline between competing positions – differing poles or axes should be used to help debate and stimulate developments, rather than prevent communication. As Robertson (1974) argues, while supporting a 'widespread agreement on parameters of general sociological enquiry' the 'basic axes of analytic variation in sociology past and present' deserve 'illumination' as 'a positive contribution to the establishment of a working consensus among sociologists'. While some consensus is needed (on '*categories* of variables'), this should not imply that 'the view that perspectival consensus on substantive issues can or should be the collective goal of sociologists'. Thus, I would agree with Robertson that a '*sociological pluralism*' should be cherished since 'it is mainly through clashes of ideas – through some form of intellectual tension – that disciplinary progress is accomplished' (Robertson 1974: 108; original emphasis). Also as Benton and Craib point out, different approaches have their particular strengths:

Weber's ideas are perhaps the most generally applicable in setting out the task of understanding and the criteria it must meet; Schutz offers us a way of studying the processes of consciousness and the taken-for-granted world; interactionism gives us a way of looking at the social generation of meaning; and rational choice theory is perhaps most appropriate to looking at certain economic decisions. (Benton and Craib 2001: 91)

It has not been the intention in the book to produce a broad 'micro social theory' – some unification of the various theories within the 'cluster' of approaches described. My intention has been to show a commitment to 'micro social theory', in general, for the insights it gives into the 'micro' aspects of the lives of individuals and groups and their social interactions. I have also pointed out that while it is analytically possible, and theoretically beneficial, to see 'micro social' theory as a separate level – 'micro social' theory (in its various guises) commonly recognises (although some approaches more than others) its relations with other 'levels'. Thus, we can have a dynamic approach that traces the connective influences each way between the micro local level of individual and group experience, localised knowledge, and other features, with meso (intermediate) and macro (society) 'strata'. While not attempting to formulate some combined approach to the 'micro' elements of social life – or reduce important differences between micro social theories – I have sought to outline a number of areas or ideas from the accounts discussed that 'lead' us into common aspects of the micro social. These key areas or ideas, I would argue, have a 'suggestability' – they will continue to be important sources for theorisation and research at the micro social level:

- the Chicago School's ideas on groups in their social situation, social distance and the ecological setting (Chapter 2)
- notions of the generalised other (or social audience), the importance of role and the individual–society relation in Mead's work (Chapter 3)
- the developments in later symbolic interaction on the definitions of situation and of 'settings' of social interactionism (Chapter 4)
- Goffman's idea of the 'interaction order' and his discussions of 'the presentation of self', and drama, ritual and game in social life (Chapter 5)
- the attention to shared knowledges and accountability in social context as found in the phenomenological approaches (Chapter 6)
- the inscription of broader social structures in localised experience (i.e. gender inequality) in the micro social work of various feminist writers, and the focus on cultural formation and social categorisation (e.g. of 'gender') in poststructuralist feminist writers (Chapter 7)
- the continued influence of a number of key ideas on the formation and continuance of social relations, such as exchange, rational choice, network, disciplinary power and structuration (Chapter 8)

- and finally, the rising amount of substantive research on new or renewed areas at the micro social 'level', including community and place, time, emotions and the body in relation to individual and group local and daily experience (Chapter 9). These areas both contribute to and reflect a new vigour in micro social theorisation – and its range of key ideas such as the self, social interaction, individual and group experience and local context that are fundamental to daily social living.

Conclusion: Micro Social Theory and Sociological Imaginings

Following Craib, we can say that social theory – including micro social theory – can be considered along four dimensions (Craib 1992a). First, along a 'cognitive dimension' 'as a way of establishing knowledge about the social world'; there are ' "cognitive fault lines" in social theory which help us to make sense of the process of fragmentation' in its development. Secondly, there is an 'affective dimension' since 'the sociologist is caught up with the problem she is trying to theorize, not just as a sociologist but as a person'. Here Craib argues that a 'strong case' can be made that the personal experience of social theorists of the social world has a bearing, beyond rational argument, on the theory they produce. Thus by omission and inclusion and the orientation to problems, this leads not so much to the fragmentation of theory but at times produces certain 'obscurities' and 'over-emphasis of differences' (Craib 1992a: 15–16). Thirdly, a 'reflective dimension' – sociology and social policy must reflect on its own position in terms of ongoing social changes. Finally, the 'normative dimension' has an effect on fragmentation since it relates assumptions on how the world 'ought to be' and thereby has consequences for what is accepted and possible in political action. In this view social theory is not merely concerned with social processes and social problems; 'it is also *part* of those processes, conflict and problems'. In the act of theorising and being a 'theorist' an important 'flexibility' is necessary since a theory is 'always open to being used to argue different points in different ways in different situations, and the flux of normal social and political life will ensure that most theories are pushed in different ways' (Craib 1992a: 19). In short, theories can be said to be formed, utlilised and experienced along these cognitive, affective, reflective and normative dimensions of theories.

Craib's further insight that in discussing the nature of 'theoretical thinking' 'it is less a matter of learning theory than of learning to *think theoretically*' is also an important one (Craib 1992a: 5). He likens the process to learning a new language and listening to people speak it – 'a process made easier if we have some insight into the purposes of the inhabitants and their problems'. While we 'all think theoretically' we are not always aware of this or used to 'thinking theoretically in a systematic manner' (Craib 1992a: 5). Crucial here is an additional element in theorisation – the use of imagination. The 'imaginary element in sociology' is a 'striving for something that is always just out of reach and that it is the process of reaching out rather than the completed act of grasping that is important' (Morgan 1998: 648; see Mills 1970a). It is also a realisation of the 'interdependence between the realm of ideas and theories of everyday life not simply ... in the more dramatic or epiphanal moments but also in the steady, apparently undramatic, flow of everyday life.' Crucially, here is not merely the study of 'others' in some distant fashion, as Morgan says:

> In a sense the sociological imagination is brought home; it is not simply *their* biographies and *their* histories with which we are concerned but also *our* lives and historical contexts which are woven together in the texts we produce and constitute through our readings. (Morgan 1998: 657)

Morgan is pointing here to the connections between the sociologists' life 'in the round' both in employment as researcher and theorist but also in various other relationships (e.g. in the family) and the biographical aspects of the sociological work undertaken. Micro sociology or micro social theory, when it draws attention to individual reflexivity, intimate relations, choices and decisions and as (generally) allied to various 'subjectivist' or 'qualitative' modes of research, is also applicable to the sociological 'role' and relationships in the practice of research and theorisation. In short, the practitioner of micro social theory and situational research also has an agency and a context. C. W. Mills argued for situating the individual in the wider public arena, while retaining a sense of the biographic individual and immediate social relations:

> We have come to know that every individual lives, from one generation to the next, in some society; that he lives out a biography, and that he lives it out within some historical sequence. By the fact of his living he contributes, however minutely, to the shaping of this society and to the course of its history, even as he is made by society and by its historical push and shove. (Mills 1970a: 12)

In terms of micro social theory, in 'thinking theoretically', sociologists should also explore its applicability to their conduct and relations in academic life and its interrelations with other spheres of personal and public life.

Glossary

Actor network theory

A theory which draws upon the study of human subjects, materials and equipment in scientific study, and other phenomena, as involved in the formation of knowledge.

Agency

The view that individuals have the ability to exercise choice and make decisions towards meeting their set goals. It is often associated with 'voluntarism', or the ability of the individual to act freely, or with a degree of freedom from constraint, and thereby be morally accountable in the actions he or she takes in social life. Agency is often contrasted with impositions of 'structure' or 'social forces' and approaches which stress biological, unconscious, or other factors outside the control of the individual.

Chicago sociology

A body of sociological work chiefly associated with Robert E. Park and W. I. Thomas that came into prominence in the 1920s and 1930s in the United States. It pioneered the study of urban communities, immigration, race relations, the media, crime and delinquency and a range of sociological methods.

Discourse

This commonly refers to talk or conversation, or a dissertation. Within sociology and other fields it refers to sets of knowledge which describe and define social 'reality' (e.g. on crime, gender, medical conditions). Discourse analysis involves the study of language as it is used.

Dualism

This is the division of life into polar opposites, such as agency/structure, body/mind, rational/emotional, natural/cultural, subject/object, micro/macro, and so on.

Empiricism

A notion with varied meanings but generally describing epistemological views that emphasise the observation, collection and measurement of 'facts' – attention to experiment and testing rather than theorisation.

Epistemology

This is a philosophical term that concerns the examination of the grounds and formation of human knowledge. Various 'epistemologies' set different scientific guidelines (or interpret criteria such as validity, adequacy, etc. differently) for what is considered to be scientifically acceptable knowledge.

Essentialism

In philosophy this is broadly the view that each phenomenon has an essence – a social or inner core of some kind – that can be revealed by a methodological procedure. More widely within the social sciences it is the view that there is some particular, basic set of characteristics that determine behaviour, e.g. biological and psychological determinants.

Exchange theory

This theory is based on an economic model of social behaviour that examines how individuals make decisions and relate to others' actions according to a consideration of costs and benefits. It can include an examination of 'fairness' and equality in transactions.

Feminism

There are many versions of feminism and it includes a range of theoretical, research and political involvement. At its most general it includes those who focus on the exploitation of women in society and challenge, in a variety of ways, dominant structures which categorise and exclude women, place them in a subordinate position or even deny their experience.

Feminist methodology

An approach to social studies which foregrounds women's experience and argues against the separation of feminist research, theory and political action.

Indexicality

This is an ethnomethodological term that indicates the contextual nature of meaning given in human action. Why individuals act in a certain manner, therefore, can only be properly understood by examining their decisions with the social context in which it occurs.

Interactionism

An interpretive sociological approach based largely on the twin inheritance of symbolic interactionism and Chicagoan sociology, with an emphasis on the construction of meanings in interaction and the detailed study of differing social groups.

Narrative analysis

This is the study of life accounts according to the 'stories' people relate about their life. Particular attention is given to how experiences are sequenced in time and, in some analyses, how such accounts reveal the construction of the self.

Ontology

In general, a philosophical term relating to the origin or essence of phenomena seen in a rather abstract (metaphysical) manner. In the social sciences it refers to something that is given or a set of assumptions regarding human beings or social life on which theorisation (or research) is based, e.g. Giddens offers the idea of 'ontological security' or sense of safety regarding society upon which we rely.

Positivism

A philosophical or methodological approach based on 'positive facts' or what is observable. It is related to empiricism and the view that social life can be understood through the direct linkage between conceptions and reality.

Post-modernism

This term originally came into the social sciences from arts and architecture. It stresses the elements of fragmentation, change and the irrational in society, which are disrupting traditional social patterns and senses of identity. While 'postmodernism' has often been used to describe the character of society as a whole, postmodern theorists argue that 'grand narratives' or general theories are not possible.

Pragmatism

A philosophy founded in the United States that had a 'practical' approach to such issues of truth by a focus on the actions of individuals.

Rational choice theory

An approach to social behaviour, which assumes that individual action can be examined according to the exercise of 'rational choices'.

Rationality

The priority given to the rational or 'calculative' basis of individual behaviour in social life – as opposed to 'emotionality' (or irrational) aspects of the actions of human beings.

Reflexivity

A term used in various senses but commonly referring to the consideration of one's own actions, based on the ability to take oneself as an 'object' through a self-conscious, critical reflection.

Sociological theory

Sociological theory or theorisation seeks the explanation of social phenomena, which goes further than our own daily experiences and assumptions.

Structuralism

This term may refer to 'traditional' structuralist accounts in sociological theory, e.g. structural functionalism or Marxism, which focus on 'macro structures'. It is also applied, rather differently, specifically to describe a development within the social sciences in the late 1960s and early 1970s which sought to find deeper 'structures' in social phenomena (e.g. in myths). 'Poststructuralism' has some similarities with 'postmodernism' in drawing attention to 'difference' and 'fragmentation' in social life.

Structure

Structure, within sociological work, usually comprises social institutions and social stratification (e.g. social class) at a 'macro' or 'intermediate' level; however, structure can also be understood at the 'micro level' in various ways (e.g. as ritual). Structure is commonly conceived (by 'structuralist theory') as constraining or shaping the social behaviour of individuals and groups, as opposed to their use of 'agency'. Giddens (and others) have sought to overcome this 'dualism' in sociological theory.

Symbolic interactionism

An approach derived initially from the work of George Herbert Mead and pragmatist philosophy, which explains human behaviour with reference to social life as the product of individuals as social beings consciously acting, reflecting and taking account of others' actions.

Verstehen

A term which is associated with understanding or interpreting the intentions, shared meanings and actions of individuals. It is derived from the 'interpretive tradition' in German philosophy and was particularly brought into sociology by Weber.

Bibliography

Abbott, P. (2000) 'Gender', in Payne, G. (ed.), *Social Divisions*. Basingstoke: Palgrave Macmillan.

Abbott, P. and Wallace, C. (1997) *An Introduction to Sociology: Feminist Perspectives*. 2nd ed. London: Routledge.

Abercrombie, N. (2004) *Sociology*. Cambridge: Polity.

Abercrombie, N. and Warde, A. (with Deem, R., Penna, S., Soothill, K., Urry, J., Sayer, A. and Walby, S.) (2000) *Contemporary British Society*. 3rd ed. Cambridge: Polity.

Abercrombie, N. and Warde, A. (eds.) (2001) *The Contemporary British Society Reader*. Cambridge: Polity.

Adam, B. (1990) *Time and Social Theory*. Cambridge: Polity.

Adam, B. (1995) *Timewatch: The Social Analysis of Time*. Cambridge: Polity.

Adam, B. (2004) *Time*. Cambridge: Polity.

Adkins, L. (2005) 'Feminist Social Theory', in Harrington, A. (ed.), *Modern Social Theory: An Introduction*. Oxford: Oxford University Press.

Allan, S. and Thompson, A. (1999) 'The Time-Space of National Memory', in Brehony, K. J. and Rassool, N. (eds.), *Nationalisms Old and New*. Basingstoke: Macmillan.

Anderson, B. (1983) *Imagined Communities*. London: Verso.

Anderson, N. (1923) *The Hobo*. Chicago: University of Chicago Press.

Atkinson, P. and Housley, W. (2003) *Interactionism*. London: Sage.

Attewell, P. (1974) 'Ethnomethodology since Garfinkel', *Theory and Society*, 1(2): 179–210.

Baker, P. J. (ed.) (1973) 'The Life Histories of W. I. Thomas and Robert E. Park', *American Journal of Sociology*, 79(2): 243–60.

Barbalet, J. M. (2001) *Emotion, Social Theory and Social Structure*. Cambridge: Cambridge University Press.

Barnes, B. (2003) 'The Macro/Micro Problem and the Problem of Structure and Agency', in Ritzer, G. and Smart, B. (eds.), *Handbook of Social Theory*. London: Sage.

Bauman, Z. (2003) *Liquid Love: On the Frailty of Human Bonds*. Cambridge: Polity.

Bauman, Z. and May, T. (2001) *Thinking Sociologically*. 2nd ed. Oxford: Blackwell.

Becker, H. S. (1963) *Outsiders*. New York: The Free Press.

Becker, H. S. and McCall, M. M. (eds.) (1990) *Symbolic Interaction and Cultural Studies*. Chicago: University of Chicago Press.

Bendelow, G. and Williams, S. J. (eds.) (1998) *Emotions in Social Life: Critical Themes and Contemporary Issues*. London: Routledge.

Benmayor, R. and Skotnes, A. (eds.) (1994) *Migration and Identity*. Oxford: Oxford University Press.

Benson, D. and Hughes, J. A. (1983) *The Perspective of Ethnomethodology*. London: Longman.

Benton, T. and Craib, I. (2001) *Philosophy of Social Science*. Basingstoke: Palgrave.

Berger, P. L. and Luckmann, T. (1971) *The Social Construction of Reality: A Treatise in the Sociology of Knowledge*. Harmondsworth: Penguin.

Bernstein, B. (1973) *Class, Codes and Control*, Vol. 1. St Albans: Paladin.

Blau, P. M. (1964) *Exchange and Power in Social Life*. New York: John Wiley.

Blau, P. M. (1969) 'The Structure of Social Associations', in Wallace, W. L. (ed.), *Sociological Theory*. London: Heinemann.

Blau, P. M. (1971) 'Social Exchange', in Thompson, K. and Tunstall, J. (eds.), *Sociological Perspectives*. Harmondsworth: Penguin.

Blumer, H. (1937) 'Social Psychology', in Schmidt, E. P. (ed.), *Man and Society*. New York: Prentice-Hall.

Blumer, H. (1954) 'What is Wrong with Social Theory?', *American Sociological Review*, 19(1): 3–10, reprinted in Blumer, H., *Symbolic Interactionism*. Chicago: University of Chicago Press, 1969.

Blumer, H. (1956) 'Sociological Analysis and the "Variable"', *American Sociological Review*, 21: 683–90, reprinted in Blumer, H., *Symbolic Interactionism*. Chicago: University of Chicago Press, 1969.

Blumer, H. (1966) 'Sociological Implications of the Thought of George Herbert Mead', *American Journal of Sociology*, 71: 535–48, reprinted in Blumer, H., *Symbolic Interactionism*. Chicago: University of Chicago Press, 1969.

Blumer, H. (1969) *Symbolic Interactionism*. Chicago: University of Chicago Press.

Blumer, H. (2003) *George Herbert Mead and Human Conduct*, ed. and intro. Thomas J. Morrione and T. Morrione. Walnut Creek, CA: AltaMira.

Boden, D. and Zimmerman, D. H. (eds.) (1991) *Talk and Social Structure: Studies in Ethnomethodology and Conversation Analysis*. Cambridge: Polity.

Bott, E. (1957) *Family and Social Network*. London: Tavistock.

Bourdieu, P. (1977) *Outline of a Theory of Practice*. Cambridge: Cambridge University Press.

Box, S. (1971) *Deviance, Reality and Society*. London: Holt, Rinehart & Winston.

Branaman, A. (1997) 'Goffman's Social Theory', in Lemert, C. and Branaman, A. (eds.), *The Goffman Reader*. Oxford: Blackwell.

Branaman, A. (2001) 'Erving Goffman', in Elliott, A. and Turner, B. S. (eds.), *Profiles in Contemporary Social Theory*. London: Sage.

Braude, L. (1970) ' "Park and Burgess": An Appreciation', *American Journal of Sociology*, 76(1): 1–10.

Bredemeier, H. C. (1979) 'Exchange Theory', in Bottomore, T. and Nisbet, R. (eds.), *A History of Sociological Analysis*. London: Heinemann.

Brehony, K. J. and Rassool, N. (eds.) (1999) *Nationalisms Old and New*. Basingstoke: Macmillan.

Brooks, A. (1997) *Postfeminisms*. London: Routledge.

Bruner, J. (1986) *Actual Minds, Possible Worlds*. Cambridge, MA: Harvard University Press.

Bruner, J. (1990) *Acts of Meaning*. Cambridge, MA: Harvard University Press.

Bryant, C. G. A. and Jary, D. (eds.) (1991) *Giddens' Theory of Structuration: A Critical Appreciation*. London: Routledge.

Bryant, C. G. A. and Jary, D. (eds.) (1997) *Anthony Giddens: Critical Assessments*. 4 vols. London: Routledge.

Bryant, C. G. A. and Jary, D. (eds.) (2001) *The Contemporary Giddens: Social Theory in a Globalizing Age*. Basingstoke: Palgrave Macmillan.

Bulmer, M. (1981) 'Charles S. Johnson, Robert E. Park and the Research Methods of the Chicago Commission on Race Relations, 1919–22', *Ethnic and Racial Studies*, 4(3): 289–306.

Bulmer, M. (1983) 'The Polish Peasant in Europe and America: A Neglected Classic', *New Community*, 10(3): 470–6.

Bulmer, M. (1984) *The Chicago School of Sociology*. Chicago: University of Chicago Press.

Bulmer, M. (1985) 'The Rejuvenation of Community Studies? Neighbours, Networks and Policy', *Sociological Review*, 33(3): 430–48.

Bulmer, M. (1986) *Neighbours: The Work of Philip Abrams*. Cambridge: Cambridge University Press.

Bulmer, M. (1987) *The Social Basis of Community Care*. London: Allen & Unwin.

Burkitt, I. (1997) 'Social Relationships and Emotions', *Sociology*, 31(1): 37–55.

Burkitt, I. (1999) *Bodies of Thought: Embodiment, Identity and Modernity*. London: Sage.

Burns, T. (1992) *Erving Goffman*. London: Routledge.

Butler, J. (1990) *Gender Trouble*. London: Routledge.

Button, G. and Lee, J. R. E. (eds.) (1987) *Talk and Social Organisation*. Clevedon: Multilingual Matters.

Cavan, R. S. (1928) *Suicide*. Chicago: University of Chicago Press.

Chamberlayne, P., Bornat, J. and Wengraf, T. (eds.) (2000) *The Turn To Biographical Methods in Social Science*. London: Routledge.

Charon, J. (ed.) (1992) *Symbolic Interactionism*. 4th ed. Englewood-Cliffs, NJ: Prentice-Hall.

Chodorow, N. (1978) *The Reproduction of Mothering*. Berkeley, CA: University of California Press.

Cicourel, A. V. (1968) *The Social Organization of Juvenile Justice*. New York: John Wiley.

Cicourel, A. V. (1973) *Cognitive Sociology*. Harmondsworth: Penguin.

Clandinin, D. J. and Connelly, F. M. (1994) 'Personal Experience Methods', in Denzin, N. K. and Lincoln, Y. S. (eds.), *Handbook of Qualitative Research*. London: Sage.

Cohen, A. (1985) *The Symbolic Construction of Community*. London: Tavistock.

Cohen, I. J. (1987) 'Structuration Theory and Social *Praxis*', in Giddens, A. and Turner, J. (eds.), *Social Theory Today*. Stanford, CA: Stanford University Press.

Cohen, I. J. (1991) *Stucturation Theory*. London: Macmillan.

Cohen, I. J. (1998) 'Anthony Giddens', in Stones, R. (ed.), *Key Sociological Thinkers*. Basingstoke: Macmillan.

Cohen, S. (1972) *Folk Devils and Moral Panics*. London: MacGibbon & Kee.

Cohen, S. and Taylor, L. (1978) *Escape Attempts: The Theory and Practice of Resistance to Everyday Life*. Harmondsworth: Penguin.

Coleman, J. S. (1990) *Foundations of Social Theory*. Cambridge, MA: Harvard University Press.

Collins, R. (1994) 'Erving Goffman on Ritual and Solidarity in Social Life', *The Polity Reader in Social Theory*. Cambridge: Polity.

Connell, R. W. (1987) *Gender and Power: Society, the Person, and Sexual Politics*. Cambridge: Polity.

Connell, R. W. (1995) *Masculinities*. Berkeley: University of California Press.

Cook, K. S. and Whitmeyer, J. (2000) 'Richard M. Emerson', in Ritzer, G. (ed.), *The Blackwell Companion to Major Social Theorists*. Oxford: Blackwell.

Cooper, D. (1994) 'Productive, Relational and Everywhere? Conceptualising Power and Resistance within Foucauldian Feminism', *Sociology* 28(2): 435–54.

Coser, L. A. (1977) *Masters of Sociological Thought*. 2nd ed. New York: Harcourt Brace Jovanovich.

Coser, L. S. (1979) 'American Trends', in Bottomore, T. and Nisbet, R. (eds.), *A History of Sociological Analysis*. London: Heinemann.

Coulter, J. (ed.) (1990) *Ethnomethodological Sociology*. Aldershot: Edward Elgar.

Craib, I. (1992a) *Modern Social Theory*, 2nd ed. New York: St Martin's Press.

Craib, I. (1992b) *Anthony Giddens*. London: Routledge.

Craib, I. (1995) 'Some Comments on the Sociology of Emotions', *Sociology*, 29: 151–8.

Cressey, P. G. (1932) *The Taxi Dance Hall*. Chicago: University of Chicago Press.

Crow, G. (2002) *Social Solidarities: Theories, Identities and Social Change*. Buckingham: Open University.

Crow, G. and Allan, G. (1994) *Community Life: An Introduction to Local Social Relations*. Hemel Hempstead: Harvester Wheatsheaf.

Crow, G., Allan, G. and Summers, M. (2002) 'Neither Busybodies nor Nobodies: Managing Proximity and Distance in Neighbourly Relations', *Sociology*, 36(1): 127–45.

Crow, G. and McLean, C. (2000) 'Community', in Payne, G. (ed.), *Social Divisions*. Basingstoke: Palgrave.

Cuff, E. C., Sharrock, W. W. and Francis, D. W. (1990) *Perspectives in Sociology*. 3rd ed. London: Unwin Hyman.

Cutting, G. (ed.) (1994) *The Cambridge Companion to Foucault*. Cambridge: Cambridge University Press.

Czarniawska, B. (2004) *Narratives in Social Science Research*. London: Sage.

Danaher, G., Schirato, T. and Webb, J. (2000) *Understanding Foucault*. London: Sage.

Deegan, M. J. (2001) 'Introduction', in *G. H. Mead: Essays in Social Psychology*. London: Transaction.

Deegan, M. J. and Hill, M. R. (eds.) (1987) *Women and Symbolic Interaction*. London: Allen & Unwin.

Delamont, S. (2003a) *Feminist Sociology*. London: Sage.

Delamont, S. (2003b) 'Titans, Silverbacks and Dinosaurs'. *Sociological Research Online*, 8(4) (http://www.socresonline.org.uk/8/4/delamont.html).

Denzin, N. K. (1970) 'Symbolic Interactionism and Ethnomethodolgy', in Douglas, J. (ed.), *Understanding Everyday Life*. Chicago: Aldine.

Denzin, N. K. (1984) 'On Interpreting an Interpretation', *American Journal of Sociology*, 89(6): 1426–33.

Denzin, N. K. (1989) *Interpretive Biography*. London: Sage.

Denzin, N. K. (1992) *Symbolic Interactionism and Cultural Studies*. Oxford: Blackwell.

Denzin, N. K. (2001) *Interpretive Interactionism*. 2nd ed. London: Sage.

Denzin, N. K. and Lincoln, Y. S. (eds.) (2000) *Handbook of Qualitative Research*. 2nd ed. London: Sage.

Desmonde, W. H. (1970) 'The Position of George Herbert Mead', in Stone, G. P. and Farberman, H. A. (eds.), *Social Psychology Through Symbolic Interaction*. Waltham, MA: Xerox College.

Dickens, P. (1990) *Urban Sociology*. London: Harvester Wheatsheaf.

Ditton, J. (ed.) (1980) *The View from Goffman*. London: Macmillan.

Douglas, J. D. (1984) 'Introduction', in Douglas, J. D. (ed.), *The Sociology of Deviance*. London: Allyn & Bacon.

Downes, D. and Rock, P. (1995) *Understanding Deviance*. 2nd ed. Oxford: Clarendon Press.

Drew, P. and Heritage, J. (eds.) (1992) *Talk at Work*. Cambridge: Cambridge University Press.

Drew, P. and Wootton, A. (eds.) (1988) *Erving Goffman: Exploring the Interaction Order*. Cambridge: Polity.

Duncombe, J. and Marsden, D. (1993) 'Love and Intimacy: The Gender Division of Emotion and "Emotion Work" ', *Sociology*, 27(2): 221–41.

Durkheim, E. (1954) *The Elementary Forms of Religious Life*. New York: The Free Press.

Elliott, A. (2001) 'Anthony Giddens', in Elliott, A. and Turner, B. S. (eds.), *Profiles in Contemporary Social Theory*. London: Sage.

Elliott, A. and Turner, B. S. (eds.) (2001) *Profiles in Contemporary Social Theory*. London: Sage.

Elster, J. (1994) 'Rational Choice Theory', in *The Polity Reader in Social Theory*. Cambridge: Polity.

Etzioni, A. (ed.) (1998) *The Essential Communitarian Reader*. Lanham, MD: Rowman & Littlefield.

Evans, M. (2003) *Gender and Social Theory*. Buckingham: Open University.

Faris, R. E. L. (1967) *Chicago Sociology 1920–1932*. Chicago: University of Chicago Press.

Featherstone, M., Hepworth, M. and Turner, B. S. (eds.) (1991) *The Body: Social Processes and Cultural Theory*. London: Sage.

Ferguson, H. (2003) 'Phenomenology and Social Theory', in Ritzer, G. and Smart, B. (eds.), *Handbook of Social Theory*. London: Sage.

Fine, G. A. and Manning, P. (2000) 'Erving Goffman', in Ritzer, G. (ed.), *The Blackwell Companion to Major Contemporary Social Theorists*. Oxford: Blackwell.

Fine, G. A. and Smith, G. W. H. (eds.) (2000) *Erving Goffman*. 4 vols. London: Sage.

Finnegan, R. (1998) *Tales of the City: A Study of Narratives and Urban Life*. Cambridge: Cambridge University Press.

Fisher, B. M. and Strauss, A. L. (1979) 'Interactionism' in Bottomore, T. and Nisbet, R. (eds.), *A History of Sociological Analysis*. London: Heinemann.

Flaherty, M. G. and Fine, G. A. (2001) 'Present, Past, and Future: Conjugating George Herbert Mead's Perspective on Time', *Time and Society*, 10(2/3): 147–61.

Fonow, M. M. and Cook, J. A. (1991) *Beyond Methodology: Feminist Scholarship as Lived Research*. Bloomington: Indiana University Press.

Foucault, M. (1967) *Madness and Civilisation*. London: Tavistock.

Foucault, M. (1970) *The Order of Things*. London: Tavistock.

Foucault, M. (1972) *The Archaeology of Knowledge*. London: Tavistock.

Foucault, M. (1973) *The Birth of the Clinic*. London: Tavistock.

Foucault, M. (1977) *Discipline and Punish: The Birth of the Prison*. Harmondsworth: Penguin.

Foucault, M. (1978, 1985, 1986) *The History of Sexuality*. 3 vols. Harmondsworth: Penguin.

Foucault, M. (1980) *Power/Knowledge*. Ed. C. Gordon. Brighton: Harvester.

Freedman, J. (2001) *Feminism*. Buckingham: Open University.

Frith, H. and Kitzinger, C. (1998) ' "Emotion Work" as a Participant Resource: A Feminist Analysis of Young Women's Talk-in-Interaction', *Sociology* 32(2): 299–320.

Gardiner, J. K. (ed.) (2002) *Masculinity Studies and Feminist Theory: New Directions*. New York: Columbia University Press.

Garfinkel, H. (1967) *Studies in Ethnomethodology*. Englewood Cliffs, NJ: Prentice-Hall.

Garfinkel, H. (1994) 'What is Ethnomethodology?', in *The Polity Reader in Social Theory*. Cambridge: Polity.

Gelsthorpe, L. (1992) 'Response to Martyn Hammersley's Paper "On Feminist Methodology" ', *Sociology*, 26(2): 213–18.

Gershenson, G. and Williams, M. (2001) 'Nancy Chodorow', in Elliott, A. and Turner, B. S. (eds.), *Profiles in Contemporary Social Theory*. London: Sage.

Giddens, A. (1979) *Central Problems in Social Theory*. Basingstoke: Macmillan.

Giddens, A. (1984) *The Constitution of Society*. Cambridge: Polity.

Giddens, A. (1987a) 'Structuralism, Post-structuralism and the Production of Culture', in Giddens, A. and Turner, J. (eds.), *Social Theory Today*. Stanford, CA: Stanford University Press.

Giddens, A. (1987b) *Social Theory and Modern Sociology*. Cambridge: Polity.

Giddens, A. (1991) *Modernity and Self-Identity*. Cambridge: Polity.

Giddens, A. (1992) *The Transformation of Intimacy*. Cambridge: Polity.

Giddens, A. (1994) 'Elements of the Theory of Structuration', in *The Polity Reader in Social Theory*. Cambridge: Polity.

Giddens, A. (ed.) (2000) *Sociology: Introductory Readings*. Rev. ed. Cambridge: Polity.

Gidlow, B. (1972) 'Ethnomethodology – A New Name for Old Practices', *British Journal of Sociology*, 23: 395–405.

Gilligan, C. (1982) *In a Different Voice*. Cambridge, MA: Harvard University Press.

Goffman, E. (1963) *Stigma*. Englewood Cliffs, NJ: Prentice-Hall.

Goffman, E. (1968) *Asylums*. Harmondsworth: Penguin.

Goffman, E. (1970) *Strategic Interaction*. Oxford: Basil Blackwell.

Goffman, E. (1971a) *The Presentation of Self in Everyday Life*. Harmondworth: Penguin.

Goffman, E. (1971b) *Relations in Public*. New York: Basic Books.

Goffman, E. (1972) *Interaction Ritual: Essays on Face-to-Face Behaviour*. Harmondsworth: Penguin.

Goffman, E. (1974) *Frame Analysis*. New York: Harper & Row.

Goffman, E. (1979) *Gender Advertisements*. London: Macmillan.

Goffman, E. (1981) *Forms of Talk*. Philadelphia: University of Pennsylvania Press.

Gouldner, A. (1970) *The Coming Crisis of Western Sociology*. New York: Basic Books.

Green, P. (1990) *The Enemy Without: Policing and Class Consciousness in the Miners' Strike*. Milton Keynes: Open University Press.

Hall, S., Critcher, C., Jefferson, T., Clarke, J. and Roberts, B. (1978) *Policing the Crisis: Mugging, the State and Law and Order*. Basingstoke: Macmillan.

Hall, S. and Jefferson, T. (eds.) (1976) *Resistance through Rituals: Youth Subcultures in Post-war Britain*. London: Hutchinson.

Hammersley, M. (1989) *The Dilemma of Qualitative Method: Herbert Blumer and the Chicago Tradition*. London: Routledge.

Harding, S (1986) *The Science Question in Feminism*. Milton Keynes: Open University Press.

Harding, S. (ed.) (1987) *Feminism and Methodology*. Milton Keynes: Open University Press.

Hatch, J. A. and Wisniewski, R. (eds.) (1995) *Life History and Narrative*. London: Falmer.

Heath, S. and Cleaver, E. (2003) *Young, Free and Single*. Basingstoke: Palgrave Macmillan.

Heckathorn, D. D. (2003) 'Sociological Rational Choice', in Ritzer, G. and Smart, B. (eds.), *Handbook of Social Theory*. London: Sage.

Heritage, J. (1984) *Garfinkel and Ethnomethodology*. Cambridge: Polity.

Heritage, J. (1998) 'Harold Garfinkel', in Stones, R., (ed.), *Key Sociological Thinkers*. Basingstoke: Palgrave Macmillan.

Heritage, J. C. (1987) 'Ethnomethodology', in Giddens, A. and Turner, J. (eds.), *Social Theory Today*. Stanford: CA: Stanford University Press.

Herman, N. J. and Reynolds, L. T. (eds.) (1994) *Symbolic Interaction: An Introduction to Social Psychology*. Walnut Creek, CA: AltaMira.

Hindess, B. (1972) 'The Phenomenological Sociology of Alfred Schutz', *Economy and Society*, 1: 1–27.

Hindess, B. (1988) *Choice, Rationality and Social Theory*. London: Unwin Hyman.

Hirschi, T. (1969) *Causes of Delinquency*. Berkeley, CA: University of California Press.

Hochschild, A. (1983) *The Managed Heart*. Berkeley, CA: University of California Press.

Hoggett, P. (ed.) (1997) *Contested Communities: Experiences, Struggles, Policies*. Bristol: Policy Press.

Homans, G. C. (1974) *Social Behavior: Its Elementary Forms*. New York: Harcourt, Brace, Jovanovich.

Hoy, D. C. (ed.) (1986) *Foucault: A Critical Reader*. Oxford: Blackwell.

Hughes, E. C. (1969) 'Robert E. Park', in Raison, T. (ed.), *The Founding Fathers of Social Science*. Harmondsworth: Penguin.

Hutchinson, J. and Smith, A. D. (eds.) (1994) *Nationalism*. Oxford: Oxford University Press.

Jackson, P. and Penrose, J. M. (eds.) (1993) *Constructions of Race, Place and Nation*. London: UCL Press.

Jackson, S. (1993) 'Even Sociologists Fall in Love: An Exploration in the Sociology of Emotions', *Sociology*, 27(2): 201–20.

Jamieson, L. (1999) 'Intimacy Transformed? A Critical Look at the "Pure Relationship" ', *Sociology*, 33(3): 477–94.

Jenks, C. (ed.) (1998) *Core Sociological Dichotomies*. London: Sage.

Joas, H. (1985) *G. H. Mead: A Contemporary Re-examination of His Thought*. Cambridge: Polity.

Joas, H. (1987) 'Symbolic Interactionism', in Giddens, A. and Turner, J. (eds.) *Social Theory Today*. Stanford, CA: Stanford University Press.

Joas, H. (2003) 'The Emergence of the New: Mead's Theory and Its Contemporary Potential', in Ritzer, G. and Smart, B. (eds.) *Handbook of Social Theory*. London: Sage.

Jones, C. and Porter, R. (eds.) (1994) *Reassessing Foucault*. London: Routledge.

Katz, S. (2001) 'Michel Foucault', in Elliott, A. and Turner, B. S. (eds.), *Profiles in Contemporary Social Theory*. London: Sage.

Kellas, J. G. (1991) *The Politics of Nationalism and Ethnicity*. London: Macmillan.

King, A. (2005) 'Structure and Agency', in Harrington, A. (ed.), *Modern Social Theory: An Introduction*. Oxford: Oxford University Press.

Kraidy, M. M. (2002) 'The Global, the Local, and the Hybrid: A Native Ethnography of Glocalization', in Taylor, S. (ed.), *Ethnographic Research: A Reader*. London: Sage.

Lassman, P. (1974) 'Phenomenological perspectives in sociology', in Rex, J. (ed.), *Approaches to Sociology*. London: Routledge & Kegan Paul.

Layder, D. (1994) *Understanding Social Theory*. London: Sage.

Layder, D. (2004) *Emotion in Social Life*. London: Sage.

Lee, D. and Newby, H. (1983) *The Problem of Sociology*. London: Hutchinson.

Lemert, C. (1997) 'Goffman', in Lemert, C. and Branaman, A. (eds.), *The Goffman Reader*. Oxford: Blackwell.

Lemert, C. and Branaman, A. (eds.) (1997) *The Goffman Reader*. Oxford: Blackwell.

Lemert, E. (1967) *Human Deviance, Social Problems and Social Control*. Englewood Cliffs, NJ: Prentice-Hall.

Lengermann, P. M and Niebrugge-Brantley, J. (2003) 'Classical Feminist Social Theory', in Ritzer, G. and Smart, B. (eds.), *Handbook of Social Theory*. London: Sage.

Lengermann, P. M and Niebrugge-Brantley, J. (2004) 'Contemporary Feminist Theory', in Ritzer, G. and Goodman, D. J. *Sociological Theory*. 6th ed. London: McGraw-Hill.

Letherby, G. (2003) *Feminist Research in Theory and Practice*. Buckingham Open University.

Lewis, J. D. and Smith, R. L. (1980) *American Sociology and Pragmatism*. Chicago: University of Chicago Press.

Lichtman, R. (1970) 'Symbolic Interactionism and Social Reality: Some Marxist Queries', *Berkeley Journal of Sociology*, 15: 75–94, reprinted in Plummer, K. (ed.), *Symbolic Interactionism II: The Future of Contemporary Issues*. London: Edward Elgar, 1991.

Lieblich, A., Tuval-Mashiach, R. and Zilber, T. (1998) *Narrative Research*. London: Sage.

Lindenberg, S. (2000) 'James Coleman', in Ritzer, G., *The Blackwell Companion to Major Social Theorists*. Oxford: Blackwell.

Lorde, A. (1984) *Sister Outsider: Essays and Speeches*. Freedom, CA: The Crossing Press.

Loyal, S. (2002) *The Sociology of Anthony Giddens*. London: Pluto.

Madge, J. (1963) *The Origins of Scientific Sociology*. London: Tavistock.

Maines, D. R., Sugrue, N. M. and Katovich, M. A. (1983) 'The Sociological Import of G. H. Mead's Theory of the Past', *American Sociological Review*, 48(2): 161–73.

Manis, J. G. and Meltzer, B. N. (1967) *Symbolic Interaction: A Reader in Social Psychology*. London: Allyn & Bacon.

Manning, P. (1992) *Erving Goffman and Modern Sociology*. Cambridge: Polity.

Martindale, D. (1961) *The Nature and Types of Sociological Theory*. London: Routledge & Kegan Paul.

Matthews, F. H. (1977) *Quest for American Sociology*. Montreal: McGill-Queen's University Press.

Matza, D. (1964) *Delinquency and Drift*. New York: John Wiley.

Matza, D. (1969) *Becoming Deviant*. Englewood Cliffs, NJ: Prentice-Hall.

May, T. (1996) *Situating Social Theory*, Buckingham: Open University.

McAdams, D. (1997) *The Stories We Live By: Personal Myths and the Making of the Self*. London: Guilford Press.

McHoul, A. and Grace, W. (1995) *A Foucault Primer: Discourse, Power and the Subject*. London: Routledge.

McKenzie, R. D. (1933) *The Metropolitan Community*. Chicago: University of Chicago Press.

McNay, L. (1994) *Foucault: A Critical Introduction*. Cambridge: Polity.

Mead, G. H. (1929) 'The Nature of the Past', in Coss, J. (ed.), *Essays in Honor of John Dewey*. New York: Henry Holt.

Mead, G. H. (1932) *The Philosophy of the Present*. La Salle, IL. Open Court.

Mead G. H (1936) *Movements of Thought in the Nineteenth Century*. Ed. M. H. Moore. Chicago: University of Chicago Press.

Mead, G. H. (1938) *The Philosophy of the Act*. Ed. C. W. Morris. Chicago: University of Chicago Press.

Mead, G. H. (1964) *On Social Psychology*. Ed. and intro. A. Strauss. Chicago: University of Chicago Press (first published 1956).

Mead, G. H. (1967) *Mind, Self and Society*. Ed. C. W. Morris. Chicago. University of Chicago Press (first published 1934).

Mead, G. H. (2001) *Essays in Social Psychology*. Ed. and intro. M. J. Deegan. London: Transaction Books.

Meltzer, B. N., Petras, J. W. and Reynolds, L. T. (1975) *Symbolic Interactionism: Genesis, Varieties and Criticism*. London: Routledge & Kegan Paul.

Merton, R. K. (1957) 'Social Structure and Anomie', in *Social Theory and Social Structure*. Rev. ed. New York: The Free Press.

Mills, C. W. (1964) *Sociology and Pragmatism*. Oxford: Oxford University Press.

Mills, C. W. (1970a) *The Sociological Imagination*. Harmondsworth: Penguin.

Mills, C. W. (1970b) 'Social Psychology: Model for Liberals', in Stone, G. P. and Farberman, H. A. (eds.), *Social Psychology Through Symbolic Interaction*. Waltham, MA: Xerox College.

Mills, P. J. (1982) 'Misinterpreting Mead', *Sociology*, 16(1): 116–31.

Mitchell, W. J. T. (ed.) (1981) *On Narrative*. Chicago, IL: University of Chicago Press.

Molm, L. D. (2003) 'Theories of Social Exchange and Exchange Networks', in Ritzer, G. and Smart, B. (eds.), *Handbook of Social Theory*. London: Sage.

Morgan, D. (1998) 'Sociological Imaginings and Imagining Sociology', *Sociology*, 32(4): 647–63.

Morris, C. W. (1967) 'Introduction', in Mead, G. H., *Mind, Self and Society*. Ed. C. W. Morris. Chicago. University of Chicago Press (first published 1934).

Muller, J. H. (1999) 'Narrative Approaches to Qualitative Research in Primary Care', in Crabtree, B. F. and Miller, W. L. (eds.), *Doing Qualitative Research*. London: Sage.

Nisbet, R. (1967) *The Sociological Tradition*. London: Heinemann.

Oakley, A. (1998) 'Gender, Methodology and People's Ways of Knowing', *Sociology*, 32(4): 707–31.

Park, R. E. (1915) 'The City: Suggestions for the Investigation of Human Behavior in the Urban Environment', *American Journal of Sociology*, 20(5): 577–612.

Park, R. E. (1922) *The Immigrant Press and its Control*. New York: Harper.

Park, R. E. (1928) 'Human Migration and the Marginal Man', *American Journal of Sociology*, 33(6): 881–93, reprinted in: Park, R. E., *On Social Control and Collective Behavior*. Ed. and intro. R. H. Turner. Chicago: University of Chicago Press, 1967.

Park, R. E. (1936) 'Human Ecology', *American Journal of Sociology*, 42: 1–15, reprinted in R. E. Park, *On Social Control and Collective Behavior*, ed. R. H. Turner, Chicago: University of Chicago Press, 1967.

Park, R. E. (1939) 'Symbiosis and Socialization', *American Journal of Sociology*, 45(1): 1–25.

Park, R. E. (1952) *Human Communities*. Glencoe, IL: The Free Press.

Park, R. E. (1967) *On Social Control and Collective Behavior*. Ed. and intro. R. H. Turner. Chicago: University of Chicago Press.

Park, R. E. and Burgess, E. W. (eds.) (1969) *Introduction to the Science of Sociology*. Chicago: University of Chicago Press (first published 1921).

Park, R. E., Burgess, E. W. and McKenzie, D. (eds.) (1969) *The City*. Chicago: University of Chicago Press (first published 1925).

Parker, J. (2000) *Structuration*. Buckingham: Open University.

Payne, G. (ed.) (2000) *Social Divisions*. Basingstoke: Palgrave Macmillan.

Petras, J. W. (ed.) (1968) *George Herbert Mead: Essays on His Social Philosophy*, New York: Teachers College Press, Columbia University.

Pivcevic, E. (1970) *Husserl and Phenomenology*. London: Hutchinson.

Plummer, K. (1983) *The Documents of Life*. London: George Allen and Unwin.

Plummer, K. (1991a) 'Introduction', in Plummer, K. (ed.), *Symbolic Interactionism, I: Foundations and History*. London: Edward Elgar.

Plummer, K. (1991b) 'Introduction', in Plummer, K. (ed.), *Symbolic Interactionism, II: Contemporary Issues*. London: Edward Elgar.

Plummer, K. (ed.) (1991c) *Symbolic Interactionism, I: Foundations and History*. London: Edward Elgar.

Plummer, K. (ed.) (1991d) *Symbolic Interactionism, II: Contemporary Issues*. London: Edward Elgar.

Plummer, K. (1998) 'Herbert Blumer', in Stones, R. (ed.), *Key Sociological Thinkers*. Basingstoke: Macmillan.

Plummer, K. (2000) 'Symbolic Interactionism in the Twentieth Century', in Turner, B. S. (ed.), *The Blackwell Companion to Social Theory*. Oxford: Blackwell.

Plummer, K. (2001) *Documents of Life 2: An Invitation to a Critical Humanism*. London: Sage.

The Polity Reader in Gender Studies (1994) Cambridge: Polity.

The Polity Reader in Social Theory (1994) Cambridge: Polity.

Polkinghorne, D. E. (1988) *Narrative Knowing and the Human Sciences*. Albany: State University of New York Press.

Polkinghorne, D. E. (1995) 'Narrative Configuration in Qualitative Analysis', in Hatch, J. A. and R. Wisniewski, R. (eds.), *Life History and Narrative*. London: Falmer.

Pollner, M. (1987) *Mundane Reason*. Cambridge: Cambridge University Press.

Psathas, G. (ed.) (1973) *Phenomenological Sociology*. New York: John Wiley.

Putnam, R. (2001) *Bowling Alone: The Collapse and Revival of American Community*. New York: Simon & Schuster.

Rabinow, P. (ed.) (1984) *The Foucault Reader*. London: Pantheon (Harmondsworth: Penguin, 1991).

Ramazanoglu, C. (1992) 'On Feminist Methodology: Male Reason Versus Female Empowerment', *Sociology*, 26(2): 207–12.

Ramazanoglu, C. with Holland, J. (2002) *Feminist Methodology: Challenges and Choices*. London: Sage.

Reckless, W. C. (1933) *Vice in Chicago*. Chicago: University of Chicago Press.

Reinharz, S. (1992) *Feminist Methods in Social Research*. Oxford: Oxford University Press.

Reynolds, L. T. (1993) *Interactionism: Exposition and Critique*. New York: General Hall.

Reynolds, L. T. and Herman-Kinney, N. J. (eds.) (2003) *Handbook of Symbolic Interactionism*. Walnut Creek, CA: AltaMira.

Ricoeur, P. (1981) 'Narrative Time', in Mitchell, W. T. J. (ed.), *On Narrative*. Chicago: University of Chicago Press.

Ritzer, G. (ed.) (2000) *The Blackwell Companion to Major Contemporary Social Theorists*. Oxford: Blackwell.

Ritzer, G. and Goodman, D. J. (2004) *Sociological Theory*. 6th ed. London: McGraw-Hill.

Roberts, B. (1999) 'Welsh Identity in a Former Mining Valley', in Fevre, R. and Thompson, A. (eds.), *Nation, Identity and Social Theory*. Cardiff: University of Wales Press.

Roberts, B. (2002) *Biographical Research*. Buckingham: Open University.

Roberts, H. (ed.) (1981) *Doing Feminist Research*. London: Routledge & Kegan Paul.

Robertson, R. (1974) 'Towards the Identification of the Major Axes of Sociological Analysis', in Rex, J. (ed.), *Approaches to Sociology*. London: Routledge & Kegan Paul.

Rock, P. (1973) *Deviant Behaviour*. London: Hutchinson.

Rock, P. (1979) *The Making of Symbolic Interactionism*. Basingstoke: Macmillan.

Rock, P. (1991) 'Symbolic Interaction and Labelling Theory', in Plummer, K. (ed.), *Symbolic Interactionism, I: Foundations and History*. London: Edward Edgar.

Rogers, M. (2000) 'Alfred Schutz', in Ritzer, G. (ed.), *The Blackwell Companion to Major Social Theorists*. Oxford: Blackwell.

Rogers, M. F. (2003) 'Contemporary Feminist Theory', in Ritzer, G. and Smart, B. (eds.), *Handbook of Social Theory*. London: Sage.

Roshier, B. (1989) *Controlling Crime: The Classical Perspective in Criminology*. Milton Keynes: Open University Press.

Sacks, H. (1992) *Lectures on Conversation*. Oxford: Blackwell.

Sandstrom, K. L., Martin, D. D., and Fine, G. A. (2003) 'Symbolic Interactionism at the End of the Century', in Ritzer, G. and Smart, B. (eds.), *Handbook of Social Theory*. London: Sage.

Sarbin, T. (ed.) (1986) *Narrative Psychology: The Storied Nature of Human Conduct*. New York: Praeger.

Schutz, A. (1970) *On Phenomenology and Social Relations*. Ed. H. Wagner. Chicago: University of Chicago Press.

Schutz, A. (1971) *Collected Papers 1: The Problem of Social Reality*. Ed. A. Wagner. The Hague: Martinus Nijhoff.

Schutz, A. (1972) *The Phenomenology of the Social World*. London: Heinemann.

Scott, J. (1991) *Social Networks: Theory and Analysis*. London: Sage.

Scott, J. (2000) *Social Network Analysis: A Handbook*. 2nd ed. London: Sage.

Seidman, S. (2004) *Contested Knowledge: Social Theory Today*. Oxford: Blackwell.

Sennett, R. (1998) *The Corrosion of Character: The Personal Consequences of Work in the New Capitalism*. New York: Norton.

Sennett, R. (2002) *The Fall of Public Man*. Harmondsworth: Penguin.

Sharrock, W. (2003) 'Fundamentals of Ethnomethodology' in Ritzer, G. and Smart, B. (eds.), *Handbook of Social Theory*. London: Sage.

Sharrock, W. and Anderson, R. J. (1986) *The Ethnomethodologists*. Chichester: Ellis Horwood.

Shilling, C. (1993) *The Body and Social Theory*. London: Sage.

Shilling. C. (2003) 'The Embodied Foundations of Social Theory', in Ritzer, G. and Smart, B. (eds.), *Handbook of Social Theory*. London: Sage.

Short, J. F. Jr. (1971a) 'Introduction', in Short, J. F., Jr. (ed.), *The Social Fabric of the Metropolis: Contributions of the Chicago School of Urban Sociology*. Chicago: University of Chicago Press.

Short, J. F. Jr. (ed.) (1971b) *The Social Fabric of the Metropolis; Contributions of the Chicago School of Urban Sociology*. Chicago: University of Chicago Press.

Silverman, D. (1998) *Harvey Sacks*. Cambridge: Polity.

Sim, S. (ed.) (1998) *Postmodern Thought*. Cambridge: Icon.

Simmel, G. (1906) 'The Sociology of Secrecy and of Secret Societies', *American Journal of Sociology*, 11(4): 441–98.

Small, A. W. and Vincent, G. E. (1894) *An Introduction to the Study of Society*. New York: American Book Co.

Smart, B. (1983) *Foucault, Marxism and Critique*. London: Routledge.

Smart, B. (1985) *Michel Foucault*. Chichester: Ellis Horwood.

Smith, A. D. (1986) *The Ethnic Origins of Nations*. Oxford: Basil Blackwell.

Smith, A. D. (1991) *National Identity*. Harmondsworth: Penguin.

Smith, D. (1988) *The Chicago School: A Liberal Critique of Capitalism*. Basingstoke: Macmillan.

Smith, D. E. (1987) *The Everyday World as Problematic*. Milton Keynes: Open University Press.

Smith, D. E. (1990) *Texts, Facts, and Femininity: Exploring the Relations of Ruling*. New York: Routledge.

Smith, G. W. H. (ed.) (1999) *Goffman and Social Organization: Studies of a Sociological Legacy*. London: Routledge.

Smith, M. P. (2001) *Transnational Urbanism: Locating Globalization*. Oxford: Blackwell.

Sparkes, A. C. and Smith, B. (2003) 'Men, sport, spinal cord injury and narrative time', *Qualitative Research*, 3(3): 295–320.

Stacey, M. (1969) 'The Myth of Community Studies', *British Journal of Sociology*, 20(2): 134–47.

Stanley, L. and Wise, S. (1983) *Breaking Out: Feminist Consciousness and Feminist Research*. London: Routledge.

Stone, G. P. and Farberman, H. A. (eds.) (1970) *Social Psychology Through Symbolic Interaction*. Waltham, MA: Xerox College.

Stones, R. (ed.) (1998) *Key Sociological Thinkers*. Basingstoke: Palgrave Macmillan.

Stones, R. (2005) *Structuration Theory*. Basingstoke: Palgrave Macmillan.

Strauss, A. (1964) 'Introduction', in Mead, G. H., *On Social Psychology*. Chicago: University of Chicago Press.

Taylor, I., Walton, P. and Young, J. (1973) *The New Criminology*. London: Routledge.

Taylor, L. (1973) *Deviance and Society*. London: Nelson.

Thomas, W. I. (1907) *Sex and Society*. Chicago: University of Chicago Press.

Thomas, W. I. (ed.) (1909) *Source Book for Social Origins*. Chicago: University of Chicago Press.

Thomas, W. I. and Znaniecki, F. (1958) *The Polish Peasant in Europe and America*, 2 vols. New York: Dover Press (first published 1918–20).

Thomson, A. (1999) 'Moving Stories: Oral History and Migration Studies', *Oral History*, 27(1): 24–37.

Thrasher, F. (1927) *The Gang*. Chicago: University of Chicago Press.

Titmuss, R. (1970) *The Gift Relationship*. London: Allen & Unwin.

Tolson, A. (1977) *The Limits of Masculinity*. London: Tavistock (London: Routledge, 1990).

Tong, R. (1989) *Feminist Thought: A Comprehensive Introduction*. London: Unwin Hyman.

Turner, B. S. (1984) *The Body and Society*. Oxford: Blackwell.

Turner, B. S. (1992) *Regulating Bodies*. London: Routledge.

Turner, R. (ed.) (1974) *Ethnomethodology: Selected Readings*. Harmondsworth: Penguin.

Turner, R. H. (1967) 'Introduction', in Park, R. E. (1967), *On Social Control and Collective Behavior*. Chicago: University of Chicago Press.

Urban Life (1983) 'The Chicago School: The Tradition and the Legacy', Special Issue, 11(4), January.

Urry, J. and Gregory, D. (eds.) (1985) *Social Relations and Spatial Structures*. Basingstoke: Macmillan.

Uttley, S. (1980) 'The Welfare Exchange Reconsidered', *Journal of Social Policy*, 9(2): 187–205.

Vincent, J. A. (2000) 'Age and Old Age', in Payne, G. (ed.), *Social Divisions*. Basingstoke: Palgrave Macmillan.

Waddington, D., Wykes, M. and Critcher, C. (1991) *Split at the Seams? Community, Continuity and Change after the 1984–5 Coal Dispute*. Buckingham: Open University.

Wallace, W. L. (1969) *Sociological Theory*. London: Heinemann.

Walsh, G. (1972) 'Introduction', in Schutz, A., *The Phenomenology of the Social World*. London: Heinemann.

Washington, B. T. and Park, R. E. (1984) *The Man Farthest Down*. London: Transaction Books.

Whitehead, S. (2002) *Men and Maculinities*. Cambridge: Polity.

Whitehead, S. and Barrett, F. (eds.) (2001) *The Masculinities Reader*. Cambridge: Polity.

Williams, R. (1998) 'Erving Goffman', in Stones, R. (ed.), *Key Sociological Thinkers*. Basingstoke: Palgrave Macmillan.

Williams, S. J. (1998a) ' "Capitalising" On Emotions? Rethinking the Inequalities in Health Debate', *Sociology*, 32(1): 121–39.

Williams, S. J. (1998b) 'Modernity and the Emotions: Corporeal Reflections on the (Ir)rational', *Sociology*, 32(4): 747–69.

Williams, S. J. (2001) *Emotion and Social Theory*. London: Sage.

Willmott, P. (1986) *Social Networks, Informal Care and Public Policy*. London: Policy Studies Institute.

Wirth, L. (1938) 'Urbanism as a Way of Life', *American Journal of Sociology*, 44(1): 1–24.

Wise S. and Stanley, L. (2003) Review Article: 'Looking Back and Looking Forward: Some Recent Feminist Sociology Reviewed', *Sociological Research Online*, 8(3) (http://www.socresonline.org.uk/8/3/wise.html).

Wolff, K. (1979) 'Phenomenology and Sociology', in Bottomore, T. and Nisbet, R. (eds.), *A History of Sociological Analysis*. London: Heinemann.
Young, J. (1971) *The Drugtakers*. London: MacGibbon & Kee.
Zeitlin, I. M. (1973) *Rethinking Sociology*. Englewood Cliffs, NJ: Prentice-Hall.
Zorbaugh, H. (1929) *The Gold Coast and the Slum*. Chicago: University of Chicago Press.

Journals

American Journal of Sociology
Auto/Biography (Hodder Arnold)
Body and Society (Sage)
British Journal of Sociology (Blackwell)
Feminist Review (Palgrave Macmillan)
Social Problems (University of California Press)
Sociological Research Online (http://www.socresonline.org.uk/home.html)
Sociological Review (Blackwell)
Sociology (Sage)
Symbolic Interaction (Elsevier)
Symbolic Interaction (University of California Press)
Time and Society (Sage)

Index